VISITOR'S GUI

World Travel... ....

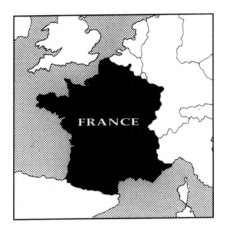

FRANCE

VISITOR'S GUIDE
FRANCE

Tony Astle

MPC
HUNTER
PUBLISHING INC

Published by:
Moorland Publishing Co Ltd
Moor Farm Road West
Ashbourne
Derbyshire
DE6 1HD
England

British Library Cataloguing in
Publication Data:
A catalogue record for this book is
available from the British Library

ISBN 0 86190 466 4

Colour origination by:
P&W Graphics Pte. Ltd, Singapore

Printed in the UK by:
Bath Press Colourbooks

Published in the USA by:
Hunter Publishing Inc,
300 Raritan Center Parkway,
CN 94, Edison, NJ 08818
ISBN 1-55650-529-9

Cover photograph: Sarlat Market,
Dordogne (*International Photobank*)

Illustrations have been supplied as
follows: Tim Hughes: pages 10, 11,
27, 31, 118, 166, 186, 187; Hedley
Alcock: 71 (top), 74 (lower), 75
(both), 95, 98, 99 (both), 122 (both),
126 (lower), 146 (top), 222; MPC
Picture Library: 22. All other
illustrations were supplied by the
author.

MPC Production Team:
Editor: Tonya Monk
Designer: Dan Clarke
Cartographer: Alastair Morrison
Typesetting: Christine Haines

Acknowledgements

To Geoff Miles and Paul Schola for
the use of illustrations.

To Muriel and Terry Latimer for
their help and support during visits
to France.

To my wife, daughters and their
husbands for their help and
forbearance during the research for
this guide.

CONTENTS

Key to Symbols Used in Text Margin and on Maps

♠	Church/Ecclesiastical site	🚶	Recommended walk
🐟	Aquatic interest	⊞	Building of interest
⋂	Archaeological site	♜	Castle/Fortification
⛰	Beautiful view/Scenery, Natural phenomenon	🦌	Nature reserve/Animal interest
🏛	Museum/Art gallery	🦆	Birdlife
☀	Other place of interest	✳	Garden
⛏	Cave	⛵	Watersports
🎾	Sports facilities		

Key to Maps

●	Town/City	— · — ·	National boundary
═══	Motorway	— — — —	Provincial boundary
━━━	Main road		Rivers/Lakes

How To Use This Guide

This MPC Visitor's Guide has been designed to be as easy to use as possible. Each chapter covers a region or itinerary in a natural progression which gives all the background information to help you enjoy your visit. MPC's distinctive margin symbols, the important places printed in bold, and a comprehensive index enable the reader to find the most interesting places to visit with ease.

At the end of each chapter an Additional Information section gives specific details such as addresses and opening times, making this guide a complete sightseeing companion.

At the back of the guide the Fact File, arranged in alphabetical order, gives practical information and useful tips to help you plan your holiday — before you go and while you are there.

The maps of each region show the main towns, villages, roads and places of interest, but are not designed as route maps and motorists should always use a good recommended road atlas.

FOREWORD

T his guide is aimed at the 'traveller' rather than the 'tourist'. It is for those who like to find their own way around, to make their own arrangements and discover the delights of out-of-the-way places for themselves, rather than relying on 'prepacked' holidays. While suggesting possible tours or itineraries, this book enables you to plan your holiday with your own needs and interests in mind. It aims to give you a range of relevant and up-to-date information to help you make your choices; but those choices will be yours.

One of the areas where you will have a wide choice is accommodation. No other country offers a greater variety: *hôtels, logis, pensions, gîtes,* private homes, camp-sites, even châteaux. Modes of travel are almost equally varied, with excellent road, rail and canal networks, and opportunities for walking, cycling, horse-riding, boating and canoeing. But perhaps the most exciting area of choice is in gastronomy, and here the guide aims to help you to choose both where and what to eat and drink.

As an independent traveller, you will be warmly greeted by the French. More than most, they are a nation of individualists who are suspicious of too much regimentation and have a soft spot for the rebel or the loner. They will respect your independence, but when you need help they will be only too eager to offer it. Their initial formal politeness will soon give way to friendly interest when they come to know you; and if you stay among them for any length of time, you will make firm friends.

You cannot 'do' France on a short whistle-stop tour. It is a country to be lingered over, to be savoured like a good wine. It has a paradox at its heart: although much of it is so well-known by travellers and tourists, it keeps its own mystery. To the French, there is a 'secret' France that the hurrying tourist passes by — a conservative land, clinging to its way of life in the face of relentless progress, valuing its little-known beauties and its deep-rooted traditions. The discerning traveller will come upon some of these, and may discover that at the heart of the mystery lies the French concern with the quality of life.

Tours In The French Regions

France is more than the sum of its parts; but they are what make it such a fascinating and rewarding country to explore. To discover these parts, the astute traveller will soon abandon the whistle-stop tour and concentrate on one region at a time. This section aims to help you to do just that. It offers a number of tours in some of the more attractive, unusual or rewarding areas, with suggestions as to what to see and do while you are there.

Nine tours are described in detail. Each tour starts with brief comments on the area you are visiting, followed by an outline of the tour. Your attention will be drawn to items of interest along the way, including natural scenery, buildings, settlements, links with the past, places to eat, drink and sample the local produce, and amenities in the area. The items of interest will be selective rather than exhaustive — it is not aimed to cover the whole of France with these tours, but to give you a glimpse of her many faces. The tour itineraries will be loosely based on French provinces or administrative regions, but will not correspond exactly to them.

A further ten tours are suggested but not described in detail.

Introduction

The Country

The French are justifiably proud of their country and have a variety of scenery and climate that are unrivalled in Europe, if not the world. Without leaving home they can climb Europe's highest mountains, bask in the Mediterranean sun, ramble through the hills of the Massif Central or wind-surf among the Atlantic rollers. They have the deep, sandy inlets of Brittany, the coves among the chalk cliffs of the north coast, the windswept beaches and high sand-dunes of Aquitaine and the beautiful and dramatic coast of the Côte d'Azur. They have the rich, well-watered pastures of Normandy, so reminiscent of England with their orchards, lush grass and fat cattle and they have the arid hills, limestone uplands and clear blue skies of Provence, with their vines, olive trees, lavender beds and *primeur* fruits and vegetables.

Above all, they have the space. It is the second largest country in Europe, with an area of 547,026sq km (211,207sq miles). It has a land and sea border of roughly 4,830km (3,000 miles) and stretches from 42° to 51° North latitude and from over 8° East to nearly 5° West longitude. Though there are large cities with dense populations — Paris, Marseille, Lyon and Toulouse — other areas are sparsely populated, and the countryside in general is less 'crowded'. Distances between towns are longer and the towns themselves are smaller. Roads are generally straighter, except in hilly districts, and there is less traffic. Yet there are few completely deserted areas and most of the land is productive.

Land Use

France is a country rich in produce of the land. Perhaps one of the reasons for their pre-eminence in the field of gastronomy is the quality and variety of their raw materials. They may be ruefully aware of their lack of mineral resources compared to other countries but they have a range of agricultural products second to none.

When one thinks of France one thinks of wine. Although it has rivals, particularly in the New World, it still holds number one position in viticulture. It is not the leader in quantity produced — Italy beats it here — but it is the acknowledged leader in quality and variety. Vineyards, producing about 1,300 million gallons of wine a year, account for about $2^1/_2$ per cent of agricultural land.

Other agricultural products are too numerous to mention. Its wealth of orchard fruits is prodigious. In Normandy and the north, the apple, plum and pear predominate, while in the south you will see thousands of acres of warmer-climate fruit trees — peach, apricot, nectarine, orange, lemon and kiwi fruit. You will also see orchards of olive, almond and chestnut trees. The French are Europe's leading producers of butter and soft cheeses, rice, sugar beet and many other fruits of the land.

France is still the country of the small farm. Over 10 per cent of the workforce work on the land and, although there are fewer farm-units than there used to be, the small family farm is still the norm. This is a result of the traditional French practice, derived from the Napoleonic Code, of dividing estates equally amongst all children.

About one-third of French land is cultivated. Of the rest, one quarter is permanent pasture, one quarter forest, and the remaining 10 per cent barren. The unproductive land is either vertiginous mountain terrain, deserted and windswept limestone plateau, or marsh and heathland, as in the Camargue in the Rhône delta or the Brière in southern Brittany.

One feature which soon strikes a visitor to France is the extent and variety of the forests. In the north, particularly in the Île de France encircling Paris, are a series of wonderful deciduous forests of broadleaved trees: Fontainebleau,

The French landscape to many encapsulates the essence of romance

Compiègne, St Germain and Chantilly are the best known. In the Ardennes, on the Belgian border, conifers have been widely planted to replace trees damaged in two World Wars and the hill forests of both the French and Belgian Ardennes are now well-managed and attractive to the visitor. The lower slopes of the Vosges mountains in Alsace-Lorraine are densely covered with conifers and a huge coniferous forest of very tall trees has been developed in the flat, sandy area of south-west France south of Bordeaux. This is Les Landes de Gascogne, an area with a rather eerie ambience all its own. In Limousin, Perigord and Provence the *chêne vert* or green oak predominates. This is truffle-hunting country: those exquisitely-scented and wildly-expensive delicacies can be tracked down to the roots of these trees with the aid of a keen-nosed pig or dog. Limousin oak provides the wood for the brandy barrels of Cognac and Armagnac, and for those richly-flavoured wines aged in *fût de chêne*. The forest land towards the Mediterranean coast becomes a

Ochre, quarried from cliffs at Rousillon, has been used on many an artists' palette

scrubby mixture of oak, pine, myrtle, laurel, olive, stunted evergreens and herbs, such as thyme and lavender. This is the *maquis*, which gave its name to the French underground movement in World War II, and its herbs provide the *herbes de Provence*, which give that distinctive flavour to southern French cuisine.

The pasture-land provides grazing for domestic animals: the Limousin and Charolais cattle, providing the cream and butter of Normandy and the *boeuf bourguignonne* in Burgundy; the sheep of the *causses* or limestone plateaux of the Massif Central which provide the milk for Roquefort cheese; and the goats, for the *fromage de chèvre* that is so popular in France.

Topology

One of the attractions of France for the visitor is the variety of region and climate. Generally, the north and west are low-lying and fertile, and the south and east mountainous, but marked differences occur within these two broad areas. The flatness of the north and west varies from the very flat lands of the Pas-de-Calais, the Vendée, Charente-Maritime and Les Landes to the undulating pastures of Normandy, the gentle granite uplands of Brittany and the vast prairies of the central corn-belt south and south-east of Paris. The northern plains are cut by river valleys. Some are broad and shallow, like the mighty Loire, the longest river in France, with its magnificent, fairy-tale châteaux and pretty riverside wine-villages; others are more deeply cut, as in Burgundy and the Dordogne.

The mountains of the south and east form three distinct groups: the Alps, on the east and south-east border, which are high, rugged, snow-bound and spectacular; the Pyrénées on the Spanish border in the south-west, which are not quite so high and slightly gentler in aspect, but still spectacular in their way; and the Massif Central. This region is one of the joys of France. Less well-known than the other two, it is larger in area and has a greater variety of scenery. The Auvergne, in the north, is a bare, open region of volcanic peaks and broad valleys studded with *puys* or volcanic cones, giving the terrain a strange moon-like quality. In the centre is the Cantal, an area of hills and wooded valleys with a Swiss aspect. In the south-east are the Cévennes mountains, thickly-wooded granite slopes of wild aspect and singular beauty; and in the south-west are the Causses, high limestone plateaux cut with deep gorges, which provide some of the most spectacular scenery in France. The Tarn gorge or the Cirque de Navacelles are perhaps the nearest that Europe can approach to the Grand Canyon in the USA.

The three massifs are divided by valleys. The Alps are divided from the Massif Central by the Rhône Valley, famous for its wines, its delta, and as a gateway to the south. As you drive down it, a little south of Lyon, look to your left. On a clear day, amid magnificent views of the snow-clad Alps, you will enjoy for mile after mile the breathtaking sight of the highest mountain in Europe, Mont Blanc, towering 4,811m (15,781ft) into the sky. The south-west Massif Central is divided from the Pyrénées by the Valley of the Aude. This is the region of the Midi, with its capital, Toulouse, connected to the Mediterranean by the Canal du Midi — although the whole of France south of the Massif Central is also known as the Midi. This is the 'other' France, with its own language, the Langue d'Oc, its own customs, and its sense of separateness dating back to the days of the Kingdom of Provence and the Cathar heresy.

Language and Culture

Unlike some of its EEC partners, France is not a union of kingdoms nor a federal state. It is a single republic with a strong sense of national identity. Nevertheless, it is made up of constituent parts with varying language, culture and tradition and though these parts normally live together in harmony, they do not always see eye-to-eye with each other or with the central government on every issue. There is a growing sense of cultural identity in several regions, and a desire for more regional autonomy.

The French are a mixture of races, and their history is one of frequent invasion or immigration by different ethnic groups. In Celtic times, the country was called Gaul and this word still has strong emotional overtones. The word 'gallic' is popular in describing French culture and attitudes. The Romans, who first conquered and then intermingled with the Gauls, gave them their language and basic culture. French is a Romance language based on Latin and Roman civilisation is still the basis of their way of life.

Oddly enough, the name of their country was given to them by the Germans. The Franks were a Germanic tribe who conquered and established a ruling dynasty after the fall of the Roman Empire. If the Franks left few traces of Nordic influence, the same cannot be said of the Vikings, or Norsemen, who conquered and settled the region of Normandy in the ninth century. This is the area, after Alsace, where Germanic culture has left its strongest impression, and where the physical appearance of the inhabitants, their buildings and settlements, even their hearty appetite for rich food, are distinctly Nordic.

Paris and the Île de France are the home of the national French culture. This was the cradle of the modern French nation — in its early years France consisted of little more than the area around Paris. Gradually it extended its sovereignty to surrounding territories — Burgundy, Normandy, Provence, Languedoc, Aquitaine, Brittany, Savoy, Flanders, parts of Catalonia and the Basque country — until it reached the boundaries of present-day France. Because of this gradual process of expansion, the areas on the outer fringes of modern France are where the most divergent influences are. This is where people speak in strange dialects, patois and languages. Though they will speak French, they may do it imperfectly and with a strong accent.

In the Nord department and part of the Pas-de-Calais, near the border with Belgian Flanders, Flemish is still spoken, mainly by older village people. The names of towns and villages (Dunkerque, Hazebrouke) are often Flemish. Brittany is still strongly Celtic: the Breton language, akin to old Cornish, is still widely spoken, and the Celtic culture is very much alive. At a folk evening, when the cider is flowing free, you can join in one of the Celtic dances to the music of traditional instruments, including a kind of bagpipes. Breton traditional dress is still worn, and very attractive, particularly the women's high coiff headdresses. In the south-west live one-third of the Basque-speaking people whose language is strange and whose origins obscure (the other two-thirds live across the border in northern Spain). The Pays-Basque is a popular holiday region partly because of its strong local culture — unique forms of architecture and design, colourful folk dances, and the exciting, athletic game of *pelota*.

At the other end of the Pyrénées, in the old province of Roussillon, the predominant language is Catalan, as it is in neighbouring Spanish Catalonia and the principality of Andorra. The island of Corsica, which is a French possession, has its own language, called *Corse*. In the Midi, there is a movement based on Toulouse to revive the language and literature of the old Langue d'Oc, once the dominant culture of southern France. Names of towns and villages and other road signs in this part of the world are now printed in both French and Languedocian. In the south-east, the closely-related Latinate language of Provençal is in a similar process of revival. Provence is well aware of the fact that it has a proud tradition as an independent state. In the Middle Ages it was a centre of European culture, and produced the troubadours who spread that culture throughout Christendom.

An Italian patois is widely spoken along the French Riviera from Nice to Menton, a reminder of the fact that this area's history is closely linked to Italy, and that Nice only became a French possession in 1860. This was also the date when France annexed the proud independent duchy of Savoy. This mountainous province in the northern Alps still guards its own traditions and culture. Long linked in the past to the Italian province of Piedmont, it had a fluctuating history as an independent state until it decided to throw in its lot with France in 1860. When it did so, it insisted on keeping its name and traditions: in these parts, a man is a Savoyard first, a Frenchman second. Further north, in the eastern province of Alsace, the difference between this region and the rest of France is the most striking of all. The Alsatians speak a patois based on German; place-names and personal names are German and the countryside is picture-book German with a softening overlay of French.

Even some of the provinces nearer to the centre of France have a strongly regional flavour. Burgundy has a style of its own: its rich, earthy culture of good food and superlative wine is the product of a long, proud independence. The flat, marshy land of the Vendée keeps its own royalist, strongly catholic traditions. The Franche-Comté (or the Jura) is legendary for its fierce independence and its adherence to local custom while the Auvergne, that citadel in the very heart of France, was for many years the natural refuge of non-conformists.

History

Prehistory

Some of the most popular sights in France are the cave-paintings of the Palaeolithic Era. The people who painted these magnificent works of art were perhaps some of the earliest settlers in France — refugees from the last Ice Age. They were hunters of reindeer and bison, and covered cave-dwellings with representations of the animals they were pursuing, possibly in the belief that this would give them magical powers over the beasts. They seem to have settled mainly in the Aquitaine basin.

Napoleon Bonaparte (1769-1821), French military and political leader

More settled communities followed in the Neolithic Era. The amazing sets of megaliths at Carnac and other places in Brittany, and the many dolmens in the Midi, are testimony to the people who first cleared forests and introduced an agricultural economy. They settled first in the northern plains, later in the mountain massifs, and began to use copper and pottery. Eventually, from about 1000BC, they were subdued and dominated by successive waves of invaders from the East, the Celts.

This Indo-European race gave the name of Gaul to this territory and established their Gallic pattern of life. They set up raised and fortified townships, introduced the basic pattern of agriculture which we still see in France today, and buried their dead in burial mounds which are a common feature of the landscape. Later these were succeeded by flat tombs in which they placed ashes of the dead, whereby they have been called the 'urn-field civilisation'. Many relics of this civilisation, including fine examples of their highly-developed pottery and bronzeware, can be seen in French museums.

The Roman Era

From about the sixth century BC the Greeks established trading posts on the Mediterranean coast. Then, in the second century BC, the Roman legions marched into southern Gallia and established the *Provincia Romana*, the basis of modern Provence. It was nearly a century before they conquered and subdued the various warring kingdoms of Celts and other tribes in the rest of the country and south-eastern France was always more thoroughly colonised than the rest. Today, this part of France retains strong Roman influences in its language, customs, style of architecture and way of life.

Many signs of Roman civilisation are apparent today, particularly in the south-east: the arenas and other buildings at Arles, Nîmes and Fréjus, the Roman theatre at Orange, above all the extensive remains of the Roman city at Vaison-la-Romaine. In other parts of France, remains are fewer, but can still be seen at such places as Autun, Narbonne, Lyon and Vienne.

The Romans built roads, bridges, aqueducts — of which the most impressive is the Pont du Gard near Nîmes — theatres, arenas and galleries. They also established some of the vineyards still in use today. But their civilisation, to which France owes its legacy of arts and good living, began to decline in the fifth century. When the Roman legions were withdrawn to defend Rome itself, Gaul was vulnerable to attack from a succession of Germanic invaders from the east. The most ferocious of these were the Huns, led by Attila, whose forces were defeated in AD451 by a combined force of Romans, Franks and Visigoths at a battle near Troyes. More and more the German tribes took control, and in AD481 the Franks, under their leader Clovis, then converted to Christianity and joined forces with the already-Christianised Provence to defeat the Visigoths, who had captured Aquitaine. He subdued the other dominant Germanic tribe, the Burgundians, was baptised by St Remi at Reims in AD496 and established a new hereditary Frankish kingdom, the Merovingian dynasty. Thus was modern France born.

The Feudal Period

The Franks assimilated with the romanised Celts and adopted their language and customs, so France retained many of the features of its Gallic and Roman past. Clovis chose Paris as his capital and died there in AD511 and his successors enlarged and beautified the city. The Merovingian dynasty gradually declined and a new threat, the Saracens, appeared in the south. Parts of the Mediterranean coast were seized and Arab communities established. Influences of Moorish culture can be seen in the lower Rhône Valley and parts of southern Provence.

A new hero appeared to save and unite France — Charles Martel (The Hammer) — who defeated and drove out the Saracens in AD732. His son Pepin 'The Short' accepted the resignation of the last Merovingian king in AD751, and established a new dynasty. On Pepin's death in AD768, his son Charles (the great Charlemagne) became sole king of the Franks and extended the Frankish empire over most of Western Europe. The Carlovingian dynasty thus became the basis for the Holy Roman Empire. Charlemagne was crowned as its first Emperor in Rome in AD800.

After his death in AD814, Charlemagne's empire began to disintegrate. It was divided among his sons, and soon fell apart in rebellion and war. But Pepin and his great son established the Feudal System and this continued as a more or less viable structure throughout the Middle Ages.

France was now beset by attacks from Viking raiders, who sacked Paris four times and could only be appeased by being given their own kingdom in the north, which they christened Normandy. People abandoned their weak king and looked to their feudal lords for protection. Gradually, however, the French kings began to re-assert their authority. Hugh Capet was crowned King of all France in AD987, and for the next 400 years the kings gradually built up their authority, establishing Paris as the political, economic and cultural capital of the country. Under Philip Augustus (1180–1223), the Louvre, the University of the Sorbonne and Notre-Dame Cathedral were built, and Paris became an admired and envied centre of justice and sound administration.

Religion And War
The Middle Ages were a time of religious fervour. France became covered in a 'white mantle' of new churches, and pilgrimages became the rage. People undertook great journeys to Jerusalem, to Rome and to the tomb of St James at Compostela in north-western Spain. Miracle-working relics and venerated shrines were eagerly sought out, causing great movement of people and bringing prosperity to religious centres. Four major pilgrimage routes led across France to Compostela, each marked by pilgrimage churches, monasteries and hostelries. Many of these can be seen today, often rich in ornament and architectural beauty. Two holy orders of knights, the Templars and Hospitallers, were founded to protect the pilgrims and the holy places, and they became rich and powerful.

One less salutary aspect of this religious fervour was the Crusade. Crusading began as a defence against Saracens invading southern France and Spain in the eighth century, and by the eleventh century it had become a holy war to recapture Jerusalem and hold it against the infidel. Embarking from Marseille or Aigues-Mortes on the French Mediterranean coast, the crusaders fought and pillaged their way across Europe to the Holy Land. Later, in the thirteenth century, France suffered an internal crusade directed against the

Cathar heresy in the south-west. This shameful episode destroyed the power and civilisation of Toulouse and the Midi, and its scars — the ruined castles, churches and towns — have become a tourist attraction in France today.

The Middle Ages were also a period of constant warfare of feudal lords, either against the king or between one another. The Hundred Years War between England and France was essentially a feudal war, in that the English kings were fighting as feudal lords of lands in France. They laid claim both to the French throne and to the overlordship of their Plantagenet lands in Anjou, Maine and Aquitaine. Other French feudal lords, particularly those of Burgundy, Orleans and Brittany, joined in on one side or the other, mainly to maintain the balance of power.

This bitter struggle devastated much of France. But in the end it was beneficial to the development of the modern nation. The feudal nobility were exhausted and had to submit to the authority of the king and the war threw up a rallying point that was to unite the nation as never before and provide for the spiritual birth of French national consciousness.

The English seemed to have won in 1420 when, after Charles the Dauphin had fled Paris, England allied itself with Burgundy and Henry V of England married the French King's daughter. He was then recognised as regent and heir to the throne of France. Then Henry died young, quickly followed by the French king, Charles VI, and the scene changed. A peasant girl from Lorraine appeared with a divine mission to drive the English out of France. The story of Joan of Arc is too well-known to need repeating, but St Joan is the patroness of France and a potent symbol of French national pride.

The Age Of Reform

The fifteenth and sixteenth centuries were a time of reform in the state, the arts and religion. Joan of Arc had given the impetus for the monarchy to strengthen and consolidate itself: following her lead, Charles VII drove the English out of France, established a permanent army, and used the services of rich bourgeois merchants to enrich his state and defeat enemies. His son, Louis XI, an able and astute monarch nicknamed 'the spider', continued the process. He strengthened his civil service, and effectively ended the power of the feudal nobility by outmanoeuvring and defeating his chief enemy and rival, Charles the Bold (or Rash) of Burgundy. Other medieval fiefdoms soon succumbed, and by the end of his reign, Louis had founded an absolute monarchy which continued to grow in wealth, power and influence up to the Golden Age of the Sun King, Louis XIV. By the end of the fifteenth century, France was peaceful, united and growing in prosperity. It was ready to experience the two momentous movements that were sweeping through Europe — the Renaissance and the Reformation. The Renaissance had profound effects in France. This flowering of the arts showed itself most strikingly in the rich carpet of châteaux that sprang up everywhere, most thickly in the Loire Valley. These buildings, which together constitute one of the greatest glories of France or indeed the civilised world, are an astounding marriage of late medieval, gothic traditions with the new, classically-influenced ideas of the Italian architects and artists brought back from the Italian wars. The monarchy led the way. Under François I, the court became a tool of government. It fixed etiquette, transformed nobles into courtiers, made French the official language of the nation, and led the way in fashion and the arts.

The other arts also flourished at this period, influenced by the new Humanism that was replacing the religious civilisation of the Middle Ages. This Renaissance Humanism led to a questioning of established thought and produced a new type of society — secular, monarchical, capitalist. It also led to demands for religious reform and a return to fundamentals. Following the ideas of Huss, Luther and Calvin, the Protestant Reformation spread throughout Europe and entered France, gaining a particularly strong hold in the south. By 1560, many French people had embraced the Protestant faith, mainly its more extreme Calvinist form. They became known as Huguenots.

The last 40 years of the sixteenth century were a bloody period of French history. This period of religious civil wars ended the Renaissance and threw the country into turmoil. At first the Huguenots seemed to be gaining the upper hand, but Catholicism maintained its hold on the country, and a series of atrocities during the Regency of Catherine de Medicis culminated in the St Bartholemew's Day massacre in 1572, when 2,000 Huguenots were murdered in Paris. The wars were political as well as religious, with the nobility trying to reassert its authority over the crown, and they became ever more bloody and unprincipled. When Henry III was assassinated in 1589, the Calvinist Henry of Navarre succeeded to the throne but found Paris barred to him; he was not officially crowned until 1594, and then only after he had renounced his faith and become a Roman Catholic.

Henry IV was a wise, strong and tolerant king and was able to re-establish the authority of the monarchy under a new dynasty, the Bourbons. He ended the war with Spain in 1598 and in 1599 he ended the period of religious strife with the Edict of Nantes, which guaranteed freedom of worship to French Protestants. Several towns in the south-west were allocated to the Huguenots, and parts of the south remain Protestant to this day.

Unfortunately the Edict of Nantes was revoked in the reign of Louis XIV in 1685, and privileges to Huguenots were abolished. This led to further religious strife, particularly in the south, and many Huguenots emigrated to Britain and elsewhere. A rebellion, called the War of the Camisards, was waged for some years in the Cevennes mountains.

The Golden Age

Following the reign of Henry IV was a period of rule by three Bourbon kings, Louis XIII (1610-1643), Louis XIV (1643-1715) and Louis XV (1715-1774). Known as the *Ancien Régime*, this was the most glorious period of the French monarchy. The country prospered under a succession of great civil servants — Sully, cardinals Richelieu and Mazarin, and Colbert. These were astute and ruthless men who systematically destroyed the power of the regional nobility and gathered all power and privilege into the hands of the monarchs. Louis XIV in particular, who had experienced humiliation as a boy-king during a civil war, was determined when he came of age to rule absolutely and, with the aid of Cardinal Mazarin and Colbert, he achieved his ambition. He compared himself to the sun, established himself in probably the most splendid palace ever built, at Versailles, and encouraged his subjects to worship him as a God.

The *Ancien Régime* had its splendours and its drawbacks for France. The arts, architecture and philosophy flourished while the country prospered and extended its frontiers. Paris became the world centre of taste, sophistication, pleasure and worldliness and the privileged classes threw themselves into a life of hedonistic pleasure which kept them diverted in the absence of any real power or responsibility, but which eventually brought about their own downfall. But there were drawbacks too. The provinces stagnated and declined; industry, agriculture and trade deteriorated; the repressive legislation against Protestant dissidents drained the country of many of its skills (to the benefit of those countries that received them); and the combination of wars abroad and luxury at home frittered away much of the wealth. Above all, the eighteenth-century 'Enlightenment' led to a questioning by philosophers of the whole basis of the monarchist state. As the century progressed, resentment at the privilege and idleness of the nobility, and their exemption from the taxes which were crippling the rest of the people, grew ever stronger.

Revolution

The decisive year was 1789. During the reign of Louis XVI, demands for social and constitutional reform grew, and finally came to a head throughout France. The three estates — nobles, clergy and commons — met together to demand action, as did the Estates General. The Third Estate then met at Versailles to swear the 'Tennis Court Oath', declaring itself a National Assembly and vowing not to disband until France had a constitution. Finally, on 14 July, in Paris the Bastille was stormed by an angry mob looking for arms. Its seizure and the release of its seven prisoners became a new symbol — the overthrow of monarchical tyranny and the establishment of the Republic. *Liberté, égalité, fraternité (liberty, equality, fraternity)* became the cry, echoing throughout Europe. Unfortunately the bliss did not last for long. Liberty turned to tyranny, equality to the savage terror of mob-rule, and brotherhood to the fratricidal conflict between its leaders that ended with the execution of the last and most vicious of them, Robespierre.

The collapse of the Revolution led to dictatorship by the victorious general, Napoleon Bonaparte. A brilliant and bold commander, he led the revolutionary forces to victory all over Europe and established a new absolute order in France itself. Modelling himself on Charlemagne, he went further than the kings of the *Ancien Régime*. In 1804, he was proclaimed Emperor, making the Pope watch while he placed the crown on his own head. As well as a great general, he was an organisational genius, and left a soundly-organised, centralised administration. He introduced the greatest social, administrative and legal reforms that France had ever known, giving land and freedom to peasants, restoring the Catholic state, and introducing a new civil, criminal and rural code known as the Code Napoléon. But eventually Napoleon overreached himself. After his disastrous failure to take Moscow, he was defeated by the Anglo-Austrian alliance in 1814, and after a brief comeback finally broken at Waterloo in 1815.

Empires And Republics

After Napoleon's downfall and exile, the Bourbon kings were reinstated, but their return was short-lived as liberal and radical movements gained strength. In 1830 Charles X was deposed, and the popular Louis Philippe elected as a 'people's' monarch. He was forced to abdicate in 1848, the 'year of revolutions'. The workers' movement that overthrew him declared a Second Republic, but this was soon crushed. Napoleon's nephew, Louis-Napoleon, came to power by a coup d'état in 1852 and restored the Second Empire, ruling as Emperor Napoleon III. This introduced a period of bourgeois stability as France became an industrial nation and grew prosperous. The wealth of the Second Empire produced a flowering of the arts, not in a single movement but in the revival of previous forms (neo-Romanesque, neo-Gothic, neo-Classical, neo-Renaissance). Building and urban design developed apace, the greatest achievement of this period being the creation of the Paris we know today by Baron Haussmann. He was commissioned by Napoleon III to clear the narrow streets that provided such a breeding ground for dissent and rebellion, and the radical Parisian working classes were moved out to the suburbs, where they remain today. The spacious boulevards, grand avenues and parks that make Paris such a beautiful city are largely Haussmann's work.

But the luxury, frivolity and corruption of the Second Empire led to the weakening of France's power. This led to an ignominious defeat by Prussia in the Franco-Prussian war of 1870, the French forces being routed at Sedan. Paris collapsed after a winter under siege, the Emperor fled to England, and Alsace and much of Lorraine were ceded to Germany. After an uprising in the capital had been suppressed, the Third Republic was narrowly voted into power. This was to last until 1940, giving France a period of unparalleled stability. The arts flourished again, and a colonial empire was founded.

World War And Its Aftermath

During the period of the Third Republic, France's allegiances changed. Germany rather than Britain became the enemy, and power was balanced between two rival blocs — Britain, France and Russia against Germany and Austro-Hungary. Thus were both France and Britain dragged into World War I (1914-18). Though she was on the winning side, France was devastated in 1918, with nearly 1.4 million men lost and her industries ruined. Germany was forced into a humiliating peace and Alsace returned to French sovereignty; but this, and the pacifist stance adopted by the French, contributed to the rise of Nazism in Germany and World War II (1939-1945).

France was quickly defeated in 1940, one half being occupied and the other becoming a satellite state of Germany (Hitler reclaimed Alsace as German territory). An underground resistance movement, the *Maquis*, developed and in 1942 the Vichy government was removed and the whole country occupied. A Free French government was formed in England under the leadership of General Charles de Gaulle, whose forces joined those of the other Allies in the Normandy D-Day landings of 6 June 1944. This led to the liberation of France in under a year, and in 1945 the Fourth Republic was declared with de Gaulle as its leader.

Post-war France was beset by problems left by the war. The years of occupation were followed by hostility between the resistance fighters and the collaborators, and these tensions persist today. The government of the Fourth Republic was inherently unstable. De Gaulle soon resigned in despair at his lack of presidential powers and 26 cabinets fell within the 14 years of the Republic's life. Furthermore, war and dissention were rife in the colonies, particularly in Indo-China and North Africa. The French forces were ignominiously defeated in Indo-China, and withdrew in 1954 but in Algeria dissention led to rebellion, then war.

The unstable and troubled Fourth Republic collapsed in 1958 and General de Gaulle was reinstated as President of the Fifth Republic with almost dictatorial powers. He engineered the ending of the Algerian war of independence in 1962, and for a while brought stability, but was forced out of office by the student riots and general strike of 1968. These events shook the complacency of a country that had been growing in prosperity and self-confidence as a founder-member of the European Common Market. The Gaullist party eventually gave way as the ruling group to the Socialists under Francois Mitterand, who was elected President in 1981. Today France maintains a centralist domestic policy and, in the EEC, is an advocate of closer economic and political co-operation, supporting moves towards a federation of European states.

France Today

Today, France is one of the world's major economic powers, with thriving industries and a large agricultural output. It has a stable government and secure frontiers, and is a founder member of, and a major participant in, the European Economic Community. It has both a strong sense of its own identity and a desire to see a more closely-integrated Europe, politically as well as economically.

The magnificent scenery of the Alps is one of the main reasons why France has an impressive tourist industry

Government And Politics

The French Fifth Republic is governed under a constitution adopted in 1958 and amended in 1962. This provides for a strong President, directly elected for a 7-year term, a Prime Minister appointed by the President, and a parliament of two chambers, the Senate and the National Assembly. National policy is decided by the Council of Ministers, which meets weekly and is usually attended by both the President and the Prime Minister. Much of the administration is devolved to the country's 95 departments and 21 regions, and these are sub-divided into *arrondissements, cantons* and *communes.*

Economy And Industry

Many of the key elements of the French economy are nationally-owned. Railways, utilities, many banks and some key industries are nationalised. The railways, which are heavily subsidised, are universally admired for their efficiency and widely used for freight transport.

In spite of its increasing productivity and improved efficiency, agriculture remains a problem in France. French farmers seem to the outsider to be in perpetual revolt and to some of her EEC partners France appears to be both over-benefitting from, and abusing, the Common Agricultural Policy. However, agricultural output is still an important part of the general national profit.

French industry has always suffered from lack of coal and oil. Coal deposits in the north-east supply less than 75 per cent of what is needed. But a number of hydro-electric plants have been developed. Most of these can be found in the Rhône and Durance valleys and in Savoy. However, the construction of nuclear power stations is a more contentious issue, and 'Non au Nucléaire' signs can often be seen daubed on walls, bridges and the sides of buildings.

France's main industrial products include metals, chemicals, natural gas, motor vehicles, aircraft and textiles. Key industries are foods (particularly cheese) and wine. Tourism is an important and highly-developed industry, as are fashion and the production of luxury goods. Iron ore and bauxite are the leading minerals produced.

The European Community

The European Community is the brainchild of three statesmen, two of them French. Jean Monnet, Robert Schuman and Paul Henri Spaak had a vision of a unified Europe which is nearer realisation today than when six countries formed the European Coal and Steel Community in 1952 and the European Economic Community in 1958. The six nations are now twelve and France has always played a leading part in its development. The home of the European Parliament is Strasbourg, the capital of Alsace.

The Arts and Entertainment

As a discerning visitor to France, you will not be content merely to eat, drink and lie in the sun. Its exceptional cultural heritage will beckon you, whichever part of the country you are visiting. In towns, villages and the open countryside you are likely to come across splendid churches, châteaux and other buildings; and every town of any size boasts a museum containing beautiful works of art and fascinating relics of the past. Few countries can offer more than France to satisfy the appetite of the 'culture-vulture'.

Architecture

While not aspiring to the quantity of interesting buildings (whether intact or in ruins) that Greece and Italy can offer, France must rival or even surpass them for variety. From the prehistoric to the ultra-modern, examples of man's attempts to build himself a civilised environment can be found in various shapes and sizes throughout the country. Buildings vary in two ways: according to the age in which they were produced and according to the region they were produced in.

Regional Styles

One of the pleasures of travelling through France is remarking changes in the style of buildings from region to region. This applies both to domestic archtiecture and to more grandiose buildings such as churches and castles. In the extreme north-east, the dominant style is Flemish. Ordinary houses tend to be squat and sturdy (probably as protection against the winds sweeping across the northern plains), the materials used are brick and stone, with unusually-shaped orange roof tiles, and larger buildings have a distinctly Dutch appearance, with high patterned gables. Normandy has its own quite different style — buildings tend to be tall, half-timbered in brown and cream, and Germanic (or English Tudor) in appearance. Brittany, on the other hand, has a distinctly 'Welsh' ambience: stone cottages have stone or slate lintels and grey slate or thatched roofs.

The changes in style continue as you go south. Buildings in Paris and around the Île de France often have an air of Second Empire grandiloquence, with tall, decorated stone fronts and high, domed blue slate roofs. These disappear when you move into Burgundy, to be replaced by a more rugged, Romanesque type of building of rough-faced stone, round towers with turrets and, on the more important houses and châteaux, those distinctive brightly-patterned, multi-coloured slate roofs. If you cross the Vosges into Alsace, you are in a different world of Germanic half-timbered buildings with overhanging gables, decorative carved beams and painted plaster fronts. The Jura has a noticeably Swiss appearance, with chalet-type buildings and trim mountain villages. Other regions, such as the Basque Country, the Alps, the Vendée and the Auvergne, also have their own regional variations in building style.

Provence and the Midi provide the greatest contrast with the rest of France, however — not only in architecture but in landscape, climate and *mode de vie*. Here the style is Roman, from the pantiles on the roofs to the shaded inner courtyards, from the dusty public squares with their inevitable *boules* parks to the ornate cemeteries with their curtain-walls of cypress trees. The French Mediterranean basin has more in common, in architectural terms, with its neighbouring territories of Italy and Spain than with France north of the Massif Central.

Historical Styles

Architecture changes in time as well as place, and the various epochs of French history have each produced their own styles. The large stones or megaliths of prehistoric times are the earliest evidence of man's desire to build. The most impressive of these are in Brittany, around Carnac, where large numbers of them are laid out in patterns like the foundations of primitive temples. Their function was probably religious, as they seem to have been placed in accordance with the position of the sun's axis.

Little is left of pre-Roman buildings, though some sites have been excavated and artefacts found. Most of the Roman remains are to be found in Provence. Though nothing like as extensive as in Italy, there are some impressive buildings to be seen. The most perfect is the Maison Carrée in Nîmes, a Roman temple built on pure classical proportions. The amphitheatres at Nîmes, and Arles are well preserved, and still used today for bull-fights and other spectacles. The Roman theatre at Orange, built in the reign of Augustus, is the best-preserved in existence — its stage wall is classified the ninth monument in the world. Triumphal arches can be found at Orange and St Rémy-de-Provence and the layout of an almost complete Roman town has been unearthed at Vaison-la-Romaine. In other parts of France Roman remains are less numerous, and much of their stone has been used for later building.

Medieval Churches

The 'dark ages' of the Frankish dynasties has left little to see — the frequent barbarian invasions destroyed most of the early Christian buildings, and those that survived were replaced in the Middle Ages. The medieval period was the great age of church building, and has provided a wealth of examples to delight the lover of church architecture.

The Middle Ages can be divided into two distinct periods, the Romanesque and the Gothic. Romanesque churches are found mainly in the centre and south of France, with Burgundy claiming some of the greatest examples while the largest and most magnificent examples of Gothic architecture are in northern France.

Romanesque churches are the glory of France. They date from the eleventh to the thirteenth centuries, and equate to the Norman style in England, though they are usually more ornate and have a greater variety of styles. The name 'Romanesque' expresses their derivation from the Roman basilica, particularly in their overall pattern, their use of the rounded arch and barrel vaulting. They are fascinating in their variety, their liveliness and their individuality. One of their joys is the personal touch given to them by local builders, particularly in the carvings on the capitals, around the arches, on the tympana above the doorways, and under the eaves. For the unlettered medieval congregation, these were their picture-books, telling the Christian story of man from Genesis to Judgement Day. The figures and scenes are down-to-earth, irreverent, sometimes vulgar, and always based on the reality of the times. These churches, and the sculptures within them, are perhaps the greatest artistic heritage of the areas where they predominate.

The peak of Romanesque architecture was the twelfth century. Different regions evolved their own styles — for instance, the Romanesque churches of Aquitaine are domed, those in Provence are most closely modelled on Roman monuments. Many churches were built along the pilgrimage routes to Santiago da Compostela, and they display the influence of the monastic order prevalent in their area.

A revolution in church architecture occurred in the thirteenth century. This was a great age of expansion, with population increasing, old towns being renewed and new ones, such as the *bastide* towns of the south-west, being built, and with royal control and influence spreading. The new style reflected this royalist, centralising trend, and soon spread across France from Paris and the cities of the north. It sharply contrasted with the old in many ways: it was urban, metropolitan and monarchical rather than rural, regional and domestic; and it was impressive, calculated and intellectual rather than homely, charming and exuberant. It was a revolution in construction techniques: the churches had pointed arches, ribbed vaulting, flying buttresses, high, slender pillars, and large windows filled with stained glass and they were often immensely tall.

This was the new Gothic style that was to dominate Western Europe for the next three centuries. In France, the earliest examples are perhaps the most magnificent: Notre-Dame and the Sainte-Chapelle in Paris, and the 'big four' of Chartres, Reims, Amiens and Beauvais. In these, the architecture is all of a piece. The French Gothic cathedrals present the visitor with some of the most awe-inspiring sights that man has created, while the later Gothic style, called flamboyant from its characteristic flame-shaped stonework, is less impressive, a sign of the decadence of a troubled age.

Châteaux and Town Houses

The French word is used rather than 'castle' as it has a wider connotation, including large country houses as well as fortified medieval buildings. In the Middle Ages most large secular buildings (and indeed some churches, such as the castle-churches in the Thiérache), were fortified, for defence in the constant wars. The French crown had little control outside the Île de France, and local lords and their communities had to defend themselves. Early castles are often situated on rocky strongholds, such as those of the Cathar heretics in the Midi. Often whole towns were fortified, for instance Carcassonne, probably the finest example of a medieval walled city in Europe. The new *bastide* towns of the south-west were all fortified, as this was front-line territory in the Hundred Years War and both the English and the French were trying to entice loyal subjects to live in them. The Papal palace at Avignon is fortified, as is the Royal fort on the other side of the Rhône at Villeneuve lés Avignon.

Some of these fortifications are now in ruins, either decaying naturally or having been deliberately destroyed to avoid the threat to central authority. Many of the modern 'survivals' are in fact heavily restored, mainly in the nineteenth century when medievalism became fashionable. The architect Viollet-le-Duc was responsible for most of this restoration of Romanesque and Gothic buildings. His greatest achievement was rebuilding Carcassone. However, he is sometimes criticised for being too simplistic in his approach.

As the need for fortification died away in the sixteenth century, fortresses changed into châteaux, and the classicism of the Renaissance replaced or modified medieval Gothic as the prevailing style. In the towns, citizens began to build fine private houses and town councils erected grandiose Hôtels de Ville with fine belfries, such as the one at Arras. In the countryside, new châteaux were built with some of the features of medieval castles, though now for their decorative value rather than for defence. The Loire Valley, the playground of the French kings, was where some of the most extravagant of these were sited, often with a royal mistress in residence. The best of the châteaux are remarkable works of art — unique combinations of late Gothic form and classically-inspired ornament. They are fantasies in stone, and have a magnetic attraction for the visitor.

The artistic inspiration for the sixteenth-century châteaux came from Italy. King Charles VIII brought back from the disastrous Italian wars a cohort of architects and artists, to reproduce in French buildings the wealth of decoration and ornament he had seen there. Later, François I went even further, inviting Leonardo da Vinci, Titian and other Italian artists to come and make his court as lavish and extravagant as any in Italy. The early châteaux were a stylistic blend of Flamboyant Gothic (in their layout, towers and roofs) and Renaissance (in their decoration, arcades and gardens). Renaissance style was

The fairytale châteaux of France help to create a dream-like atmosphere

inspired by the architectural rules of ancient Greece and Rome: symmetry, harmony and balance. Gradually, as the century progressed, the Renaissance style took over and Gothic disappeared.

During the next three centuries, the ornate style of the Renaissance developed into Baroque, neo-Classical and Rococo. Styles tended to reflect the taste of the ruler of the time, and are usually given the king's name: Louis XIII, Louis XIV, Louis XV and so on. This trend started with François I, whose magnificent royal palace at Fontainebleau began the new, elaborate 'Fontainebleau' style. Baroque was the style of the Wars of Religion and Counter-Reformation, reflecting in its turbulent forms the turmoil of the times. The Louis XIII period was one of sober, restrained neo-Classicism while the Louis XIV style reflected the imposing, rich but ordered grandeur of his reign. The Louvre, and the palace and park of Versailles, are the buildings which give the fullest expression to the splendour of the Sun-King. Classicism became less formal in the later eighteenth century with the flowery, delicate Louis XV style of Rococo. But overall, classicism in one form or another held sway throughout this period.

Louis XIV's reign was not one of universal peace, however, and a valuable heritage of the constant wars of the period are the military fortresses of Vauban. Most of these are found around the perimeters of France, and were intended for the defence of the country against invaders. Vauban was Louis XIV's military architect and engineer, and he built 33 new fortresses and redesigned 300 during his period of office. Examples of these models of defence and urban planning can be seen at Belfort, Briançon and Colmar.

The period before the French Revolution saw a return to the stricter principles of Classicism. But the Revolution itself did little to develop architecture or the arts: it was a time of destruction rather than building. The Empire style of Napoleon was a continuation of the Classical style with a heavier overlay of Egyptian themes. The Second Empire, under Napoleon III, was a period of luxury and display, when the strict restraints of Classicism were abandoned in favour of heavy ornamentation.

After the Second Empire, Classicism lost its hold on French artistic taste. This was the age of borrowing and restoration, when heavy, grandiloquent versions of every style — Romanesque, Gothic, Renaissance, Classical, as well as various Oriental forms — were tried out, and when medieval buildings were rediscovered and, often crassly, renovated by Viollet-le-Duc and others.

Modern Architecture

The first modern French building is perhaps its most famous monument—the Eiffel Tower. Love it or hate it, it has become a symbol of France, and replicas of it of various sizes are sold in their millions. Built for the Paris Exhibition of 1889, it is 300m (984ft) high and dominates Paris. It was an early example of the ostentatious use of steel and other metals in architecture, a striking and controversial example of which is the Pompidou Centre in Paris. Gustave Eiffel was a great and daring engineer who also built bridges and viaducts.

The Eiffel Tower was an early example of the Art Nouveau which was to captivate Paris at the turn of the century. Meaning simply 'new style', it was a compound of Japanese art with the ideas of an English designer, William

Morris, a Belgian architect, Baron Victor Horta, and a Czech artist, Alphonse Mucha. It was an extreme reaction against Classicism, abhoring straight lines and symmetrical forms and characterised by twisting, swirling flower and hair motifs. They can be seen today in some of the older Métro signs, in bistros and restaurants (often in designs on wall and ceiling glass panels) and in the Petit and Grand Palais exhibition halls.

French architecture since World War I is a matter of taste. It is perhaps more extreme and starkly functional than 'modern' style in any other country, owing to the dominating influence of Le Corbusier. He is a major figure in modern architecture, and one reason for its unpopularity today. He believed that a house was a 'machine for living in', and was fond of using concrete as a building material. His buildings are in the main cheerless and uninviting, though there are exceptions — his commemorative chapel at Ronchamp, in Alsace, is warmly expressive of the surrounding Vosges mountains. Le Corbusier's ideas on architecture and town planning have influenced post-war urban reconstruction in towns like Le Havre and Royan, whose identical wide, straight streets and anonymous concrete blocks make them some of the less attractive towns in France. On the other hand, some of the ultra-modern new holiday developments, like La Grande Motte on the Languedoc coast, have a certain weird fascination.

The Visual Arts

Museums

France is rich in museums and art galleries housing works of art from many countries and periods of history. Every town of any size will have at least one. Sometimes they are housed in buildings that are works of art in themselves and the setting may on occasion provide a richer aesthetic experience than the contents!

If Paris's claim to be the cultural capital of the world is disputed, she certainly has the finest and most famous museum. The Louvre is a vast storehouse of great works of art from all over the world (far too much to take in at one visit), containing the best collection of Leonardo da Vinci's works as well as such acknowledged masterpieces as the *Mona Lisa* and the *Venus de Milo*. Museums in the rest of France cannot equal those of Paris in quality or variety, but can still be superb at their best.

French Painting And Sculpture

French visual art begins at the dawn of time, with the cave paintings in the Dordogne and Pyrénées. At their best, these sacred representations of animals are remarkable for their realism and brilliance of colour. You may be disappointed when you visit as the figures are often drawn over and difficult to decipher, and the caves crowded, cramped and uncomfortable.

A few sculptures, pieces of mosaic and other artefacts survive from Greco-Roman times, but France is not rich in Roman art. The first works of art that can be called truly French are the sculptures in the Romanesque churches. These can be found on the capitals and around the doorways of churches in Burgundy and the Midi, and, at their best are sublime examples of folk art.

Though painting was an important art in the Romanesque period, few traces remain.

The early Gothic period was the age of stained glass and statuary, not of painting. French stained glass is a major art form, seen at its best at Chartres, Amiens, Bourges, Laon, Le Mans, Notre-Dame and the Sainte-Chapelle in Paris. The medieval art-form of manuscript illumination produced a late flowering and portraits and other easel pictures began to appear for the first time. Some of the finest art of the period was seen on tapestry hangings.

Renaissance art was dominated by Italian influences. Style in painting was mannered, while in sculpture more realistic forms, based on Classical models, began to appear. Mythological figures began to replace saints and virgins, and for the next two centuries palaces and parks were populated with them. But the greatest artistic products of this period are to be found in the parish closes of Brittany, with their triumphal arches and sculpted calvaries. These wonderful examples of local folk art are unique in form and content, fusing Romanesque, Gothic and Renaissance styles with a touch of the Celtic.

Baroque art swept across Europe with the Counter-Reformation, but had less influence in France than elsewhere. The age of Louis XIV reinforced stricter classical discipline and it was in this period that the first really French artistic movement emerged. French Classicism flourished in this reign, producing a number of great painters: Georges de La Tour, Claude Lorrain and Nicolas Poussin. The classical tradition continued into the eighteenth century, though Baroque tried to make a comeback. This led to the exotic style of Rococo, with its grottoes, gardens with 'follies', fake shepherds and shepherdesses and romantic ruins. Watteau was the foremost painter of this century, with Boucher and Fragonard in the same tradition.

Though the Revolution produced no great architecture, it did throw up one painter of stature — some say the greatest artist France has produced. Jacques-Louis David was the leading artist of the stern neo-Classical movement which overthrew Rococo in the later eighteenth century. But during the Revolution, he became the virtual art dictator of France. His most famous painting *The Assassination of Marat* (1793), is a moving memorial to a revolutionary martyr. He later became Napoleon's first painter.

The early nineteenth-century Romantic movement was a reaction against three centuries of Classicism. Its watchword was freedom, revolting against convention, tradition and social order, and extolling emotion, imagination, nature and the medieval past. Its two greatest representatives in painting are Géricault and Delacroix. Against them, Ingres maintained the strict classicism of his master, David.

Following the Romantics, French art always tended to be 'agin the government'. In the later nineteenth century, movement followed movement, each one challenging established values and authority. Authors and artists were seen as 'anti-establishment' or 'bohemian', living unconventional lives. A number of trials of artists took place — Balzac, Flaubert, Zola, Manet. In painting the first of these movements was Realism, led by Courbet and Manet. Manet's painting *Déjeuner sur l'Herbe*, showing a naked woman picnicking with two fully-dressed men, scandalised the nation.

Manet's work led to the next, and perhaps the greatest and best-known of French art movements, Impressionism. The Impressionists were trying to record visual sensation in its pure state, and were in effect the first 'modern' painters, in moving away from a natural representation of things as they are towards a subjective 'inner' view of them. The first wave of these — Monet, Pisarro and Sisley — were the 'pure' Impressionists, followed by those with a more personal and eccentric vision — Renoir, Degas, Toulouse-Lautrec, Cézanne, Gauguin and Van Gogh.

The work of the later Impressionists led to three early twentieth-century movements: Fauvism (Vlaminck, Dufy, Matisse); Cubism (Braque, Picasso); and Abstractionism. These were followed in the inter-war years by Dadaism, Surrealism and Pure Abstract art. Other French artists, like Douanier Rousseau, Bonnard, Rouault, Léger and Chagall, chose to develop their own individual styles.

Artistic Haunts

Many places in France have associations with French artists. The most obvious one is Montmartre, in Paris, that crazy art colony on the hill (La Butte) where many Impressionist painters lived and worked, and where Cubism was born. Today it is full of less illustrious artists and their hangers-on, but still happy and thriving on its memories. Provence is also Impressionist terrain, particularly round Arles, where Van Gogh spent his last days going mad in the sun, and in the countryside of Mont St Victoire near Aix-en-Provence, where Cézanne painted many of his masterpieces. You can visit his studio in Aix, preserved just as it looked when he died in 1906. At least four Paris museums are dedicated to individual artists: Delacroix, Moreau, Picasso and Rodin; and Monet's house and garden at Giverny, preserved as a museum, is a most popular tourist attractions of northern France. Here, where the Epte joins the Seine, you can see the water-garden, with its Japanese bridge and luminous water-lilies, that inspired his most impressionist works.

Scenes like the Tunnels de Fayet waterfall have given inspiration to artists

THE OTHER ARTS

Literature

If you are a lover of French literature, there are a number of 'pilgrimages' you can make to literary 'shrines'. You can visit the houses in which writers were born, lived or died; or you can visit the town or countryside in which they set their novels or plays, or which inspired them to write their poems or philosophical treatises. You may come across these accidentally in your travels, or you may seek them out according to your literary enthusiasms. A visit to the home of a favourite author, especially if it has been turned into a museum, can be the high point of a holiday.

Sometimes a region has become associated with a particular writer or work of fiction. The area round Chinon in the Loire Valley is Rabelais territory — he was born on the estate of La Devinière nearby (where there is a museum), and all his place-names are derived from the neighbourhood. If you have read Zola's *Germinal*, the mining villages of the north-east near Lille will forever recall the grim scenes in that novel. Other associations are more tenuous: D'Artagnan was a companion of the Three Musketeers in the Alexander Dumas novel, and was known by them as Le petit Garçon. He was apparently based on a real person born at Castelmore in the Armagnac, and he has become a symbol of the region.

Music

France has always had a lively musical tradition, from the polyphonic music of the Middle Ages to modern composers like Milhaud and Poulenc. In the summer season, concerts of various kinds are widely held in churches and public halls throughout France, especially in tourist areas. Music festivals are held mainly in the summer, the best-known ones outside Paris being at Bordeaux and Strasbourg. There is a Berlioz festival in Lyon in September. One very popular musical form is jazz. Since the days of Le Hot Club de Paris in the 1930s, with its legendary gipsy guitarist, Django Reinhardt, and violinist, Stephane Grapelli, France has always had a strong jazz tradition, and its summer jazz festivals attract musicians from all over the world. The best-known jazz festivals are at Antibes (in July) and Paris (in October).

Theatre And Film

Paris is the centre of the French theatre. Though there are many avant garde and experimental theatres, the classical theatre maintains its exacting standards at its traditional home, the Comédie Française. Here the works of the three great playwrights — Corneille, Racine and Molière — are regularly performed. More international works are staged at the Odéon on the Left Bank. The theatres on the *grands boulevards* are the home of popular, long-running plays, while the tiny *café-théâtres* provide satirical cabaret or controversial drama.

The famous Opéra (de Paris-Garnier) is now the seat of the National Ballet company, while the National Opera performs at the Opéra-Bastille. At the other end of the spectrum is Pigalle, with its famous (or notorious) nightclubs. Some of these are now even sleazier than they used to be, but in the heart of Montmartre remains the glorious Moulin Rouge, still staging its boisterous and irreverent floor-shows. The days of Toulouse-Lautrec and the Belle Époque may have gone, but the world's most famous *boite de nuit* soldiers on. The famous music halls, the Folies-Bergère and the Casino de Paris, continue drawing their audiences in the same tradition.

Provincial theatre is alive and well but, as in Britain, the cinema is more popular with the masses. In Paris alone there are over 200 cinemas, most of them well patronised–queues are common, but you can usually get in. Though foreign films are widely shown, the French film industry is buoyant, and there are plenty of opportunities to sample the home-grown product. Festivals of both theatre and film are of world-wide repute: for the theatre, the Avignon Festival, held in July, is popular with the avant garde, while the Cannes Film Festival every May is the most prestigious event in the world of the cinema.

1

THE NORTH-EAST

The inhabitants of this flat area of north-east France are fiercely proud of their land and sentimental about its attractions. It is not a land that immediately reveals its charms to the visitor, yet it is worth exploring for its own sake. The strip between Béthune and Valenciennes on the Belgian border, the coal-mining country of Zola's *Germinal*, is still France's 'black country' and unappealing to the tourist, though some of the towns and villages are giving themselves a face-lift and new technology is replacing some of the smoke-stacks and blast furnaces. But the rest of the region has a variety of scenery, and a wealth of culture and history, that make it worth a prolonged stay.

The far north-east, towards the Belgian border, is the true flat country of French Flanders. Broken only by the 175m (574ft) high Mont Cassel, it is dotted with windmills and criss-crossed with dykes, blending forest with agricul-tural land. Its towns are built in Flemish-style red brick, with canals running alongside the streets reminiscent of Venice. West of this, between Calais and Boulogne, is the Boulonnais, part of the Regional Park of the Pas de Calais. It is chalk downland country, undulating and open, with a coastline of fine chalk cliffs and sandy beaches called, poetically, the Opal Coast. Further south is the undulating, sparsely-populated farmland of Artois, crossed by valleys of the rivers Canche, Authie and Somme. In the south-east, south of the Lille-Valencienne industrial belt, is the Avesnois, a charming area of green fields and hedges, flowered villages, pretty churches and water-mills.

The region has its architectural splendours, from the superb high Gothic cathedral at Amiens to the magnificent Flemish-style centre of Arras with its belfried Town Hall and squares of gabled houses. Its museums include one of the richest art museums in France, the Palais des Beaux-Arts in Lille. It is rich in folklore too, with its famous 'Giants' — immense wickerwork figures representing legendary local heroes, which appear in processions on feast-days. The people of the north are in some ways a race apart from other Frenchmen, who regard them as 'honorary Belgians'. They play darts and skittles instead of *boules*, drink beer instead of wine, and even keep pigeons!

Above all, this region is the cock-pit of Europe, ravaged by war throughout the centuries. The countryside is itself a museum of man's inhumanity to man, with medieval battlefields jostling for attention with the vast graveyards of two World Wars. It is a place for the traveller to stop and reflect.

The tour begins and ends at **Calais**. This is the most popular landing point for British invaders past and present, and its history is interwoven with England's. It was an English possession for over 200 years, only lost in Mary

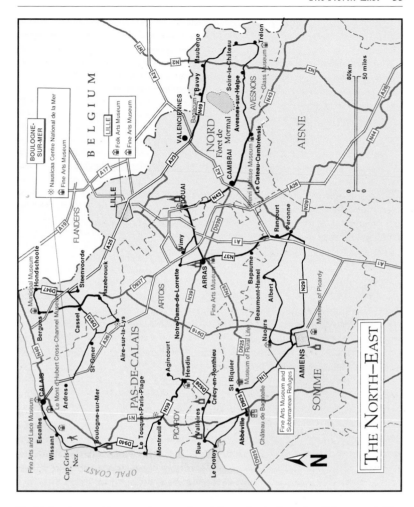

Tudor's reign and its most impressive sight today is the splendid memorial by Rodin to the Burghers of Calais who offered their lives to save the city after Edward III,s conquest in 1347 (he spared them). Today Calais is a busy passenger port and industrial centre, specialising in lace and other textiles. The Fine Arts Museum has a section on the city's English-inspired lace industry. Also English-inspired is the town church of Notre Dame, the only example of English Perpendicular Gothic in France.

The Opal Coast
Avoid the rather drab suburbs by heading for the *centre ville*. The Rodin group statue is in front of the imposing Town Hall with its 75m (246ft) high belfry, built this century in Flemish Renaissance style. Take the coast road D940 past a long stretch of fine sandy beach with many facilities and begin your drive along the most scenic part of the Opal Coast (so named on account of its white waves). In 6km (3 miles) is Sangatte, where the Flanders plain becomes the

hilly Boulonnais and where the Channel Tunnel emerges. There is a Eurotunnel information centre just beyond Sangatte. Further on, at Cap Blanc Nez, is a memorial to the unsuccessful cross-channel aviator H. Latham and a monument to the Dover Patrol, with fine views across the channel to Dover. Just behind, on the Mont d'Hubert near the village of **Escalles**, is a curious small museum dedicated to 'the Mad Adventure of the Dover Straits'. Called the Cross-Channel (Transmanche) Museum, it tells the story of the attempts to cross that treacherous stretch of water since earliest times. It has a restaurant with a panoramic view, and a small display of Calais lace.

Wissant is an attractive, flowery village with some good restaurants, a small museum in the old mill and a fine beach. Nearby, just off the main road, **Cap Gris-Nez** is the highest point on the cliffs and has a coastal path with good views. This is where the Channel becomes the North Sea. Inland, **Audinghen** has a curious modern church in the shape of a boat. The whole of this part of the Opal Coast is riddled with foxholes, bunkers and other fortifications from the last war — this is where Hitler thought the Allies would land, and built his defences accordingly. Just beyond Audinghen, near an attractive camp-site, is a former blockhouse housing the Museum of the Atlantic Wall, and evocative site whose structure, equipment, claustrophobic atmosphere and musty smell recall those grim times. Beyond here the coast flattens out, and the quiet holiday villages of Audresselles and Ambleteuse, nestling in the dunes, precede the busy resort of **Wimereux**, with its air of slightly-faded charm. Just beyond, on the outskirts of Boulogne, is the new, ultra-modern Nausicaa national sea-life centre, claimed to be one of the most important in the world. It has a tropical lagoon, a shark-viewing aquarium, and a 3,000m (9,840ft) deep marine observation tank.

Boulogne-sur-Mer is a more attractive town than Calais on account of its setting and upper town. The old walled upper town stands on a hill behind the port, the medieval ramparts enclosing a château, some fine old houses, a splendid Gothic belfry and the huge Basilica of Notre-Dame, whose enormous dome is the town's great landmark. Just below the walls is a Fine Arts Museum with a splendid collection of Greek vases and other antiquities. This was the port from which Julius Caesar sailed to invade Britain and from which Napoleon more recently planned a similar invasion. The museum contains details of this, including English cartoons ridiculing his attempt. Boulogne is a thriving town, proud of its position as the major fishing port of the EEC. One of its attractions is an excellent range of fish restaurants to suit all pockets.

Continue on the D940 out of Boulogne towards Le Touquet. You pass through pine-wooded sand dunes, by-passing the resorts of Equihen-Plage and Hardelot-Plage and a long, windswept sandy beach which is much-frequented by windsurfers and sand-yachters. Reaching **Étaples**, a colourful fishing port beloved of artists, turn right for **Le Touquet-Paris-Plage**. This elegant sea and health resort at the mouth of the Canche was once fashionable with British visitors, who virtually created it. It is now more cosmopolitan and less trendy than earlier in the century, though still smart and expensive. It consists largely of large mock-gothic or mock-tudor villas half-hidden in the woods, but has a stylish shopping centre and extensive sports facilities. The nearby resort of **Berck-Plage** is much more down-market, attracting hordes of visitors on summer weekends from the industrial towns of Picardy.

The Picardy River Valleys

Back in Étaples, turn inland and follow the N39 along the flowery Canche valley to **Montreuil**. This was once *sur mer* until the sea receded, leaving it impressively sited on a bluff above the river. It is a charming small town completely contained within the brick ramparts built by Vauban as a defence for Louis XIVs armies; the town was later used as a base of operations by the Allies. It has an imposing seventeenth-century citadel, an attractive central square and a grassy, wooded walk around the ramparts, with fine views and some good restaurants. Continue along the Canche valley to **Hesdin**, a small town with a wide cobbled market square, on one side of which is the town hall with a magnificently ornate seventeenth-century bay-window, and inside a small museum with Flemish tapestries. A short detour north along the D928 towards St Omer brings you to the battlefield of **Agincourt**. Sadly, but understandably, there is little to see at the site of this most ignominious of French defeats by the English in 1415 — only a cross marking the ground and, in the nearby church of Auchy-lès-Hesdin, the tombs of some of the French knights who fell in the battle.

Return to Hesdin and continue south on the D928 for 15km (9 miles), then turn right on the D938. This will shortly bring you to the site of another famous English victory over the French, **Crécy-en-Ponthieu**. Again there is little to commemorate the battle of Crécy in 1346, which started the Hundred Years War and gave England 200 years of domination over the French: only a cross dedicated to the blind king of Bohemia who died in the battle and an old mill, the Moulin Edouard III, giving views over the battlefield. Much more interesting is the nearby Cistercian abbey of **Valloires**, nestling in the Authie Valley about 12km (7 miles) north of Crécy. Founded in the twelfth century, it was rebuilt in the eighteenth century in a harmonious blend of brick and stone, and contains some lovely wood panelling and wrought-iron work in the splendid interior. Return to the D938 and continue westwards to **Rue**, an attractive small town near the Somme estuary. This has old streets with half-timbered houses, a pretty market square with a fine fifteenth-century belfry above the town hall, and, in front of the parish church, the marvellous Gothic Chapel of St Esprit. Inside are three finely-carved vaults, to the Father, Son and Holy Spirit, and two treasury rooms, one on top of the other: the upper one with marvellous carvings of biblical scenes, the lower with a beautiful painted sculpture of the Virgin and Child on the wall.

Rue was once a seaport, and is now the principal town of the reclaimed broad coastal plain between the Somme and Authie estuaries called the **Marquenterre**. It is a wild, marshy land of lakes and ditches, a refuge for birds and a haunt of bird-watchers. Cross the plain on the D940 to the Somme estuary, where the two attractive old fishing ports of **Le Crotoy** and **St Valéry-sur-Somme** face each other across the bay. Much of the estuary has now silted up and you can walk across and fish in the pools at low tide. St Valéry has a pleasant promenade walk and a ramparted upper town. This was where Duke William of Normandy sailed from in 1066 to attack the forces of King Harold of England (whom he had saved from a shipwreck here 17 years before) at Hastings, an event that changed the course of English history. Continue from here alongside the Canal de la Somme to **Abbéville**, a sizeable town on the N1 trunk road. Once beautiful, with many old buildings, it was almost com-

One of the faster ways of travelling to France is by hovercraft

Wissant, with its charming buildings, makes a popular stop for the tourist

The Château-folly of Bagatelle was allegedly built for a king's mistress

pletely destroyed in World War II and is now unattractive; but it has a fine Flamboyant Gothic church of St Wulfram with carved doorways and, nearby, a museum with collections of birds and prehistoric objects. But Abbéville's jewel is the small, exquisite building on the south side of town, the Château-folly of **Bagatelle**. This bijou pink and white château was built about 1750, reputedly for a king's mistress. Open to the public in summer, it has period furniture inside and a pretty garden.

From Abbéville, take the D925 east to **St Riquier**. Here, in a sleepy village, in a square set back from the road, stands a stunningly ornate Flamboyant Gothic abbey church, all that remains of a once-important Benedictine monastery. The richly and delicately-carved white stone façade matches the imposing interior, which has a splendid Renaissance baptistery, seventeenth-century furnishings in the choir, and a treasury. St Riquier also has a small museum of rural life in the old abbey buildings, a beautiful chapel in the old hospital, and a small, squat sixteenth-century belfry in the square, quaintly housing the local Syndicat d'Initiative.

From here, follow the Somme upstream to **Amiens**, the capital of Picardy. A thriving textile town known for fine velvet, Amiens is large and busy. Much rebuilt after being 60 per cent destroyed in World War II, it is generally lacking in tourist appeal: an ultra-modern centre surrounded by drab suburbs. But it has one great attraction which was mercifully not destroyed in the war — the Notre-Dame Cathedral in the city centre. This is one of the architectural wonders of France, if not the world, a high-Gothic building of rare beauty and breathtaking proportions. It is the largest cathedral in France, and the purest in style, having been mainly completed in 50 years in the thirteenth century. As you turn from a busy street into the cathedral square the impact is staggering. The richly-ornate façade, decked with beautiful sculptures, takes your eye soaring up to the twin towers of uneven heights but perfect proportion, the one with its small gabled spire balancing the flatness of the other. Inside, the effect of the huge, high nave (the longest in France) is breathtaking and the church is a treasure-house of statuary, stained glass, carving in wood and stone, and goldsmith's work. The carved figures in the choir are particularly fine. Amiens also boasts the fine Museum of Picardy, with a unique collection of sixteenth-century altar-paintings on wood.

The Killing Fields

The Somme Valley between Amiens and Péronne, and the land to the north towards Arras, are dotted with villages whose names are all-too-familiar to students of World War I. This area of Artois and Picardy is the world's chief battlefield and though souvenirs of the many battles fought over the centuries are thick on the ground, it is well to be selective. The spirit can be overwhelmed by the sadness and futility of so much suffering and wasted life.

North of Amiens, near the mud-walled village of **Naours**, is a large network of underground refuges, dug out by hand through the centuries by local people to hide from the wars that raged around them. There are 2km (1 mile) of long rooms, able to hold up to 3,000 people, in this subterranean city 30m (98ft) below ground. Inside is a folklore museum (open daily). The Memorial Park of Beaumont-Hamel, between Albert and Bapaume, has World War I trenches still in their original state, giving a graphic picture of army life under trench warfare. The park also contains a 'caribou' monument to the Canadian Newfoundland regiment; while nearby, at Thiepval, is a huge 15-pillared memorial arch, bearing 73,000 names, to the British soldiers killed here in World War I. Of the many cemeteries in the region, all distinguished in their nationality by the colour or shape of the memorial crosses or gravestones (the German ones have black crosses), those at Rancourt, Bray-sur-Somme and Villers-Bretonneux are typical and moving examples.

Further north, between Arras and Lens in Artois, is the site of one of the bloodiest of World War I battles — **Vimy Ridge**. The whole of this region north of Arras was the scene of particularly violent fighting both in 1915 and 1940, and the sites on the crests overlooking the town (Les Crêtes du Sacrifice) have been well preserved. Vimy Ridge itself has a massive memorial to the 74,000 Canadians who died in France, and below, on the wooded south slope of the ridge, the original World War I trenches can still be seen. Nearby, at **Notre-Dame-de-Lorette**, is a French national cemetery and a large ossuary containing the remains of 26,000 unidentified soldiers. The ossuary houses a small museum and just below this desolate site, near the Cabaret-Rouge cemetery outside Souchez, is an informative Museum-Diorama of the Battlefields.

The region west and north of Amiens is not only of interest for its war memorials. **Péronne** has an attractive town centre and has retained some of its ancient ramparts; **Bertangles** has a pretty eighteenth-century stone château; at **Vaux** there is a belvédère with a fine view over the Somme and its many green islets covered with market-gardens, many dating from the Middle Ages; and then there is **Arras** itself. This town, the capital of Artois, has a dingy exterior but a glorious interior — the old centre with its two arcaded, cobbled squares, the Grand Place and the Place des Héros, overlooked by its Gothic

Town Hall and splendid belfry, surmounted by its town lion. Happily Arras, unlike most towns in the region, has preserved its old centre from the devastations of war; as a consequence you can enjoy one of the most complete and harmonious town ensembles in Europe. The seventeenth-century Flemish-style houses with pilasters and elegant curving gables are arcaded at ground level and give a distinctly Dutch appearance to the town. Below ground are the deep cellars, used as hiding places during the various wars. The narrow streets lead to the huge Cathedral of St Vaast, containing enormous statues of saints, with a richly-endowed Fine Arts Museum in the Benedictine abbey. Other interesting buildings are an eighteenth-century theatre and an old Fisherman's Guild building, decorated with sirens and fish.

On leaving Arras, one excursion into the nearby mining belt is worth making. In 25km (15^1/$_2$ miles) on the N50 is **Douai**, capital of the coal country and a university town. It is famed for two things: its Gothic belfry and its wickerwork giant, called *Gayant*. The former is claimed to be the handsomest of all the northern bell-towers, and it is certainly the best-known, thanks to a famous Corot painting. Grey, spiky, with yet another Flanders lion on top, it has a 62-bell carillon, the largest in Europe. The latter is renowned in local folklore, being based on one Jehan Gelon who saved the town from a band of brigands in the Middle Ages. 'Gayant de Douai' is the best known *géant* in France, and appears on feast days, running and dancing among the people by day and retiring at night accompanied by fanfares and fireworks. Douai has a number of fine buildings, including an old charterhouse housing a fine museum with Flemish primitives.

The Avesnois

The tour now heads east on the N43 towards the Avesnois, arriving first at **Cambrai**, the 'town of three towers' (two churches and a belfry). It has a pleasant central square, built largely of white limestone, a reasonable art museum and a Rubens in the church of St Géry. Further on, **Le Cateau-Cambrésis** was the birthplace of the modern painter Matisse, and an exhibition of his paintings can be seen in the former Archbishops' Palace. The old Town Hall has a charming bell-tower. On by the D959, at Landrecies you skirt the vast Forêt de Normal, the largest forest in northern France and a good place for walks and picnics. At Maroilles, famous for its delicious but smelly cheese, take the D962 to **Avesnes-sur-Helpe**, capital of the pastoral Avesnois. This was an old fortified frontier town perched high on the river bank, and some of Vauban's strong walls remain. It has an elegant town hall and a church with beautiful altar-pieces, and is a good base to explore the surrounding area.

The **Avesnois**, tucked into a fold of the Belgian border, is reminiscent of southern England or Normandy. It has green fields, hedges, grazing cattle producing milk for that Maroilles cheese, water-mills still working, and charming villages bedecked with flowers. Strongly catholic, it is dotted with oratories and shrines. The area has good leisure facilities, with many woods and lakes. A suggested route is through **Fourmies**, an important textile centre with an Ecomuseum in an old cotton mill; **Ohain** with a beautiful statue of Christ scourged in the sixteenth-century chapel; **Trélon**, a former glass-making town with a Glass Museum; **Moustier-en-Fagne**, with a sixteenth-century priory and charming manor-house; **Eppe-Sauvage**, passing the man-made lake of Val Joly; **Liessies**, with its church full of treasures from a nearby abbey; **Soire-le-Château**, a lovely old town with many fine buildings; and **Sars-Poteries**, an important earthenware, ceramic and glass centre with a fascinating museum, and with a barrel-making museum at nearby **Felleries**. From here, return to Avesnes or go north to Mauberge.

Mauberge is an industrial centre but has buildings of interest: the Mons Gate (1665), the fortified church of St Pierre, a Baroque Jesuit College, a regional museum, and a zoo. Turning west on the N49, you reach **Bavay**, a town interesting for its long history as the legendary capital of Gallo-Roman Belgium. Excavations have revealed the foundations of the ancient city of *Bagacum*, on the intersection of seven Roman roads. A small museum holds many of the findings. The final call before heading back north is **Le Quesnoy**. This is a rare example of an intact Vauban citadel with a complete system of town walls, once a strong defence for the town and now a pleasant walk. At their foot is a leisure centre with two small lakes. The fifteenth-century Town Hall has a striking eighteenth-century tower, and nearby is the small thirteenth-century moated château of Potelle.

Amiens Cathedral, one of France's greatest examples of Gothic architecture

French Flanders

The route north-west along the Belgian border passes first through **Valenciennes**, an industrial town but the birthplace of many artists, including Watteau, to whom it has dedicated a square and fountain. It has two interesting churches, two museums, and a library with some rare old manuscripts. After that you pass through the Lille-Roubaix-Tourcoing industrial belt. Fortunately motorways can take you speedily through this region; but you should at least make one stop, to visit **Lille**, the capital of French Flanders. Lille has diversified and is prospering in its central position at the EEC crossroads. It has its own proud traditions, and much to impress the visitor. It has the finest and best-preserved Vauban citadel along the whole Franco-Belgian border. Amongst its treasures are the impressive seventeenth to eighteenth-century Flemish-style buildings in the old town, notably the Old Stock Exchange, a modern Palais de Justice, a Flamboyant Gothic church (St Maurice), and the richest Fine Arts Museum outside Paris. This has a comprehensive collection of paintings from Old Masters to Impressionists, particularly strong in the seventeenth-century Dutch and Flemish schools. There is also a fine Folk Art Museum housed in a thirteenth-century hospice.

From Lille, rejoin the A25 motorway as far as Steenvoorde. You are now in the flat Flanders plain, with its heavily-cultivated fields, dykes and windmills. Windmills can be of different shapes and materials, but are basically of two types — the 'pivot' type where the whole mill revolves to face the wind, and the solid tower type with a revolving roof. A fine example, open to visitors, is the windmill built in 1127 near **Hondschoote**, a Flemish-speaking village on the Belgian border. Nearby **Bergues** is picturesque and typically Flemish, with low houses built in brick and tile, quaint old streets, a fine but reproduction belfry, an excellent museum, and brick fortifications by Vauban. Further

---

Northern Cuisine

This is the region of the *frite*. Chips, or french fries, are eaten on their own or with any savoury dish, for instance mussels. At one of the many roadside snack-wagons, *frites* are served in conical bags with mayonnaise or mustard (optional). A popular accompaniment is a Frankfurter sausage.

Fish is a speciality of the area, both fresh and salt-water, and is often eaten pickled — salted and smoked herrings and pilchards, rollmops and *bouffi*. Eels are popular, eaten fresh, smoked or in pâtés. Shellfish are widely found — shrimps, cockles, mussels and the excellent North Sea oysters.

The north is known for two savoury dishes: the *carbonnade flamande*, a beef stew cooked in beer with a bread and mild mustard crust; and the *waterzoï*, freshwater fish or chicken in a creamy stew. Another popular stew is *lapin aux pruneaux*, or rabbit with prunes. *Andouillettes*, the tripe sausages found throughout France, are really a speciality of Troyes and the Champagne district, but are commonly made and eaten in the north too.

A popular local vegetable is the endive, or chicory and coffee is often drunk mixed with this. Sea-fennel, a marine plant which they call *passe-pierre*, is often eaten as a vegetable.

The main alcoholic drink is beer, both brewed locally and from Belgium. There is a greater variety of Belgian beers, and they are often stronger than the normal blond *Stella Artois* or *Jupiler*.

inland is **Cassel**, a little town perched on the only hill in the area (Mont Cassel, 175m, 574ft), topped by a wooden mill and giving panoramic views of the surrounding plain. Cassel is a town with a typically Flemish long central square of low painted brick houses, narrow sloping streets and flights of steps.

Two other towns in the area are worth a detour. **Hazebrouck** is a smart and busy town, with the nearby forest of Nieppe providing pleasant walks; and back in Artois, **Aire-sur-la-Lys** has an air of faded grandeur with its *Ancien Régime* style houses and streets. The classical Town hall with belfry and carillon, the Renaissance Bailiff's Court and the Flamboyant Gothic church are worthy of note. From here you rejoin the N43 back to Calais, passing through **St Omer**, a quiet but sizeable town on the Flanders-Artois border. The old town is dominated by the large but perfectly-proportioned Basilica of Notre-Dame, a beautiful ex-cathedral containing fine works of art, including an astronomical clock dated 1558. Of the many fine seventeenth- and eighteenth-century houses in the town, the Hôtel Sandelin has a monumental doorway and contains a good Fine Arts Museum. The marshes to the north, or *watergangs*, were reclaimed over 1,000 years ago by Omer, the town's founder, and his companions, and now form a network of 3,000km (1,860 miles) of canals, supporting an active community of watermen.

The road back to Calais undulates at first, then after Ardres levels out across the coastal plain. **Ardres** is worth a stop. It has a pleasant, quiet town centre and some good restaurants. From here, cross the Canal de Calais at the Pont d'Ardres and return to Calais to complete your tour.

Additional Information

Places of Interest

Calais
Fine Arts and Lace Museum
Open: 10am-12noon and 2-5pm daily.
Closed Tuesday.

Escalles
Le Mont d'Hubert Cross-Channel Museum
Open: 10am-12noon and 2-6pm daily.
Closed January.

Audinghen — Cap Gris-Nez
Museum 39/45 of the Atlantic Wall
Open: daily 1 March to 30 November in a German blockhouse.

Boulogne-sur-Mer
Nausicaa Centre National de la Mer
☎ 21 30 98 98
Open: daily 10am-8pm April to September, 10am-6pm October to March.

Fine Arts Museum
No 34 Grande-Rue
Open: 9.30am-12noon and 2-6pm
Wednesday to Sunday.

Abbéville
Château de Bagatelle
Open: 2-6.30pm, closed Tuesday July to September.

St Riquier
Museum of Rural Life
In abbey buildings
Open: 10am-12noon and 2-6pm daily June to September, 2-6pm Saturday and Sunday, April, May and October.

Amiens
Museum of Picardy
48 Rue de la République
Open: 10am-12noon and 2-6pm, closed Monday.

Notre-Dame-de-Lorette
Museum-Diorama of the Battlefields
Open: April to November daily, afternoon only; June to August 10am-6pm except Sunday morning.

Arras
Fine Arts Museum
In abbey of St Vaast

Open: 10am-12noon and 2-5pm daily, except Tuesday.

Douai
Museum
In former charterhouse
Open: 10am-12noon and 2-5pm, except Tuesday.

Le Cateau-Cambrésis
Henri Matisse Museum
In former Archbishops' Palace
Open: 3-6pm Wednesday to Saturday, closed Monday and Tuesday, 10am-12noon and 2-6pm Sunday.

Fourmies
Ecomuseum
In former cotton mill
Open: daily 9am-12noon and 2-6pm May to October.

Trélon
Glass Museum and Workshop
Open: daily Easter to 15 October.

Felleries
Barrel-Making Museum
In old mill
Open: 2.30-6.30pm Sunday and national holidays, April to June and September to November; daily July to August.

Bavay
Excavations and Museum of Ancient Bagacum
Open: 9am-12noon and 2-5pm daily except Tuesday; Sunday and national holidays 9.30am-12noon and 2-7pm (2-5pm winter).

Lille
Palais des Beaux Arts Fine Arts Museum
Open: 9.30am-12.30pm and 2-5pm, closed Tuesday and holidays.

Folk Arts Museum
In the Hospice Comtesse
Open: 10am-12.30pm and 2-5pm, closed Tuesday.

Bergues
Municipal Museum
In Mont-de-Piété
Open: 10am-12noon and 2-5pm, closed Friday.

St Omer
Fine Arts Museum
In Hôtel Sandelin
Open: 10am-12noon and 2-6pm

Wednesday and Sunday; Thursday and Friday morning only.

Tourist Information Centres

Amiens
Office de Tourisme
Rue J-Catelas
☎ 22 91 79 28

Arras
Office de Tourisme
L'Hôtel de Ville
☎ 21 51 26 95

Avesnes-sur-Helpe
Syndicat d'Initiative
41 Place Géneral-Leclerc
☎ 27 57 92 40

Boulogne-sur-Mer
Office de Tourisme
Quai de la Poste
☎ 21 31 68 38

Calais
Office de Tourisme and Accueil de France
12 Boulevard Clemenceau
☎ 21 96 62 40

Lille
Office de Tourisme and Accueil de France
Palais Rihour
☎ 20 30 81 00

Restaurants

R = With Accommodation
Haute cuisine restaurants include:

Amiens
(at Dury — 6km, 4 miles south on N1)
L'Aubergade
☎ 22 89 51 41

Arras
La Faisanderie
☎ 21 48 20 76

Boulogne
La Matelote
☎ 21 30 17 97

Dunkerque
(at Téteghem)
La Meunerie (R)
☎ 28 26 01 80

La Madeleine-sous-Montreuil
Auberge la Grenouillère (R)
☎ 21 06 07 22

Le Touquet-Paris-Plage
Flavio-Club de la Forêt
☎ 21 05 10 22

Lille
Le Restaurant
☎ 20 57 05 05

Le Flambard
☎ 20 51 00 06

A L'Huitrière
☎ 20 55 43 41

Paris
☎ 20 55 29 41

Loos
Nr Lille
L'Enfant Terrible
☎ 20 07 22 11

Lumbres
Moulin de Mombreux (R)
☎ 21 39 62 44

Montreuil
Château de Montreuil (R)
☎ 21 81 53 04

Pont-de-Briques
Nr. Boulogne
Host de la Rivière (R)
☎ 21 32 22 81

Sars-Poteries (Avesnois)
L'Auberge Fleurie
☎ 27 61 62 48

Other restaurants, offering good value
for money, include:
Ardres
Grand Hôtel Clément (R)
☎ 82 25 25

Le Relais (R)
☎ 21 35 42 00

Boulogne
La Liègeoise
☎ 21 31 61 15

La Huitrière
☎ 21 31 35 27

Calais
Le Channel
☎ 21 34 42 30

La Sole Meunière
☎ 21 34 43 01

Cambrai
La Buissonnière
☎ 27 85 29 97

Favières
(near Rue)
La Clé des Champs
☎ 22 27 88 00

Sains-du-Nord
(Avesnois)
Le Centre (R)
☎ 27 59 15 02

St Omer
Le Cygne
☎ T21 98 20 52

Host St-Hubert
(6km, 4 miles)
☎ 21 39 77 77

2

NORMANDY

Today, Normandy is a region of France with its own clear identity and 'style'. Since those Norsemen sailed up the Seine in the ninth century to claim their own territory from a weak French crown, and their duke Rollo founded a dynasty leading directly to the Conqueror of England 150 years later, they have settled down and assimilated into their adopted country as true Frenchmen.

It is an area with much to offer the visitor. It has a variety of scenery, from the high, often dramatic chalk cliffs and shingle beaches of the north-east coast to the long sandy beaches further west; from the lush farmlands of the north and the Seine valley to the harsh, granite scrubland of the south-west Brittany border; from the flat pasturelands of the Cotentin peninsula to the rolling hills of the Alpes Mancelles and the Suisse Normande. Normandy has two distinct halves and two capital cities. Rouen is the capital of the land lying to the north and east of the Seine, including the Pays de Caux, the Pays de Bray, the Vexin and the Quatre Vallées, while the larger area west of the Seine, including the Pays d'Auge, the Perche and the Cotentin, look towards Caen as their chief city. The east regards Paris and the Île de France as its spiritual centre, while the west and south have more independent traditions.

William was not only a conqueror but a born administrator, and his skills were part of the Norman legacy of firm government, as seen in the Feudal System. This is reflected in their architecture, with soundly constructed buildings sparse in decoration. The great abbeys, châteaux and manor houses which are the pride of this region have a gaunt but elegant solidity which transforms the styles of Romanesque, Gothic or Renaissance into something distinctly 'Norman'. But this sparseness is not reflected in their generosity or large appetites. They are a hospitable people who are only too willing to share the rich produce of their fertile country — butter, cream, cheese, fish, meat, vegetables, fruit, cider and apple brandy — with the visitor.

One legacy of the more recent past has scarred the region, however. If north-east France has suffered from the ravages of World War I, Normandy has been battered by World War II. The D-Day Landing of 6 June 1944 and its aftermath destroyed many of its northern towns, leaving for the visitor the more sombre tourist attractions of invasion beaches, graves and war museums.

This is not a circular tour, nor does it cover the whole of the region. It starts in the north-east, at Le Tréport, and takes a winding course through some of the more attractive or interesting parts of Normandy, ending in the south at Alençon.

The Alabaster Coast

Le Tréport is not the most picturesque spot to start the tour. However, it has a pleasant harbour and an impressive church overlooking the port, and a calvary on the cliffs above (the cable car up to it is out of action) giving a fine view.

For a more attractive town, travel 4km (2 miles) down the industrial Bresle estuary to **Eu**. This has a pretty, pedestrianised centre with some good shops (excellent oysters at the fishmonger's), the fine Gothic Collegiate church of Notre Dame and St Laurent O'Toole (the Primate of Ireland who died here in the twelfth century), a College chapel, château and museum. A stone in the main square commemorates the fact that the future William the Conqueror was married here. The nearby large Eu forest is pleasant for picnics, with some beautiful beech glades.

Crossing the rich but monotonous coastal plateau of Caux on the D925 brings you first to **Criel-sur-Mer**, a quiet village with a pleasant fourteenth-century church, part rebuilt, and a handsome sixteenth-century manor house, the Manoir de Briançon, which houses the town hall and the Syndicat d'Initiative. Here the chalk cliffs are steep, with small shingle beaches, and the coastal villages of Criel-Plage and Val-Mesnil look rather run-down, though there are some good restaurants and camp-sites in the area. From here, turn inland to follow the pretty chalk-banked valley of the Yères, among lush fields and apple orchards, as far as the village of **St Martin le Gaillard**. This has a thirteenth-century church with a slender, flat-topped spire, typical of the region, and some quaint carved capitals inside. There are also some splendid Norman granges and a ruined feudal castle which is now used as a farm. From here cross country on the D22 to **Envermeu**, a sleepy little town with an unusual incomplete Gothic church (fine interior with lovely choir and spiral columns), and an excellent restaurant.

Leaving Envermeu by the D149, pass through St Nicholas d'Aliermont, a long straggly town known for the manufacture of precision goods, to **Arques-la-Bataille**. This is also industrial, but famous for a great battle, when Henry IV, the Protestant 'king without a kingdom', held out against and finally defeated the Catholic League in 1589. The town nestles beneath a rocky promontory topped by one of the most striking feudal ruins in northern France, now overgrown, half-demolished and slightly eerie. You can walk right round the ramparts, seeing the castle from different aspects and gaining splendid views of the coastal plain. Just off the D54 near Arques is the seventeenth-century château of **Miromesnil**, the birthplace of the master of the short story *Guy de Maupassant*. It is a stylish château with a pretty garden and a statue of the writer in the grounds. Nearby **Offranville** has a 1,000-year-old yew in the village square.

The busy seaport of **Dieppe** is only 6km (4 miles) from here. It claims to be the oldest seaside resort in France, and it is certainly a popular one, not least with the English who come across on short excursions for the shops and restaurants. It has a long shingle beach with seafront promenade, a castle on the cliff above, a deep and large harbour, and a pleasant, partly-pedestrian-ised old town, with some good fish restaurants. There are two museums: one in the château, telling of the town's maritime history and, 2km (1 mile) west, a war museum commemorating the abortive Canadian Commando raid in 1942, when 5,000 men were killed or taken prisoner. Dieppe is a pleasant resort for a short stay, though busy in summer.

Take the cliff road out of Dieppe to Pourville-sur-Mer (D75), passing the museum dedicated to 19 August 1942 en route. On the left, on entering Varengeville, is a charming sixteenth-century manor house called the Manoir d'Ango. Jean Ango, Governor of Dieppe from 1535, was shipbuilder and maritime counsellor to King Francis I, achieving wealth and fame by organ-ising a fleet of privateers to destroy the Portuguese sea power. This was his country residence, a delightful building of ornamental brick and stone, with a beautiful ornate dovecote in the central courtyard. **Varengeville** is an elegant, floral resort set in the woods behind the cliffs. There is a superb view from the church, which contains the tomb of the Cubist painter Georges Braque and some good stained glass.

Follow the cliff road through the attractively-sited **St Marguerite-sur-Mer** and a string of holiday villages set back from the sea. This is the **Alabaster Coast**, so-called for its series of dramatic chalk cliffs with fishing villages and ports nestling in the gaps between them. The beaches are shingle and often inaccessible, and the cliffs often eroded into strange shapes. There is good camping at St Aubin-sur-Mer and **St Valéry-en-Caux**. St Valéry, a port and resort that has recovered from devastation in World War II (British military memorials), has a beautiful Renaissance house and fine views from the sur-rounding cliffs. From here either continue along the tortuous cliff road or turn inland to **Cany-Barville**, with its attractive château and town square. Enter Fécamp by the cliff-top road through Senneville, passing the chapel of Our Lady of Safe Return (Notre-Dame du Salut). This is the local seamen's pilgrim-age church; from here you get a magnificent view of the town below.

Fécamp is France's leading deep-sea cod-fishing port. It has a proud herit-age of fearless mariners travelling long distances and braving the perils of the sea — a small museum on the attractive but narrow sea front, the Newfound-land Fishery Museum, tells the story of their Viking traditions and techniques and their links with the New World. In the Middle Ages, Fécamp had a large Benedictine monastery, sheltering the relic of the 'Precious Blood', and was the leading pilgrimage centre in Normandy. All that remains of this today is La Trinité Church, a massive Gothic structure with an odd classical façade, a splendid belfry, and, inside, a majestic nave and some gorgeous works of art, including a beautiful fifteenth-century sculpture, the *Dormition of the Virgin*, beside which is a footprint left in AD943 by a visiting angel! The church also houses the relic of the drops of Christ's blood reputedly collected by Joseph of Arimathea, which still attracts large numbers of pilgrims today.

Fécamp's other legacy of its monastery is the world-famous liqueur

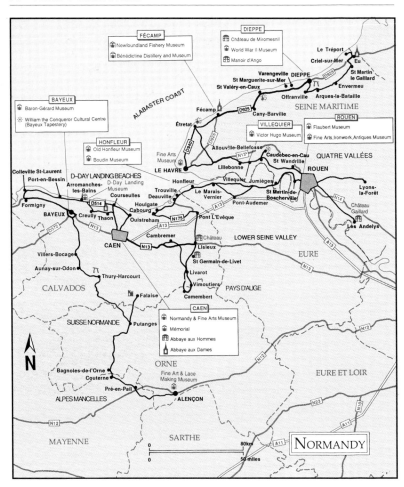

Bénédictine. This was first distilled from aromatic plants grown on the local cliffs by a monk called Vincelli in 1510, but large-scale production was only begun in the nineteenth century by a wine-merchant, Alexandre Le Grand, who blessed it with the initials D.O.M. (*Deo Optimo Maximo* — To God the Best and Greatest). He built the palace which now houses the Bénédictine Museum, a grandiose mock-Gothic and Renaissance building containing relics of the old abbey and other interesting artefacts as well as information on the manufacture of the liqueur (you get a tasting at the end of your visit). Fécamp's Municipal Museum has a good display on rural life in the Pays de Caux, and its port is lively and interesting.

Take the cliff road D940 to **Étretat.** You can go direct or on the winding cliff-top road through Yport. Étretat's main claim to fame is its setting, a narrow shingle sea-front between magnificent cliffs eroded into fantastic shapes, including arches, grottoes and a 200m (656ft) needle rock. You can see these from a cliff walk or by taking a boat trip. To the west, the Aval cliff gives the

Take a walk down the Rue du Gros Horloge and admire the façade of Rouen's famous clock

Fécamp's strong nautical past makes the harbour well-worth a visit

better view, while the eastern Amont cliff has a memorial to the first, unsuccessful attempt to fly the Atlantic (museum in the town). This small town was once the haunt of artists like Monet and Corot, and is quaint, with many fish restaurants and a pleasant covered market. The rest of the coast towards Le Havre is best avoided as it contains a large petrol port and **Le Havre** itself, after its destruction by the Allies in 1944, is a functional town built largely in reinforced concrete. It has an ultra-modern Fine Arts Museum with some good modern paintings (notably by Dufy), and a huge port, the second largest in France and third in Europe, but little else to interest the visitor.

The Lower Seine Valley

Instead, turn inland and cross the Caux plateau to **Lillebonne** on the north bank of the Seine. This small industrial town was a major port in Roman times, and has the remains of a large Roman theatre, a Gallo-Roman museum and the ruins of a castle where Duke William assembled his barons before invading England. From here join the estuary road (the views westward are of the impressive modern Tancarville toll-bridge) and travel east to **Villequier**, a pretty village squeezed between the Seine and a wooded hill topped by a castle. Here is the scene of a famous tragedy, when Victor Hugo's daughter, Léopoldine, and her husband, Charles Vacquerie, were drowned in the river 6 months after their marriage in 1843. The writer expressed his grief in his poem *Les Contemplations*. There is a charming small Victor Hugo Museum on the river bank, in the house once owned by the Vacqueries, a rich local boat-building family. The house, often visited by Hugo, is preserved with its original decor and furnishings, and contains letters written by the writer and his daughter and other family mementos. The tombs of Charles, Léopoldine and Hugo's wife are in the attractive local church.

Continue along the quay, passing the station where the river-pilots take over from the sea-pilots to **Caudebec-en-Caux**, once the capital of the region but now a smallish town. Its setting is impressive, ranged like an amphitheatre on the north bank of the majestic Seine, but its buildings are drably modern after extensive war damage. Two old buildings have survived: the splendid Flamboyant Gothic church of Notre-Dame, described by Henry IV as 'the most beautiful chapel in the Kingdom', with its finely-wrought belfry and spire, beautiful doorways and rose window surrounded by small statues. Inside it has some outstanding stained glass: the panels above the door were donated by a Shropshire knight, Fulke Eyton, who held the town from 1436 to 1448 for the English king Henry VI. There is also a fine old organ, and side chapels of the Holy Sepulchre and the Virgin Mary, the former containing a curious group of restored statues from Jumièges abbey. The other building which survived the war is the Templars' House, a handsome thirteenth-century gabled residence housing the Syndicat d'Initiative and a local history museum.

A short detour north takes you to the sleepy village of **Allouville-Bellefosse**, famous throughout France for its oak tree. Over 1,200 years old, probably the oldest in the country, it stands in the churchyard shored up by wooden planks. It has two tiny chapels inside, one on top of the other, with a wooden spiral staircase giving outside access to the upper floor. It is quaintly picturesque, especially inside but it is often closed for repairs. Back in Caudebec, take the short drive under the modern toll bridge, the Pont du Brotonne, to the **Abbey of St Wandrille**. Set in the attractive Fontenelle Valley, this famous abbey has a long history, taking its name from a seventh-century Count Wandrille, who gave up his newly-wed bride to become a hermit! He was later ordained in Rouen and founded the abbey in AD649. It was sacked by the Vikings but flourished again in the Middle Ages and became a centre of learning. After a temporary decline during the Wars of Religion, it revived until dissolved during the Revolution, after which it had a succession of owners including the English Marquess of Stacpoole. It became an abbey again only in 1931. All you can see of the original are some massive columns from the old Gothic church, and the beautiful cloisters which you can only visit on a special tour. The present church is a transported and reconstructed fifteenth-century tithe barn, with the attractively simple design of plain wooden beams supporting a wooden roof, and a shrine containing the head of St Wandrille. A mass with the Gregorian Chant is sung every morning. A nearby shop sells products made by the monks.

It is time to leave the wooded Seine Valley for a while and head for the big city. Cross country on the D22 to Pavilly, where a short motorway journey will bring you into **Rouen**, capital of Upper Normandy. A fascinating city with a long history and thriving culture, of which its citizens are so proud, Rouen has so many attractions for the visitor that you should not try to do them all in a day or two. A long weekend would be ideal. Set on both banks of a deep curve in the Seine, it is France's fourth largest port and an industrial centre, whose extensive suburbs and factories do not prepare you for the delights of the old city. This has been extensively restored, and the whole area is now virtually one big museum. You can wander at will through the pedestrianised narrow streets, flanked by old gabled, half-timbered houses; gaze in awe at the splendour of one of the most beautiful Gothic cathedrals in the world; stand in reverence in front of the national monument, a 20m (66ft) high cross, on the spot where Joan of Arc was burned at the stake; walk down the Rue du Gros Horloge and under Rouen's biggest tourist attraction, the old clock; or visit one of the many museums, perhaps one dedicated to one of Rouen's famous sons — say the dramatic poet Pierre Corneille or the novelist Gustave Flaubert. However you pass your time, you will be entranced by Ruskin's 'labyrinth of delight'.

Rouen merits a guide book to itself, and the local Office de Tourisme will be pleased to supply one. This will tell you something of its history, from the baptism here of the Viking leader Rollo, who became Robert, first Duke of Normandy to the reign of terror by the English 'Goddams', and the trial, imprisonment and execution of St Joan; through the gradual growth of trade and prosperity to modern times and the extensive damage of World War II. The old centre was badly hit, and the post-war restoration of the 'city bristling with spires and belfries' has been little short of miraculous. Some sights not to miss are: the Cathedral of Notre-Dame, whose open-work iron spire is the highest in France, with its two Gothic towers in different styles, one simple and early, the other Flamboyant and ornate, its fine south doorway and elaborately-decorated front, and its wealth of features inside, including the tombs of the cardinals of Amboise and some rich stained glass; the Abbey Church of St Ouen, a magnificent Gothic building of harmonious proportions; the beautiful late-Gothic church of St Maclou with its see-through spire, its picturesque cobbled square surrounded by timber-framed houses, and its cloister with medieval plague cemetery and charnel-house; and the old town, with its famous fourteenth-century gilt clock, its old market square where Joan of Arc came to grief, and its Law Courts and Bourgheroulde Mansion with their fine Renaissance façades. Of the museums the following are recommended: the richly-endowed Fine Arts Museum, the Antiques Museum, the Secq des Tournelles Ironwork Museum, the Corneille and Flaubert museums, and the Joan of Arc Museum, telling the story of her life.

The tour now has two optional extras — excursions to the Quatre Vallées and the Seine above Rouen. These can be done while using Rouen as a base. The Quatre Vallées is a pleasant area of wooded valleys to the east of Rouen, centred on **Lyons-la-Forêt**, a quiet town with half-timbered houses and a covered market. The Forêt de Lyons which surrounds it is perhaps the most beautiful beech forest in France. Two ruined abbeys are worth noting as you pass: Fontaine-Guérard, wild and romantic, and Mortemer, peaceful and rural. The trip upstream to **Les Andelys** and Château Gaillard is mainly for their historical assocations. The romantic, overgrown ruin of Château Gaillard, on a cliff above the twin villages of Petit and Grand Andely, was built by the English King Richard I in 1196 and lost to the French by his brother John in 1204. It was built within a year, to block the French king's passage to Rouen, and was lost after a long seige when a French soldier broke in through a newly-installed lavatory! You can walk round the castle, and the view over the Seine valley is superb.

Leave Rouen by the D982 through the Roumare Forest to rejoin the Seine valley. Turn left at Duclair for **St Martin-de-Boscherville**, to visit the second of the three great abbey churches of the lower Seine. The church of the former abbey of St Georges, built around AD1100, is the best-preserved of the three, being saved from destruction during the Revolution by becoming the parish church of St Martin. It is a fine example of Norman Romanesque, with a plain façade, geometric designs on the main door, and beautiful, delicately-carved capitals (with amusing figures) reminiscent of Romanesque churches further south. Return to Duclair, with a view on a hill to the south of the ruined castle of the legendary character Robert le Diable, which now houses a Viking museum. Follow the next meander of the Seine left to **Jumièges**. The abbey church here is perhaps the high-spot of the tour — the greatest Romanesque ruin in Europe. The abbey was founded in the seventh century, destroyed by the Vikings, rebuilt by Duke William Longsword in the tenth century, and its church consecrated by William the Conqueror in 1067. The monks were dispersed in the Revolution and part of the church later blown up, but fortunately the tall twin towers and part of the nave were saved and the ruin is now one of France's proudest national monuments. It is a beautiful, strongly 'atmospheric' place, and strangely moving, the majestic ruins half-hidden by the surrounding tall trees. You enter by the small church of St Pierre, where there is a small exhibition of relics of the abbey.

From here you can cross from the narrow Jumièges 'loop' to the Brotonne forest by the Seine *bac*, a bijou car ferry (it can just take a small caravan). On the other bank, at the edge of the forest, is a curious large oak, the Chène à la Cuve, with four trees growing out of a single trunk. You can drive through the attractive Brotonne forest on small private roads (though there are few sign-posts) to the pretty woodland village of **La Haye de Routot**. This has old thatched cottages typical of the area, their roof ridges planted with flowers — one of these is a communal bread oven, another a clog-maker's or *sabotier's* workshop, both of them housing small museums. There are two more fasci- nating trees: two old hollow yews in the churchyard, one containing a small chapel and the other a shrine to the Virgin. This village still holds its quaint traditional forest festival, the Fête de Ste Clare, on 16 July every year. The villagers build a huge spire of rough wooden staves, and dance round it through the evening, while indulging in the usual fun of the fair — side-shows and food washed down with local cider. Then, a little before midnight, the 25m (82ft) high bonfire is blessed and ignited, and when the brands are well-burned the local men snatch them from the fire and carry them away to their homes. This is supposed to protect them from fire for the next year. It is a spectacular sight, though rather hazardous to participants and spectators alike!

The ruined Château Gaillard overlooks the River Seine at Les Andelys

From La Haye de Routot join the D139 to **Pont-Audemer**, a town badly damaged in World War II but preserving some fine old half-timbered buildings in the main street and with an impressive late-Gothic church, St Ouen, which has some beautiful Renaissance stained-glass and a lovely decorated nave. From the old bridge there is a pleasant view of the River Risle. Take the N182 towards the Tancarville bridge and turn left towards **Le Marais Vernier**. You will soon have a panoramic view of this large reclaimed marsh, in an oxbow at the southern end of the Seine estuary. Its drainage was undertaken over many years, first by the monks of Jumièges, later by a team of Dutch engineers brought in by King Henry IV (it is crossed by the 'Dutchmen's Dyke'), and finally this century. It is now a green, fertile agricultural plain. Bypass the village of Marais-Vernier, with its typical thatched cottages, and just beyond St Samson-de-la-Roque is the lighthouse of Pointe de la Roque, from where is a fine view over the Seine estuary to Le Havre on the northern side.

The Pays d'Auge
Cross the Risle and take the coast road through Berville-sur-Mer (pretty converted château at La Pommeraie) to **Honfleur**. This delightful old port is the jewel of Normandy and one of its most popular tourist attractions. It is strongly picturesque, the main attraction being its central dock (the Vieux Bassin) entered by boats via a swivel bridge and lined by tall, slender houses with roofs and sometimes walls of grey slate. It was from here that Norman sailors first discovered and then colonised Canada. It has long been a haunt of painters, writers and composers, and was where the Impressionists first gathered, and some of them, like Boudin and Monet, settled — their works can be seen in the Boudin Museum. Artists are still drawn to Honfleur in droves, and the town has many art galleries. The sixteenth-century Governor's House (Lieutenance) stands at the entrance to the old dock; of the two main churches, St Stephen's on the dockside is now a Norman folk-art museum, and St Catherine's, perhaps the most interesting building in Honfleur, is built entirely of wood, with twin naves and side aisles whose roofs are supported by wooden pillars. Apparently the local shipbuilders were so relieved at the departure of the English after the Hundred Years' War that they could not wait for the stone to arrive before thanking God for their release! Across the charming St Catherine's market square, behind the Governor's House, is the separate church belfry, covered in chestnut weather-boarding.

Honfleur attracts many tourists, who love to wander round its picturesque old streets and gaze into its expensive shops, but it is not spoilt by them. It is still a busy and thriving fishing port, with some good fish restaurants at all prices. It has an air of easy opulence, of the good life, its citizens chatting by the harbour or at café tables over a beer. It has good amenities for sport and leisure, and good walks over the hills behind the town, particularly on the Côte de Grâce to the west. The view is not what it was — across the estuary are the huge oil refineries of Le Havre — but the inland scenery of the St Gatien forest is pleasant. There is good camping at nearby Equemauville, and a luxury hotel at St Siméon's farm, where the Impressionists used to meet.

This stretch of coast between the Seine and the Orne, and its hinterland, are the central and most popular part of Normandy. The coast is a string of more-or-less classy resorts with fine sandy beaches and flowery parks and gardens, called the Côte Fleurie; while inland is the lush, rich countryside of the Pays d'Auge. King of the coast is **Deauville**, the Monte Carlo of the north, with its casino, its smart people, its host of summer activities by day and night, and its 3km (2 mile) long beach with its famous path of duckboards known as *les planches*. It claims to have invented sea-bathing and the beach holiday in the nineteenth century and though its heyday was the turn of the century, it is still busy and wealthy. It has a large marina and yacht harbour, an elegant boulevard with exclusive beaches (less so towards the western end), many large hotels and villas in various pseudo styles, and facilities for every kind of sport and pastime you can think of. Among others, it is famous for its bridge, polo, golf and tennis tournaments, its horse-racing and its American film festival. The other coastal resorts are more down-to-earth. **Trouville** is unashamedly down-market, while **Cabourg** and **Houlgate** are quietly residential.

If the coast of the Pays d'Auge is busy and colourful, the hinterland is Normandy at its most typical — soft, green and peaceful. This is the garden of northern France, producing the rich cheeses of Camembert, Pont L'Evêque and Livarot, and the butter, milk and cream that enrich its cuisine. It is also its orchard, providing the apples for its cider and apple-brandy (Calvados), and in May it is white with apple blossom. The picture-book countryside is dotted with colourful, half-timbered manor houses and thatched cottages with those flowery roofs. A tour of the region should combine visits to some of these with liberal tastings of local cheese, cider and Calvados — there are established cheese and cider routes to help you do so.

Turn inland from Deauville to **Pont L'Evêque**, whose delicious cheese is made in the surrounding villages. The town was badly damaged in the last war and is unprepossessing, though with one or two old houses intact. Two roads, both attractive, take you south to **Lisieux**, the industrial centre of the Pays d'Auge whose most famous product was St Teresa. Apart from its elegant early Gothic cathedral of St Pierre, the town is completely modern after being flattened in the war; but it has become a high-place of pilgrimage on account of the young girl from Alençon, Thérèse Martin, who became a Carmelite sister at the age of 15 and died in 1897, after an agonising illness, at the early age of 24. She lived an uneventful life of saintly simplicity, and was canonised in 1925. On the edge of the town is a huge, ornate neo-Romanesque basilica, full of colourful Byzantine-style mosaics retelling the story revealed in her autobiography, *The Story of a Soul*. It is thronged with pilgrims throughout the year, who fill the souvenir shops in the town buying their holy mementos.

Lisieux is an ideal starting point for a tour of the Pays d'Auge. Of the manor houses or *mesnils*, perhaps the one 7km (4 miles) south at **St Germain-de-Livet** is the finest — a moated fifteenth- to sixteenth-century château with towers and ramparts, half-timbered façades and superb chequered stone and glazed brick decoration. Other fine examples are the château of Mesnil-Guillaume,

Bellou Manor near Livarot, and Coupesart, but there are many others that you can see as you wind your way down to Livarot and Vimoutiers. **Livarot**, which produces the third of Normandy's famous cheeses and is a leading centre of butter production, is a good place for a visit to a cheese-making plant. Further south, **Vimoutiers** has a statue in the main square of Marie Harel, the lady who, in the early nineteenth century, perfected the making of the world's best-known soft cheese at her farm 5km (3 miles) away in the village of Camembert. West of Lisieux is cider country, with many tastings round Cambremer and Beuvron-en-Auge. The latter is a historic village known as 'the cider capital of France', and has a festival every November.

The Legacy of War

So much of Normandy is scarred by the bitter fighting of World War II that no visitor can avoid seeing its remains. Though the damage was widespread, the densest concentration of these remains is in the north-west. The main interest for the visitor is on or around the D-Day Landing Beaches west of the Orne estuary, but your first port of call should be the capital of Lower Normandy, **Caen**, 40km (25 miles) west of Lisieux on the N13. This town does not have the tourist interest of the other capital, Rouen, but it is an essential starting place for your tour.

Caen was three-quarters destroyed in World War II, one of the war's heaviest casualties. Miraculously, its abbey, main churches and a few old houses were spared, and it has rebuilt itself into a thriving commercial centre. Today it is a busy and workmanlike city, with wide streets and tree-lined boulevards, and new buildings uniformly constructed in the same light-coloured local stone as the old ones. It is certainly not drab but, apart from its monuments, it appears rather like any other northern European city. It is dominated by its castle, plumb in the centre, round which the merciless traffic flows — do not try stopping your car to see it! This impressive fortress, whose medieval walls have been revealed by the destruction of encompassing buildings, was founded by William the Conqueror in the eleventh century. Its flowered terraces provide good views over the town and an oasis of calm in the surrounding bustle. It has some restored internal buildings, a war memorial and two museums, of local history and fine arts. At its foot is one of the spared churches, the mainly Gothic St Pierre, unusually ornate by Norman standards, with exuberant Renaissance decoration on the east side. Opposite is a fine old house occupied by the tourist office.

Reminders of William the Conqueror are everywhere in his favourite city. Caen's two greatest landmarks are tributes to him and his wife Matilda: the Abbaye aux Hommes and the Abbaye aux Dames, the former founded by William and the latter by his wife to win the pope's approval for their marriage. The Abbaye aux Hommes is an eighteenth-century building now used as the town hall, with a fine view of the cloisters and flank of the adjacent abbey church of St Étienne from the first floor. This church, which contains William's tomb, is a magnificent example of Norman Romanesque: massive and severely simple, with no side chapels or internal ornament. The tomb is

Normandy will always be synonymous with the D-Day Landings; a memorial at Omaha Beach

The old port at Honfleur is one of Normandy's most picturesque attractions

a simple plaque — the body has been long since pillaged. Matilda's 'Ladies' Abbey' lies on the other side of town, with the castle in between. Its church of La Trinité is smaller and more damaged than its twin, but still charming, and has retained some of its original Romanesque carved capitals.

In Caen's sprawling industrial suburbs is the Mémorial, an ultra-modern museum commemorating the town's recent sufferings. Inaugurated by President Mitterand in 1988, its aims are noble: 'to place the epic events of the Allied Landings of 6 June 1944 within the historical context of the twentieth century, and to be a place to reflect on peace'. Built over a former German command post, it has six sections, including two on pre-war and post-war developments, and a gallery on the Nobel Peace Prize and its winners. It is impressive and moving, though stronger on message and style than content (its post-war section is already out-of-date) and its 'peace' motif may be seen by some as tendentious.

Just beyond Caen's industrial suburbs to the north-east is **Bénouville**. Turn right in the village and stop where a small metal bridge crosses the Orne canal. This is Pegasus Bridge, named in honour of the British 6th Airborne Division who liberated this and the Ranville river-bridge on the night 5-6 June 1944 in preparation for the Allied landings the next morning. The small café on the bank is the famous Café Gondrée, the first house to be liberated in occupied

France, and at its side is a small museum commemorating the event. Cross the two bridges to the first-liberated village of **Ranville**, where there is a British cemetery, beautifully laid out and maintained. Returning to Bénouville, note the memorial at the crossroads to the capture of the town hall by the paratroopers at 11.45pm on 5 June — their leader, Major Howard, is said to have apologised to the mayor 'for being a few minutes late'!

A few kilometres further north is **Ouistreham**, the starting-point for a tour of the D-Day Landing Beaches. The stretch of the Calvados coast from here to **Arromanches-les-Bains** covers the three beaches — Sword, Juno and Gold — taken by various forces under British Army command. West of Arromanches are the two beaches of the US sector, Omaha and Utah. Along this littoral are a series of monuments commemorating the exploits and sacrifices of the allied forces during the Overlord operation, but the two exceptional sites are the vestiges of the artificial port known as **Mulberry Harbour** (later Port Winston) at Arromanches, with its big concrete blocks marking off a vast roadstead, and the German coastal artillery battery at **Merville**. The story of Operation Overlord is fascinating though often told, and can be recalled in the many museums of the area. Apart from those mentioned, the most impressive are

the Landing Museum at Arromanches, which has a long window overlooking the artificial port with a diorama, film and models illustrating the landing operation and the 'Battle of Normandy' 1944 Memorial Museum at Bayeux, which retraces the whole operation from 7 June to 22 August 1944.

The British and Americans differed in their practices for burying their dead. The British preferred small cemeteries near the battle sites, while the Americans chose to honour their fallen in one big cemetery. This is at **Colleville St**

Laurent on Omaha beach, a beautiful, serene and proudly-maintained park with over 10,000 white crosses. On the beach below are two memorials amid a maze of bunkers and foxholes. The German cemetery at nearby **La Cambe**, inland from Grandchamp, has 21,000 graves, while the principal Anglo-Canadian cemeteries are at Ranville, Bayeux and Banneville-la-Campagne. There is a Polish cemetery at Grainville-Langannerie.

This stretch of the Calvados coast, known as the **Pearl Coast** (Côte de Nacre), has other attractions than D-Day. It has a string of family seaside resorts, pleasant but lacking the glamour of the Côte Fleurie. It has the famous oysters of Courseulles-sur-Mer and the attractive small port at **Port-en-Bassin**. This town has a memorial and small museum commemorating the meeting of the Americans from Omaha beach with the British from Gold Beach and the establishment of joint operations. Inland from Courseulles is the lovely Renaissance château of **Fontaine-Henry**, with a steeply-sloping slate roof; and at nearby **Thaon** a beautiful small twelfth-century Roman-esque church, now deconsecrated and standing forlorn and neglected by a spring in a secluded glen outside the town. It is a perfect example of its type, with intricately-carved capitals and corbels, and in a lovely spot. Nearby, at **Creully**, is an attractive thirteenth-century fortified castle where General Montgomery stayed after the D-Day Landings.

Turn inland from the beaches to **Bayeux**. This is an ideal base for a holiday in the area, as it is a charming town with picturesque old streets round a splendid cathedral, has good accommodation, camp-sites and has the famous tapestry. The British sectors of the landing beaches were less heavily attacked than the American, and Bayeux, just inland from Arromanches, was unusu-ally spared from much damage. It is a glimpse of what Normandy towns might have looked like before the holocaust. Its cathedral is more highly decorated than usual for Normandy, and mixes Romanesque and Gothic styles in an attractive harmony. Inside it has some lovely carvings of geometric shapes and oriental figures on the arches in the nave.

The Bayeux Tapestry really needs no comment. It is Normandy's most famous possession and should not be missed. Bayeux was the cradle of the Norman dukes and the last Norse-speaking part of Normandy, so it is apt that this testament to the great feat of the Conquest should be housed here. It was probably commissioned by the Bishop of Bayeux and executed by Saxon embroiderers in wool on a linen base. It is both a rare and precious historical document and a considerable work of art. It gives a unique glimpse into life and events in the early Middle Ages, and it is a graphically-told story, beau-tifully drawn, coloured and decorated with animal and symbolic motifs. It is well displayed in the Centre Guillaume le Conquéror — take the English audio-guide and buy a fold-out reproduction as a souvenir. Your ticket gives you free entry to the Baron-Gérard Museum of local arts. You can explore the Normandy Landing Beaches, memorials and museums using *The Visitor's Guide to Normandy Landing Beaches*, refer to the advert at the back of this book.

Southern Normandy

Leave Bayeux by the D6, through Tilly-sur-Seules, Villers-Bocage and Aunay-sur-Odon to **Thury-Harcourt**. This small town, rebuilt after extensive war damage, is attractively sited on the banks of the Orne, with a fine park containing the ruins of the castle of the Dukes of Harcourt. It is a tourist centre on the northern edge of the Suisse Normande, an attractive area of rivers, woods and rolling hills, with some rocky outcrops, though as it has neither lakes nor mountains it is hardly Swiss! It is good walking, rock-climbing, canoeing and fishing country, with some fine views from the 'peaks'. Follow the river south on the D562 to St Rémy, then for a short tour of the region turn left onto the narrow Route des Crètes (D133), past the Pain de Sucre (Sugar-loaf Hill) with its fine view, and back down into **Clécy**. This small town is the tourist centre of the region, in a majestic setting on a curve of the river. Pass the Faverie Cross (another fine view) on the D168 to **Pont d'Ouilly**, a cross-roads of the Suisse Normande and a canoeing centre, and on to the **Oëtre Rock**. Behind a café at a crossroads is a rocky platform which gives a spectacular view over the wild Rouvre Gorges below. Continue south through the Gorges de St Aubert to **Putanges-Pont-Ecrepin**, the southern limit of the Suisse Normande.

Falaise, a 17km (11 miles) detour to the north, is a town with ancient and modern historical associations. Set in a wild, rocky ravine and dominated by an enormous fortress, Falaise was the birthplace of William the Conqueror, illegitimately born to a beautiful local 17-year-old girl, Arlette, and Robert, son of Duke Richard of Normandy, in 1027. It was also the centre of the bitterest battle in the World War II liberation of France, when the 'Falaise Pocket' was the scene of a bitter German fight-back with much loss of life on both sides. The old town was virtually destroyed. The fortress, with its twelfth-century keep and fifteenth-century round tower, stands massive and impregnable on its rock above the town.

Continue south from Putanges to **Bagnoles-de-l'Orne**. With its suburb of Tessé-la-Madeleine, this is the largest spa in western France, attractively set in wooded country and facing its casino across a lake. There is a fine viewpoint over the town and Thermal Baths from Le Roq au Chien, a rock in the park of the Tessé château. It is an excellent centre for woodland walks, riding and boating, as well as for its curative waters and the pleasures of the casino. Just south of Bagnoles, at **Couterne**, is a pretty château by a lake.

From Couterne, take the N176 south-east to Pré-en-Pail, and in the village turn right on the D144 for the Alpes Mancelles. This region of the Normandy-Maine Regional Park, on the southern borders of Normandy, is similar in its physical features to the Suisse Normande, though smaller in area, and has a similarly pretentious name. The 'Alps' are really hills covered in heath and broom, cut by streams running swiftly between gorges. The village of **St Céneri-le-Gérai** is picture-book pretty, with a Romanesque church and an old bridge over the Sarthe and **St Léonard-des-Bois**, on a steep-sided bend in the same river, is a good touring centre for this attractive region.

The tour ends at the nearby town of **Alençon**, on the border of Maine. It is

Norman Cuisine

A dish *à la Normande* will be cooked in butter, with cream, apples and cider, and it may be finished off with a dash of Calvados. These are the staple ingredients, and two well-known dishes of the region have them. *Poulet Vallée de l'Auge* is chicken cooked with onions, cider and cream and *Tripes à la Mode de Caen* is tripe braised in cider. The region is also known for its tender beef and tasty salt-meadow lamb. Sole and other fish from northern seas are popular.

Crème fraiche, or clotted cream, is popular throughout France, but the best is said to come from Normandy and its butter is considered the best you can buy.

Normandy produces thirty-two different varieties of cheese, the best-known being Camembert, Pont-l'Evèque and Livarot. They are usually soft, creamy and rich. Desserts include rich apple tarts and soufflé omelettes *à la Mère Poulard*.

No wine is produced in Normandy. Cider is the most common drink, usually *bouché*, in bottles with wired corks. 'Calva', or Calvados, the apple brandy that is often home-made, is drunk any time — with or in coffee, before or after a meal, or between courses to increase the appetite. This is the famous *Trou Normand*, or 'Norman Hole', that lets you take on board that little bit extra!

a market town in the rich Sarthe countryside, and a centre for dealing in the famous Percheron horses from the nearby Perche region. It is renowned for its lace, with its distinctive pattern of tiny bunches of flowers on a rectangular background. The town has a fine fourteenth-century Flamboyant Gothic church of Notre-Dame, and a museum of fine arts and lace-making. It is also a good base for exploring the attractive Perche region to the east.

Additional Information

Places of Interest

Dieppe
Château de Miromesnil
6km (4 miles) south-west
Open: afternoons only, closed Tuesday.

Château Museum
Open: daily, closed Tuesday out of season.

World War II Museum
2km (1 mile) west
Open: daily except Monday, Easter to October.

Manoir d'Ango
8km (5 miles) west
Open: afternoons only, April to November.

Fécamp
Newfoundland Fishery Museum
Open: 10am-12noon and 2-5.30pm except Tuesday. Joint ticket with two other museums.

Bénédictine Distillery and Museum
Open: daily Easter to 11 November. Tastings.

Le Havre
André Malraux Fine Arts Museum
Open: daily except Tuesday and national holidays.

Villequier
Victor Hugo Museum
Vacquerie House
Open: 10am-12.30pm and 2-6.30pm except Tuesday, April to September. 10am-12.30pm and 2-5.30pm except Monday and Tuesday, October to March.

St Wandrille
Abbey
Guided visits: 11.30am, 3 and 4pm, Sunday and holidays, 3 and 4pm weekdays.

Rouen
Fine Arts, Faience, Ironwork and Other Museums

All open: 10am-12noon and 2-6pm daily, except national holidays.

Jumièges
Abbey and Stonework Museum
Open: 10am-12noon and 2-6pm daily, except national holidays.

Honfleur
Old Honfleur Museum
In St Stephen's Church
Guided tours only; closed weekdays out of season.

Boudin Museum
Closed Tuesday and mornings out of season, except Saturday and Sunday and in January.

St Germain-de-Livet
Château
Open: daily except Tuesday and 15 December to end January.

Caen
Mémorial
Open: daily 9am-10pm June to August; 9am-7pm September to May.

Castle (Normandy & Fine Arts Museums)
Open: daily except Tuesday and national holidays.

Bénouville
Pegasus Bridge Paratroop Museum
Open: daily except Tuesday and national holidays.

Arromanches-les-Bains
6 June 1944 D-Day Landing Museum
Open: daily 9am-12noon and 2-7pm; 2-6pm winter.

Bayeux
Baron-Gérard Museum
Open: 15 May to 15 September, 9am-7pm; 16 September to 14 May 9am-12.30pm and 2-6pm.

William the Conqueror Cultural Centre (Bayeux Tapestry)
Same hours as above — joint ticket available.

Alençon
Fine Arts & Lace-Making Museum
Open: daily except Monday.

Tourist Information Centres

Alençon
Office de Tourisme
Maison d'Ozé
☎ 33 26 11 36

Bayeux
Office de Tourisme
1 Rue Cuisiniers
☎ 31 92 16 26

Caen
Office de Tourisme and Accueil de
   France
Place St Pierre
☎ 31 86 27 65

Dieppe
Office de Tourisme
Boulevard Géneral de Gaulle
☎ 35 84 11 77

Fécamp
Office de Tourisme
Place Bellet
☎ 35 28 20 51

Honfleur
Office de Tourisme
Place A. Boudin
☎ 31 89 23 30

Le Tréport
Esplanade de la Plage L. Aragon
☎ 35 86 05 69

Rouen
Office de Tourisme and Accueil de
   France
25 Place Cathédrale
☎ 35 71 41 77

Restaurants

R = With Accommodation
Haute cuisine restaurants include:
Audrieu
13km (8 miles) south of Bayeux
Château d'Audrieu (R)
☎ 31 80 21 52

Bayeux
Lion d'Or (R)
☎ 31 92 06 90

Bénouville
10km (6 miles) north of Caen
Manoir d'Hastings et la Pommeraie (R)
☎ 31 44 62 43

Caen
La Bourride
☎ 31 93 50 76

Caudebec-en-Caux
Le Manoir de Rétival (R)
☎ 35 96 11 22

Conteville
Auberge Vieux Logis
☎ 32 57 60 16

Deauville
Le Spinnaker
☎ 31 65 08 11

Dieppe
La Mélie
☎ 35 84 21 19

Honfleur
Ferme St Siméon (R)
☎ 31 89 23 61

L'Assiette Gourmande
☎ 31 89 24 88

Le Breuil-en-Auge
Auberge Dauphin
☎ 31 65 08 11

Rouen
Gill
☎ 35 71 16 14

Bertrand Warin
☎ 35 89 26 29

Beffroy
☎ 35 71 55 27

La Butte
($3^1/_2$km, 2 miles at Bonsecours)
☎ 35 80 43 11

Veules-les-Roses
Les Galets
☎ 35 97 61 33

Other restaurants, offering good value
for money include:

Balleroy
Manoir de la Drôme
☎ 31 21 60 94

Beuzeville
Auberge Cochon d'Or (R)
☎ 32 57 70 46

Caen
Le Boeuf Ferré
☎ 31 85 36 40

Criel-sur-Mer
Auberge de Briançon (R)
☎ 35 50 99 33

Drubec
Near Pont-l'Éveque
La Haie Tondue
☎ 31 64 85 00

Duclair
La Poste (R)
☎ 35 37 39 19

Envermeu
Near Dieppe
Auberge Caves Normandes
☎ 35 85 71 28

Falaise
La Poste (R)
☎ 31 90 13 14

Fécamp
Le Maritime
☎ 35 28 21 71

Fontaine-le-Dun
Auberge du Dun
☎ 35 83 05 84

Forges-les-Eaux
Le Paix (R)
☎ 35 90 51 22

Honfleur
Cheval Blanc
☎ 31 89 39 87

L'Absinthe
☎ 31 89 53 60

Deux Ponts
☎ 31 89 04 37

Au P'tit Mareyeur
☎ 31 98 84 23

La Ferrière-des-Étangs
Near Flers at Le Gué-Plat
Auberge de la Mine
☎ 33 66 91 10

Le Havre
La Petite Auberge
☎ 35 46 27 32

Villers-Bocage
Trois Rois (R)
☎ 31 77 00 32

3

Paris and the Île de France

Paris must have a good claim to be the world's most popular city. It has been immortalised through the ages in prose, verse, song and paint. It is a dazzling city, beautiful at first sight, even more beautiful on close acquaintance. To add more words to those already penned may seem superfluous — just go and enjoy it! Do not try to see it all at once — you will only give yourself spiritual indigestion and sore feet. The ideal is to spend a few days there every year or two, if you can.

It is the great heart of a great country, but can be supercilious about its 'provinces', and provincials can be suspicious of the perfidious Parisian. This 'culture gap' is partly a product of its history. For many centuries, Paris and its hinterland the Île de France were French— the rest of the country was hostile to it and belonged to somebody else. Under the *Ancien Régime* the French kings treated the rest of France as hostile territory, to be subdued and pillaged. Only in relatively recent times have capital and country become truly united.

Today Paris has almost everything, and its citizens know it. They abound in self-confidence and style, whether moving quickly but elegantly about their business or sitting at café tables watching the world go by. Their dress is either *haute couture* or studiedly casual, but never scruffy. If they seem arrogant at times, they have much to be arrogant about: their wide boulevards, spacious parks, sumptuous buildings, graceful squares and, above all, their beautiful River Seine with its bourgeois right and bohemian left bank, all belie the fact that this is the most densely populated city in Europe. It seems to be one vast pleasure ground, the acme of civilisation.

The Île de France can be considered along with Paris as it has always been part of it, culturally, spiritually and economically. The city's surrounding mantle of forests, for so long the playground and hunting ground of French king and court, was also its protective cover against the outside world and its source of nourishment. The cities of the Île de France are often, in style, miniature versions of Paris itself, and reflect its tastes and interests; and its magnificent châteaux — Fontainebleau, Versailles, Compiègne, Chantilly — were often the kings' country houses. The regions of the Île de France (Vexin, Valois, Brie, Beauvaisis) were in medieval times usually allied with France and part of its pageantry.

The landscape of the Île de France, if not covered with those magnificent forests, is either wooded river valleys, peaceful meadows or agricultural plains of wheat dotted with grain silos. It is country immortalised by landscape painters like Corot, Monet and Renoir, and at weekends is invaded by Parisians, picnicking in the fields or walking on the forest paths. The region is a living museum of Gothic art, from magnificent cathedrals like Chartres or Beauvais to hundreds of beautiful smaller churches.

Travelling In Paris and The Île de France
Do not try to see Paris by car. Parking is very difficult, and even if you find a space, you may not be able to get your car out of it when you come back. Most Parisian cars show distinct signs of minor damage — it is one of the accepted hazards of living there. The best ways of getting around are by walking, or by using Métro, bus, taxi or boat. Paris is a compact city, and much of the centre can be seen on foot. This is the most pleasant and relaxing way to do it, with occasional stops for refreshment at a pavement café. But watch out when crossing the boulevards — they are wide, and the one-way traffic moves fast!

For longer distances the Métro is efficient, clean, quiet, convenient, and quite cheap, especially if you use *carnets* of ten tickets rather than buying them one at a time (the cost is the same however far you go). If you are staying several days, you can get a tourist pass (for 3 to 5 days). Métro tickets and passes are also valid on buses, and vice-versa. There are express lines (R.E.R. — *Réseau Express Régional*) which whip you into town from the outer suburbs in about 15 minutes. The system is easy to use, with large light-up maps displayed in every station, and is open from 5.30am to 1am. Do not bother with first-class unless you travel regularly in the rush-hour.

Buses are slower and less frequent, especially on Sundays and public holidays. They are also more expensive, as you may have to use more than one ticket for longer distances — use your Métro carnet tickets whenever you can (buses do not sell them). A better way to see the sights is to use one of the Inter-Transport coaches which follow a set route round the major highspots. They go every hour, on a $2^1/_2$ hour tour, and you can hop on or off, wherever and as many times as you like, on the same ticket. A river bus, called the Batobus, operates in summer between the Eiffel Tower and the Hôtel de Ville. Special boat tours, with commentaries in English, are a pleasant way of seeing the centre, especially at night when they may include a meal.

Maps of Paris are often provided free, in tourist offices, hotels, shops and elsewhere. But for more detail, the Michelin Map 7 (Paris Tourism) is the ideal plan for the tourist sightseer. It is in English, and details the main sites, with historical and general information, and includes a Métro map.

You can visit the Île de France either by separate excursions from Paris, or by making a round tour. Organised coach excursions operate regularly from Paris to the more popular sites or you can easily get to many towns and villages by using a judicious mixture of Métro, RER, trains and buses. But a round tour using your own transport is quite a feasible alternative: there is plenty of accommodation, although prices are affected by the proximity of Paris.

Sightseeing In Paris

Paris is a compact city, logical in its layout. It is encompassed by a roughly circular ring of outer boulevards and, framing them, the *Périphérique*, or motorway ring road. Inside this ring, the city is divided into 20 *arondissements*, or administrative districts, spiralling out from the centre, with numbers 1 to 8 the central ones containing most of the sights and shops. The River Seine bisects the city, fairly straight in the centre but curving away south towards the west end. Most of the important and famous buildings are on the banks of the Seine or close to it and the oldest part of the city, the Île de la Cité, is actually an island in the middle.

This is therefore a logical place to start a tour. To avoid exhaustion and save shoe-leather it is best to concentrate on one area of the city at a time, including a balanced ration of sights in your itinerary. Four tours are suggested, with perhaps a day for each, but even these could be subdivided if they prove too demanding. It is a good idea to get a bird's-eye view first, with a guided coach or river-boat tour.

Itinerary 1— The Old City

Paris began on a boggy island in the middle of the River Seine. When Julius Caesar's army came, saw and conquered in 52BC he found a small town called *Lutetia* (meaning marshland) inhabited by a small tribe called the Parisii. The Romans enlarged and fortified the town, extending it onto the left bank as the right was too marshy. Later, the first Christian king, Clovis, chose Paris as his capital, and his Frankish successors enlarged and beautified it, until the Norman invaders reduced it again to a small island town in AD886. This is now the **Île de la Cité**, still the geographical and historical heart of Paris. It stands in the Seine like the hull of a boat, its prow breasting the water.

Start the tour on the Pont de Sully, on the eastern end of the **Île St Louis**. This quiet, charming island of gracious living lies to the east of its big brother; it used to be two islands, but was joined into one and first developed in the seventeenth century, when it was endowed with aristocratic houses, now some of the most magnificent hôtels in Paris. You can enjoy their superb façades, but only one, the Hôtel de Lauzun, can be visited. The island has an elegant church in its picturesque main street, the Rue St Louis-en-l'Île, which abounds with fashionable boutiques and gourmet food shops including the famous Berthillon ice-cream shop. At the west end of the island is a spectacular view over the river to the apse of Notre-Dame Cathedral, with its wondrous flying buttresses.

Cross to the Île de la Cité by the Pont St Louis. In front of you is the sublime **Notre-Dame Cathedral**, Paris's greatest and most famous building. This masterpiece of French Gothic architecture, built between 1163 and 1345, is a work of art, a monument and a history book. It is noble and harmonious in proportions, and richly endowed with sculptures and stained glass. Particularly fine are the three façade portals, with their finely chiseled stone figures, the central and transept rose windows, and the lovely Virgin and Child to the right of the choir entrance. It has witnessed many great events, from St Louis' lying in state in 1270 to the funeral of General De Gaulle in 1970. It is a symbol of Paris and a national shrine, and it has influenced Gothic art throughout Europe. It inspired Victor Hugo's *Notre Dame de Paris*, which caused an outcry that led to its restoration in the nineteenth century.

From its towers, looking over the spine, statues and gargoyles, are splendid views of the two islands, the river and its peaceful, tree-lined quays. Cross the wide cathedral parvis and the elegant Place Dauphine with its flower market

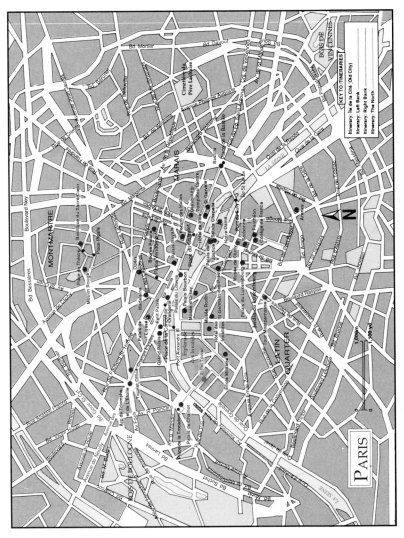

 round the Art Nouveau Métro entrance, to the **Palais de Justice**. This huge, imposing building, now France's legal headquarters, was the home (and refuge) of her earliest kings, and later the prison of the victims of the Revolution. Underneath, and reached from a side entrance on the Quai de l'Horloge, is the **Conciergerie**, a grim reminder of the Terror. After 6 April 1793 this became the 'Antechamber of the Guillotine', where Marie-Antoinette, Robespierre, Danton and many others spent their last nights before the tumbrels came to take them to their final destination. You can see Marie-Antoinette's chapel and crucifix, Robespierre's cell, a guillotine blade, and the small courtyard, the Cour des Femmes, where the 2,500-odd condemned had their last tryst with their loved ones.

Behind the Palais de Justice is a shining jewel of late Gothic architecture, the

Street-side cafés can be a welcome break from shopping and sight-seeing

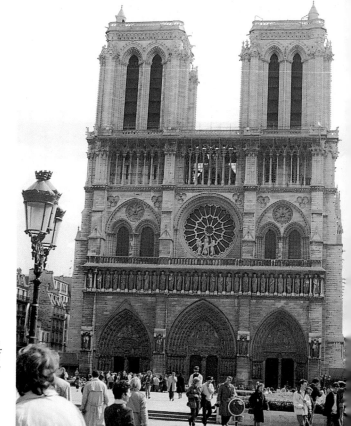

Notre-Dame Cathedral, a national monument of unrivalled splendour

Sainte-Chapelle. Built in 1248 by St Louis (the pious Louis IX) to house the relic of the crown of thorns brought back from Jerusalem, it is really two chapels — the lower one was for church dignitaries and the upper for the king and his retinue. Its fifteen stained-glass windows, most of them original, are superb, giving the two rooms a strange ethereal atmosphere, contrasting with the solidity of the surrounding buildings. These are extensive and forbidding, including the Préfecture of Police buildings on the Quai des Orfèvres, haunted by the ghost of Inspector Maigret. Finish the tour at the Pont Neuf, the oldest and finest of the thirteen bridges which connect the Île de la Cité to the riverbanks.

Itinerary 2 — The Left Bank
Crossing one of these bridges onto the southern bank of the Seine brings you onto the Left Bank, the intellectual, bohemian part of Paris. This is where Paris's university, the **Sorbonne**, has led the world in scholarship since medieval times. As the language of scholarship used to be Latin, it is called the **Latin Quarter**. The quays are lined with bookstalls and paintings, the streets full of small restaurants, cafés and jazz clubs. This is the oldest part of Paris after the Cité, and is where the Romans established their encampment of the first century BC. The remains of a Roman arena can be seen to the east and at the intersection of the area's two main axes, the Boulevards St Germain and St Michel, stands the **Musée de Cluny**, built on a vast Roman bath house the remains of which can be seen in the museum. The hill rising from the river is the **'Mountain' of Ste Geneviève**, a real student quarter with academic bookshops, cheap restaurants and rooms, and specialist cinemas. Ste Geneviève is the patron saint of Paris and on the top of the hill is a building first intended as her shrine — the **Panthéon**. This heavy, domed temple was later dedicated by the Revolutionaries to the heroes of republican liberty and houses the bodies of Voltaire, Rousseau and other great men.

Nearby in the Rue des Écoles are the university colleges, including the **Collège de France**, where the physicist Ampère researched, and the Sorbonne itself, the oldest college founded in 1253. Across the 'Boul-Miche' is the **Jardin du Luxembourg** (gardens) much frequented by students, and formally laid out with statues and the beautiful Médici Fountain. The huge Palais du Luxembourg is the home of the French Senate. Between here and the river is the fashionable Rive Gauche, the district of **St Germain-des-Prés** whose noble church is the oldest in Paris (from AD990). Opposite the church are the famous Deux Magots Café and the Café de Flore, scenes of past literary and philosophical discussion, and all around are attractive shops catering for young trendies, art galleries, and restaurants of many nationalities. This pedestrianised area either side of the Boulevard St Germain is still lively and exciting, though very popular with tourists.

Along the riverbank opposite the Louvre is the **Musée d'Orsay**. Now the most popular museum in Paris after the Louvre, its setting in the restored Orsay railway station-hotel is magnificently daring, with multi-level modern galleries suspended in the vast hall. It has a comprehensive collection of art from 1848 to 1914, including the greatest display of Impressionist works ever assembled. There is a fine view over the Seine from the top-floor café balcony.

Walk along the Quai d'Orsay to the Palais Bourbon, the home of the

Assemblée Nationale, turn left and pass through the once-aristocratic residential area of the Faubourg St Germain with its elegant mansions, one of which is the Hôtel Biron, now providing a beautiful setting for the **Musée Rodin.** 🏛 Cross the boulevard to the Hôtel des Invalides. This magnificent complex of buildings was commissioned by Louis XIV as a hospital for 4,000 'invalid' war veterans, hence the name (there are still 100 in residence). Napoleon's tomb is in its fine Baroque domed church, and the hospital itself houses the **Musée de** 🏛 **l'Armée**, possibly the finest military museum in the world. Walk down the *Esplanade* with its broad expanse of tree-lined lawns, to **Pont Alexandre III** (bridge), lavishly-decorated in Belle Époque style with winged horses and candelabras; then look back for a splendid view of the whole neo-classical complex.

Beyond the Invalides is the fine eighteenth-century **École Militaire**, and beyond that the wide grassy expanse of the Champ de Mars leading down to the **Tour Eiffel**. In Paris you cannot avoid seeing this famous symbol of French ❋ daring and technical know-how, but you should still visit it. Built by Gustave Eiffel for the 1890 World Fair, it was at its time the highest man-made structure in the world (300m, 984ft), and is still an awesome sight looking up from underneath. If you cannot face the 1,652 stairs, lifts will take you up to all three stages, though you may have to queue at each stage. Views from the top are wide and panoramic, but too high, and often hazy, to pick out much detail.

Cross the Seine by the Pont d'Iena to the **Palais de Chaillot**, avoiding the skateboarders of all ages as you walk up the slopes beside the fountains. From the balcony in front of the palace (Place du Trocadero) is a magnificent view 🎡 of the whole complex, with the Eiffel Tower straddling the Champ du Mars and the Invalides in the background. The Palais de Chaillot has two broad, curved wings, each housing a museum: Anthropology on the right, Cinema on the left. Nearby are a number of other museums, including the **Modern Art** 🏛 **Museum** and the **Musée Guimet**, a collection of oriental arts.

As an optional extra, take the Métro from Trocadero to **Montparnasse**, an inner suburb south of the Invalides. This was Paris's bohemian quarter earlier in the century, with intellectuals like Sartre and Simone de Beauvoir meeting in the La Coupole bar–restaurant. It is no longer this, but still lively and popular, particularly at night, with some good restaurants. It has a large cemetery full of the tombs of celebrities (including the Sartres) and a bleakly modern high tower whose view from the top rivals or even surpasses that of the Eiffel Tower.

Itinerary 3 — The Right Bank
This tour begins east of the Île de la Cité on the north bank of the Seine, on the site of that notorious symbol of *Ancien Régime* France, the **Bastille**. All that exists today of the prison the Revolutionaries destroyed is a wide square, the ❋ **Place de la Bastille**, with the Colonne de Juillet commemorating another failed revolution in 1830. To the east of this square is traditional lower-class Paris, where the riff-raff used to carouse at night and the *apaches* (gangsters) held sway in the dance-halls. The square itself is still a rallying point for trade-union and other demonstrations. On one side is an opera house, the **Opéra de la Bastille**, opened in 1989.

The area from here westward to the Hôtel de Ville is the **Marais**, one of the ❋

The Eiffel Tower, an engineering master-piece, now symbolises France

St Germain L'Auxerrois near the Louvre

A walk in Paris leads to the discovery of the unexpected

The Basilica du Sacré-Coeur offers some of the finest views of Paris

most fascinating areas of Paris. It was reclaimed swampland (the word means 'marsh'), later farmland, which became the city's prosperous heart in the seventeenth century, after the Court had moved there from the Île de la Cité. Some of the most elegant Renaissance-style houses, or *hôtels*, were built then, but in the eighteenth century the Court moved again and the Marais started to decline. It had almost crumbled into decay when a plan to renovate the area was introduced in 1962. Its property is now much sought-after by wealthy Parisians, and the whole area has sprung to life most attractively, with small hotels, restaurants, shops and art galleries. Many of the aristocratic old houses have become museums, libraries or archives. Its origin and heart is the **Place des Vosges,** once the Place Royale, created by King Henry IV as a model square, with thirty-eight elegant town houses built in white stone and red brick over long, symmetrical arcades. It has been delightfully restored today, and is possibly Paris's most picturesque square, a refreshing change from the areas of grandiose architecture further west.

To explore the area, take the Boulevard Beaumarchais and turn left into the Rue des Francs-Bourgeois. This brings you to the Place des Vosges, with its antique shops, bookshops, cafés and restaurants. House number 6, where Victor Hugo lived from 1832 to 1848 and wrote some of his most famous works, is now a museum to his memory. Continue on the road to see some of the architectural jewels of the sixteenth and seventeenth century. There are too many to mention them all, but note the **Hôtel Salé** (Picasso Museum nearby); **Hôtel de Lamoignon** (history library); **Hôtel Carnavalet** (Museum of French History); **Hôtel de Rouhan** (national archives); **Hôtel Soubise; Hôtel de Sully** (historic monuments); **Hôtel de Sens** (Forney library). Turn left into the Rue des Rosiers to visit the **Jewish Quarter,** a lively shopping area with an atmosphere all its own. Finish at the Flamboyant Gothic church of St Gervais, behind the town hall.

The town hall stands on the old place of execution, the Place de Grève and beyond it a busy square with an isolated tower in the middle, the Tour St Jacques, the only remaining part of an old church destroyed in the Revolution. Nearby is the **Place du Châtelet,** a central crossing place for through traffic. Châtelet is the home of popular theatre, with the Municipal Theatre and Théatre Municipal de Paris facing each other across the square. This is the area for the cheaper department stores. The larger, better-known ones like Galeries Lafayette and Au Printemps are further north on the Boulevard Haussmann.

Just north of here is the **Beaubourg,** a formerly-depressed area redeveloped in the 1970s and including the **Pompidou Centre** (known by Parisians simply as 'the Beaubourg'). President Pompidou intended this, his pet product, to be a focal point for contemporary French culture. It is undeniably modern, looking like a garishly-coloured oil refinery, and provokes strong reactions for and against. But it certainly attracts the crowds, many of whom come just to ride up and down on the escalators in long glass tubes running diagonally across the front of the building. Inside are a library, children's workshop, theatre workshop, music laboratory and, on the top floor, the **National Museum** **of Modern Art.** There is a splendid view over Paris to Montmartre from the parvis in front of the building are constant live shows of musicians, acrobats and circus performers. The Place Igor Stravinsky, at the side, has a fountain containing weird mobile machines by Tinguely.

West of Beaubourg is the rather seedy Rue St Denis with its porno shops and clubs and beyond that the vast underground commercial complex of the **Forum des Halles**, underneath the Métro and RER stations. Until the 1970s this was the famous Paris market, but pressure on space and traffic problems forced it out to the suburbs (near Orly Airport). The area is still being developed as an urban project, with streets, theatres, museums, a shopping forum, an underground greenhouse, a swimming pool, sports complex and exhibition centre. It has retained only its superb Renaissance Fountain of the Innocents and its renowned Pied de Cochon restaurant, which never closes.

From here it is only a short distance along the Rue de Rivoli to the **Louvre**. This is the largest building complex in Paris, housing the world's richest museum. As a building, it is grandly impressive but rather uniform, which is surprising as it was built over eight centuries. It was started as a fortress by Philippe Auguste in 1190, and finished in Second Empire style in the late nineteenth century. Its most attractive and oldest part is the Cour Carré, a square courtyard enclosed by superb colonnades at the east end and its newest is President Mitterand's sparkling glass pyramid over the entrance in the Cour Napoléon. Under the spectacular entrance, with its bookshops and cafés, the corridors radiate outwards to a daunting series of wings — too many to cover in one visit. The signposts are clear and will quickly lead you to the most popular exhibits: the *Mona Lisa*, or *La Joconde*, with other Leonardo da Vinci masterpieces in the Italian Gallery; the *Venus de Milo* and the *Winged Victory of Samothrace* in the Greek and Roman section and the *Crown Jewels* in the Apollo Gallery. There are lecture tours twice daily.

Cross the bridge over the Rue de Rivoli from the Cour Carré to the **Palais** **Royale**. This was originally Cardinal Richelieu's palace, rebuilt in 1763, and has a long and sometimes disreputable past. Today the arcaded palace, with its peaceful garden of limes and beeches, provides a quiet, restful enclave in the busy city centre, and the long galleries house strange little shops selling off-beat goods. Cross back to the Arc de Triomphe du Carrousel, a smaller version of the Arc de Triomphe at the east end of the **Jardin des Tuileries**. Stroll through the pleasant gardens (about 1km, $^1/_2$ mile long) or the elegant raised terraces running along the Seine and the Rue de Rivoli either side. Enjoy the flowers, statues, pools and fountains, or watch the model-boat enthusiasts and the children in the playgrounds then admire the fine perspectives to east and west.

At the west end of the Tuileries are two museums, the **Orangerie** and the **Jeu** **de Paume**. The latter is closed for improvements, but the former is a small jewel of a museum, containing, amongst a fine collection of Impressionist and twentieth-century paintings, two oval basement rooms whose walls are covered with Monet's hypnotic water-lilies murals, a masterpiece of Impressionist art. Descend its steps onto the **Place de la Concorde**, the wide and majestic central square of Paris. In its centre is a tall Egyptian obelisk, and though crossing to it can be hazardous, it has superb views in four directions: east, back to the Tuileries and the Louvre; west, down the Champs-Elysées to the Arc de Triomphe; south, across the Pont de la Concorde to the Invalides; and north, down the Rue Royale to the Madeleine.

Stroll down the **Champs-Elysées** towards the Arc de Triomphe, first on a wide, graceful, tree-lined promenade with gardens and exhibition halls, with the **Grand** and **Petit Palais** on your left and the Presidential **Palais del' Elysée** on your right; later on a broad avenue flanked by department stores, cinemas, restaurants and commercial premises. In the middle is the Rond-Point des Champs-Elysées with its graceful fountains. The tour ends at the **Place de L'Étoile**, now renamed the Place Charles de Gaulle, with its majestic **Arc de Triomphe** in the centre. Over the years this monument to France's military glories and her heroes, conceived by Napoleon and completed by Baron Haussmann, has become a symbol of the nation's pride. Built on a raised mound, it is 50m (164ft) high, 45m (148ft) wide and covered with bas-reliefs and statuary celebrating victories of the Revolution and Empire. It is the focal point for state funerals and ceremonial occasions; it is where Hitler first came to proclaim his conquest of France, and where General de Gaulle started his triumphal march of Liberation in 1944. Underneath the arch is the Tomb of the Unknown Soldier of World War I, on which a flame is kept constantly alight. On Bastille Day the arch is profusely decorated with flags and wreaths.

Finally, climb to the top for a magnificent view. Below you are twelve roads, or points of the 'star', radiating from the centre; and around you a panorama of the whole city, from Montmartre to Montparnasse and from the Eiffel Tower to the Panthéon.

Itinerary 4 — The North

This tour begins in Paris's luxury commercial area and moves out north to its legendary bohemian quarter on the Montmartre hill above the city. Start from the Place de la Concorde, and walk up the stately Rue Royale, passing Maxim's famous restaurant. You will cross the Rue du Faubourg Sainte-Honoré, the most opulent shopping street in Paris — the President lives at number 55, the Elysée Palace. At the top of the Rue Royale is the **Place de la Madeleine**, a busy square at the crux of the Grands Boulevards, with the church of **La Madeleine** in the centre. This heavy but imposing monument of a building does not look like a church — it was at first meant by Napoleon to be a temple of glory for his military victories until he decided to build the Arc de Triomphe instead. It resembles a Greek temple, and has no transept, aisles, bell tower or cross on the roof. On most days there is a flower market on and around its steps.

The **Grands Boulevards** were the only wide streets in Paris in the pre-Haussmann era, running north along the site of the old city walls from the Madeleine to the Bastille. At the turn of the century they were the centre of Parisian fashion, and though less fashionable today they still carry an air of wealth and style. The most stylish are those leading from the Madeleine to the Opéra, and it was in a house on one of these, the **Boulevard des Capuchines**, that the Impressionists had their first exhibition in 1874. The Lumière brothers held their first public moving picture show at the Hôtel Scribe here in 1895, and still today the Boulevards are the home of Paris's most popular cinemas.

Turn off from the boulevards down the Rue des Capuchines to the elegant **Place Vendôme**, centre of the most exclusive (and expensive) area of Paris. This beautiful octagonal-shaped square, built in honour of Louis XIV in 1715, is probably the most harmonious and balanced in the city, though its central column, with its spiral of bronze bas-reliefs depicting Napoleon's great battles, topped with a statue of him in Roman costume, is perhaps too grandiose.

It was introduced during the Revolution to replace an equestrian statue of King Louis, and cast from 1,250 cannons captured at the battle of Austerlitz. The area around the square abounds with expensive shops and names like Cartier, Boucheron, Van Cleef and the Ritz hotel give an idea of the opulence of its clientele.

From the Place Vendôme walk down the Rue de la Paix to the **Opéra**. This magnificently pretentious building, a tribute to the wealth and glorious bad taste of the Second Empire bourgeoisie, was begun in 1862 and completed in 1875. Its architect, Charles Garnier, wanted to give Europe's most glamorous capital its largest and most splendid theatre, and if he went over the top in its design, his creation is still loved by Parisians today — it is now called the Opéra Paris-Garnier in his honour. Its façade is ornate and its inside is sumptuous (Garnier apportioned more space to the public areas than to the theatre itself), with a marble and onyx staircase, mosaic-tiled roof in the foyer, and gigantic six-ton chandelier. It now has rather incongruous ceiling paintings by Chagall.

After the Opéra, the boulevards go down-market, with chain-stores, fast-food shops and cheap restaurants; and round the forbidding-looking temple of the Bourse, or Stock Exchange, is the dull and sedate business quarter. From here, you can either walk north along the Rue Montmartre, or take the Métro, to the **Boulevard de Clichy** and the **Place Pigalle**. This area at the foot of La Butte of Montmartre is the sleazy centre of traditional Paris nightlife, living on its reputation made in the days when Toulouse-Lautrec haunted the Moulin Rouge and immortalised it in paint. The famous windmill still twirls its sails at night, surrounded by porno-shops and sex-shows. During the day the area looks distinctly tatty, though the street markets are lively and colourful.

From here, climb the **Butte de Montmartre**, either by one of the side-streets such as the Rue des Martyrs, ending with a flight of steps, or by the long 'staircase' directly up to the Sacré-Coeur. The famous hill has become a legend both to Parisians and the world, and attracts tourists as a honeypot attracts bees. It has a long and colourful history. In Roman times it was a shrine to the god Mercury, then in AD250 renamed the Mont des Martyrs to commemorate the execution of St Denis. Another bloody event occurred in 1871, when hundreds of Communard rebels were massacred in the chalk caves — the Sacré-Coeur Basilica was built to expiate this crime. In the late nineteenth century, artists began to converge on Montmartre, creating its legend as the birthplace of modern art and the centre of La Vie Bohème. Today it is an uneasy blend of commercialism and real village life — reacting against the one, you may miss the charm of the other.

Montmartre's main attractions are its steep, narrow cobbled streets, with their arty shops and cheap, noisy bistros, its **Place du Tertre**, with its colourful pavement cafés and permanent side-show of artists haggling with their tourist models and the **Basilique du Sacré-Coeur**, with its dramatic façade. The icing-sugar domes of this grandiose but uninspired building can be seen from all over Paris, and it reciprocates by providing panoramic views of the city from the walkways round the domes. A much more interesting church lies just behind it: the Romanesque **St Pierre de Montmartre**, the oldest sanctuary in Paris, founded, some think, on a Roman temple and providing a welcome escape from the tourist melée in the nearby Place du Tertre.

There is much to see as you wander round those streets so familiar from Utrillo prints. Two windmills have been preserved, one of them the famous **Moulin de la Galette**, immortalised by Renoir. The **Vieux Montmartre Museum** has a complete old-fashioned bistro among its exhibits and the many art shops and galleries provide opportunities to see real artists at work. Above all, the atmosphere is unique — the old-fashioned street signs and lamp-posts, the cobbles, the cafés and bistros, the friendly *insouciance* (carefree, easy-going attitude) of the inhabitants, all give you the feeling of being in a nineteenth-century bohemian village. It is a shock to the senses when you descend, by steps or funicular, into the noisy modern world of the Boulevard Rochechouart below, to end your tour.

Before leaving Paris for a tour of the Île de France, three other areas out of the centre are worth a visit. The **Père Lachaise Cemetery**, to the east of the Bastille, is rewarding for a number of reasons. It is a pleasant spot — green, shaded and quiet. Nearly $1^1/_2$ million people have been buried there since it opened in 1804, including some of the world's most illustrious figures. It has a wealth of nineteenth-century sculpture in its tombs and monuments (Epstein's monument to Oscar Wilde is a fine example) and its Mur des Fédérés marks the spot where 147 Communards were shot in 1871 after making a last stand in the cemetery.

The two large parks, the **Bois de Boulogne** in the west and the **Bois de Vincennes** in the south-east, have a number of attractions for visitors. The former, simply known as 'the Bois', is a beautiful park with boating lakes, two racecourses (Auteuil and Longchamps), a miniature railway, elegant open-air restaurants, a children's garden and fun-fair, an exclusive sports club, and a superb walled English garden, the Bagatelle Park. This has the city's most magnificent display of flowers, particularly roses, grouped round a splendid 'folly'. The Bois de Vincennes, though rather less stylish and more 'popular', has many of the same attractions, plus some museums and France's largest zoo.

The Île de France

West Of Paris

The tour starts with France's most popular tourist attraction, the **Palace of Versailles,** so prepare yourself for crowds. You can reach it from Paris on the RER route C, or by car on the N10 or motorway A13. You will need a day at least to give it the attention it deserves — it is huge, with several sections, some with their own guided tours and some where you can wander at will, though you will still have to pay. The gardens and park, which you must see, are extensive and have two châteaux of their own to visit, the Grand and Petit Trianon.

Louis XIV was the Sun King and Versailles was his Sun Palace. He ruled as an absolute monarch, keeping his vast army of courtiers imprisoned here away from their own centres of power and that hot-bed of intrigue, Paris. Like the sun, radiating his own power from the centre, he even had his bed sited at the exact centre of the château! Its construction was a huge and ingenious feat, taking 21 years to complete (1661-82), and the architects (Mansart and Le

Vau), interior designer (Le Brun) and landscape gardener (Le Nôtre) all worked under his close control. The formal terraced gardens and park reflect the order Louis imposed on nature as on man, and are in perfect keeping with the palace architecture. The château was ravaged in the Revolution, and was later restored and turned into a museum.

The main attractions of the château are: the sculptured west façade overlooking the park; the superb chapel; the Grands Appartements, including the marvellous Hall of Mirrors (Salle des Glaces) and the King's Apartments; the Petits Appartements of Louis XV, Louis XVI, Marie-Antoinette and Mme DuBarry, smaller and more delicate than the grandeur of the Louis XIV style; and the Opéra Royale, built for the wedding of Louis XVI and Marie-Antoinette and magnificently restored. The gardens have geometrical flowerbeds, pools, fountains, sculptures, marble colonnades, avenues and intimate arbours. In the park beyond is an artificial Grand Canal, leading the eye away towards the horizon (boats can be hired). The gardens are brought to life in summer by two occasional events which recall the great days of Versailles: the Grands Eaux, an hour-long fountain display (2 or 3 Sundays each month), and the Fêtes de Nuit, a night-time firework show (once a month).

At the north-west edge of the park are two delightful small châteaux: the **Grand Trianon**, with its white and pink marble façade and sumptuous interior, was used by Louis XIV, and later Napoleon, as a refuge from affairs of state while the elegant **Petit Trianon**, built by Louis XV for Mme de Pompadour in 1768, was used by Marie-Antoinette and her friends for amateur dramatics. Its informal Anglo-Chinese gardens, with their make-believe rustic hamlet by a lake, were the ideal setting for playing at the simple peasant life. The town of Versailles was developed with the same controlled formality as the château, to accommodate its courtiers and dependants. It retains this elegance today, in spite of its expansion into a large residential Paris suburb.

St Germain-en-Laye, north of Versailles, is an even more affluent suburb on a hill between the Seine and the forest, 20km (12 miles) from Paris (RER route A). Its restored Renaissance château was the home of Louis XIV and his court before they moved to Versailles, and today houses the National Antiquities Museum, an important archaeological collection (prehistory to eighth-century AD). The famous terrace designed by Le Nôtre provides a fine panorama over the Seine with Paris in the distance.

Instead of the N10, take the D91 south-west from Versailles and pass through the **Chevreuse**, a pleasant area of sandy woods and river valleys, popular with Parisians for walks and picnics. **Dampierre** has an elegant seventeenth-century moated château in brick and stone, with fine interior furnishings and a spacious park. **Rambouillet** is much grander. Its château is the French President's summer residence, and it has a beautiful park and vast forest. Though the château is not particularly attractive, the park is fascinating. It has a dairy which looks like a Greek temple, established by Louis XVI for Marie-Antoinette (she liked to drink the milk), along with another of her favourite English gardens. It is home to a famous flock of Merino sheep. Louis bought them in Spain in 1786 and had them brought to Rambouillet by foot on an epic 4-month journey. Their descendants now form the basis of the **Bergerie Nationale** (National Sheep Farm) which has produced some impressive species. The splendid forest, with its oaks, birches and beeches, its

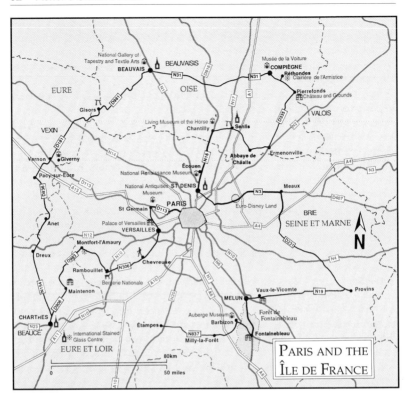

PARIS AND THE ÎLE DE FRANCE

streams, lakes, deer and wild boar, is a popular haunt of walkers (the GR1 runs right through the centre), and of cyclists and huntsmen. At its northern end is the picturesque village of **Montfort-l'Amaury**, which has a ruined castle, cobbled streets, tiled roofs, a church with some fine Renaissance stained glass, and an old charnel-house.

Continue south-west on the D906 to **Maintenon**, in the Eure Valley. Here is a curious row of arches, the remnant of an abandoned aqueduct with which Louis XIV had intended to divert the water from the Eure to Versailles to supply his fountains, but funds ran out before he could finish the job. The charming Gothic-Renaissance Château de Maintenon, with its pretty gardens by the Eure, was given by Louis to his favourite, the beautiful Mme de Maintenon. She was later his wife (but not his queen) and the power behind the throne in his later years. After Maintenon the road leaves the woods and valleys of the Île de France for the broad, open wheat-plains of the **Beauce**, France's bread-basket. From miles away you will see, soaring up before you, the majestic spires of Chartres Cathedral.

Chartres is a busy market-town, capital of the Beauce. While its medieval upper town clusters around the cathedral, its modern lower town stretches out beside the Eure. Here, from its hump-backed bridges, you can obtain wonderful views of one of Europe's most beautiful churches. Renowned for its magnificent western façade in rich golden stone, its asymmetrical twin towers, and its stained glass, probably the finest in the world, Chartres cathedral is one of the great treasures of France. It was built in the period of transition from Romanesque to Gothic, and reflects both styles. The elongated figures on the Royal Doorway (1145-55), depicting Christ in glory, contrast strongly with the more realistic later sculptures on the two side porches (1200-50), which portray Old and New Testament themes. Of the two towers, the famous south tower is Romanesque, while the Gothic northern tower and spire are ornate and elaborate.

Inside, the effect of the huge nave (the widest in France) and the ethereal colours of the stained glass is awe-inspiring. The glass tells the Biblical story in great detail, and repays long study (do not forget your binoculars); but its first impression is the lasting one — that famous Chartres blue mingling with the red and yellow to give a rich glow to the whole interior. The fourteenth-century carved stone choir screen is remarkable in its vivid detail, and the tenth-century crypt is the largest in France. Daily guided tours in English are usually given by experts and are well worth taking. The town also has an International Stained Glass Centre, a Fine Arts Museum in the Bishop's Palace, some fine old houses in the upper town, and an impressive Gothic church of St Pierre.

Turn north and take the N154 to **Dreux**. This industrial town on the border of Normandy has a church with a fine belfry, and, to the north, a stretch of attractive forest, with a charming royal hunting pavilion in the centre. On its northern edge, at **Anet**, is the remains of Diane de Poitier's Renaissance château, once the most beautiful in the land but now reduced to one wing. Follow the Eure valley to Pacy-sur-Eure, then the D181 to **Vernon**. This town is just inside Normandy, and capital of a region that straddles both provinces — the **Vexin**. This was a frequent battle-ground in the Middle Ages between

The Palace of Versailles is an irresistable attraction due to its Royal ancestry

the Crown and the Dukes of Normandy. Today it is a quiet, prosperous area of rich agricultural land and wooded hills, cut by the Seine with its broad meanders, and popular for country homes or weekend cottages. Its villages abound with châteaux and pretty churches, many of them Romanesque though often remodelled in the Renaissance.

Vernon is pleasantly situated on the left bank of the Seine, and is a good centre for exploring the area. It has a fine Gothic church and some old half-timbered houses with a Norman air, though the town's architecture is mainly Parisian. On the other bank, at Vernonnet, is a ruined medieval bridge and château. Cross the river and turn right for the village of **Giverny**, at the junction of the Epte and Seine. Monet made his home here, and his house and garden, now a museum, have become a major tourist attraction, especially for art and garden lovers (regular excursions from Paris). The gardens are ravishing, and seem to be in bloom throughout the year and the famous water-gardens beside his beloved Epte still have their Japanese bridge and hypnotic water-lilies. The house has been renovated, but retains many souvenirs of the Impressionist painter and his work.

Follow the Epte valley along the Normandy/Île-de-France border to **Gisors**. This frontier area is marked with ruined fortresses testifying to past struggles (Beaudemont, Château-sur-Epte, La Roche-Guyon), and Gisors was the main Norman stronghold on the Epte. Extensive remains of the fortress still exist, and there are attractive gardens inside the walls. The church of St Gervais-St Protais has some good Renaissance decoration.

From here take the D981 to **Beauvais**, the 'Chartres of the North'. There are some similarities between the two towns. They are both situated on a wide agricultural plain, and they both have soaring, majestic cathedrals, visible from far away. If Chartres has the most beautiful Gothic church in France, Beauvais has to have the most spectacular. Beauvais cathedral marks the limit to which Gothic can go in size, height and audacity of conception. It has the loftiest choir in the world, which has to be held up by huge double flying buttresses. The bishop who commissioned it in the early thirteenth century wanted to outdo Amiens, Paris and Chartres, and had the choir vaults built over 46m (150ft) high; but they fell down 12 years later and had to be rebuilt with strong supports. The church has always had structural problems, owing partly to poor foundations and partly to over-grandiose plans, and has never been completed. The attempt to impose a 137m (450ft) spire caused another collapse, and the nave was never finished — part of an early Romanesque building can be seen in its place. But even so, the cathedral is strikingly beautiful as well as spectacular. The transept doorways are adorned with fine late Gothic carvings, and there are good tapestries and stained glass, including a tree of Jesse in the north window. The astronomical clock is copied from the one at Strasbourg. Medieval Beauvais and its traditional industry of tapestry-making were largely destroyed by World War II bombardments. Only the cathedral remained, though its organ suffered a direct hit. There is little else to see in the town, except for a tapestry museum next to the cathedral, and the church of St Étienne with some good stained glass. Now is the time to head east on the N31.

East of Paris

Heading east from Beauvais on the N31 will bring you in 55km (34 miles) to **Compiègne**, an elegant town on the Oise whose château has been the country residence of kings from the early Frankish rulers to Napoleon III. The town has a pleasant shopping centre, an ornate late Gothic town hall, with wooden soldiers on the façade striking a carillon on the quarter-hour and the Vivenel Museum, with a fine collection of Greek vases. The château is less interesting for its grand apartments, furnished mainly in First and Second Empire styles, than for its Musée de la Voiture, which has a splendid collection of old cars, carriages and bicycles. Take the Allée des Beaux Monts from the château park into the Forêt de Compiègne. This is what attracted those monarchs over the years — one of the largest and loveliest forests in France.

The forest stretches from south-west to north-east of the town, crossed with roads and pathways, watered with streams and ponds, and ringed with hills providing splendid views. It has pretty villages, such as **St Jean-aux-Bois** and **Morienval**, which has the finest Romanesque church in the Île de France, and the small spa resort of **Pierrefonds**, dominated by its huge parody of a medieval fortress. This was simply a romantic ruin until Napoleon III, who had bought it cheaply, instructed Violet-le-Duc to restore it to its former glory in 1858, a task which took him 20 years. Today it is almost a Disneyland castle, with round towers and conical roofs overdone but great fun, especially for children. The best-known attraction of Compiègne forest is the Clairière de l'Armistice (wagon) hidden away in a clearing near **Réthondes**. Two armistices were signed in this railway carriage: one by Maréchal Foch in 1918, and the other, with ominous satisfaction, by Hitler in 1940, after which he took the original to Germany (the present carriage, a museum with wax figures, is a replica).

From Compiègne take the D932A south to **Senlis**. This quiet country town has one of the best-preserved old centres in the Île de France, and an elegant Gothic cathedral (recently restored) with a beautiful open tower and spire. It also has a wealth of Gallo-Roman remains, including a substantial portion of the town walls. There are two museums: a Museum of Art and Archaeology in the cobbled cathedral square; and the Musée de la Vénerie (Hunting Museum) in the ruins of the Château Royale. The town is surrounded by attractive forests, including the popular Fôret d'Ermenonville, which is almost one vast leisure centre, with its famous 'sea of sand', a lake, train and camel rides, and a zoo. The **Abbaye de Châalis**, within the forest, has picturesque overgrown ruins in the grounds, and its main building houses a superb art collection. Ermenonville has associations with the philosopher Jean-Jacques Rousseau, who died here.

Senlis is only 10km (6 miles) from **Chantilly**, a town famous for lace, sweetened whipped cream and horse-racing. This elegant small town has an aristocratic air, and hosts some of the most prestigious race-meetings in France (Prix du Jockey-Club, Prix de l'Arc de Triomphe) on the turf of its spacious race-course bordered by the famous eighteenth-century stables. These sumptuous buildings have now become the Living Museum of the Horse, a mecca for horse-lovers. Next to the race-course is the fairy-tale château, in an idyllic setting by a swan-lake at the edge of the forest. This was the seat of the Princes of Condé, a blue-blooded Bourbon family whose most illustrious son, the Great Condé, was a legendary war hero and entertainer of kings (his famous chef Vatel committed suicide when the fish was late). The château houses the precious Condé Collection of magnificent works of art, with paintings by many great masters and superb medieval illuminated manuscripts, including the *Très Riches Heures du duc de Berry*.

Chantilly forest is really a continuation of the Ermenonville and Halatte forests, famous in the past for deer-hunting and now popular with walkers (GR1, GR11 and GR12). On its western edge is **St Leu d'Esserent**, with a superb Romanesque-Gothic church and further south the Abbaye de Royaumont has a fine Gothic cloister and refectory, and pleasant gardens. It is now a cultural centre, providing regular concerts and exhibitions.

South of Chantilly, on the road to Paris, are two sites worthy of a detour. The first is a magnificent sixteenth-century castle, the **Château d'Écouen**. This sober, elegant creation of Anne de Montmorency (a man!) is now the National Renaissance Museum, with a splendid collection of tapestries, sculptures, ceramics, enamels and painted chimney-pieces illustrating the decorative arts of the Renaissance. A little further on, in the drab, working-class Paris suburb of **St Denis**, is the early Gothic basilica which has served through the years as the necropolis of the kings of France. All the kings were buried here, from the early Merovingians to Louis XVIII and although most of the bodies were destroyed in the Revolution, the tombs remain to give a fascinating display of the evolution of funeral art through the ages. St Denis can be reached from Paris by Métro.

East of Paris is the broad Marne Valley and the surrounding open farmland of the **Brie**, famous for its runny cheese. In this pleasant pastoral setting a new holiday development, opened in April 1992, extends over 5,000 acres of parkland on both sides of the A4 motorway 30km (19 miles) east of Paris. This is **Euro-Disneyland**, Europe's first American-style leisure-and-pleasure complex, developed by the Walt Disney Corporation on the model of Disneyland and Disney World in the USA. The aims of this vast undertaking are grandiose: the largest concentration of swimming pools in Europe; four of the continent's largest hotels; more visitors annually than the population of Greece; the biggest and most spectacular collection of funfair rides and shows ever staged and so on. The Disney family claim descent from a knight of Issigny, in Normandy, who sailed with Duke William in 1066 to conquer England. Their return to France after nearly 1,000 years offers Europeans a chance to sample the unique experience that has made their theme-parks two of America's biggest tourist attractions. Everybody can enjoy unlimited free rides once they have paid the high but not exorbitant entrance fee (go early or stay late to avoid queuing). Euro-Disney is easily accessible from Paris by RER or by motorway from channel ports, and accommodation is available through special package arrangements.

Meaux, 20km (12 miles) north-east of here on the A4, produces one of the best Brie cheeses, and is also known for its mustard. Though busy and industrial, it has an impressive Gothic cathedral with old precincts. Further south, **Provins** is a more interesting town, with well-preserved twelfth and thirteenth-century ramparts enclosing the charming old buildings and flowery gardens of the upper town. It has a long history, and was once the third largest town in France.

There are three sites worth a special visit south of Paris. The first is the magnificent seventeenth-century château of **Vaux-le-Vicomte**, east of the Seine near Melun. This was built by the same architects (Le Brun, Le Vau and Le Nôtre) who later built Versailles, and rivals it in beauty if not in size. This beauty is in harmony with its setting in a moat, surrounded by superb formal gardens, giving a unified effect to the whole scene. Its owner was Nicolas Fouquet, Louis XIV's extravagant finance minister, who entertained his master too lavishly and aroused his jealousy, thus causing his downfall. The king took over his entire team for the building of Versailles and imprisoned him for life. The château is privately owned, but open every day for visits. Special candlelight visits and fountain displays are held.

Melun is on the northern edge of the renowned and heavily-visited **Forêt de Fontainebleau**. This vast forest, with its lush vegetation, dramatic, grotesquely-shaped rocks and abundant wildlife, attracts hordes of visitors. It has the dramatic gorges of Apremont and Franchard, beloved of would-be mountaineers, and a network of clearly-marked walking and bridle-paths popular with hikers and artists have long admired and painted the landscape. One

---

Cuisine in Paris and the Île de France

There is no such thing as Parisian cuisine. It has two contributions to make to French gastronomy: to provide ample opportunity to sample the current vogue in food and eating habits, whether it be fast food, junk food, nouvelle cuisine or the latest overseas import; and to give a home to the many fugitives from the regions who have brought their culinary skills to the capital and set up restaurants here.

The Île de France is little better equipped than Paris with its own regional fare. It tends to reflect the cosmopolitan outlook of the capital it serves, both in its cuisine and its relatively high prices. It may have one or two regional specialities to offer — mustard from Meaux, soft cheese from the Brie, Chantilly cream — but no real cuisine of its own.

Restaurants

In Paris you really are spoilt for choice — but making that choice can be difficult. You will need to eat out, as most hotels do not provide meals, apart from continental breakfast and when they do, they are not usually the best places to eat. Other than taking pot luck (which is not usually a good idea), there are two ways to find out: either consult a specialist guide or ask hotel staff, local café owners or shopkeepers. Give them an idea of the sort of price you expect to pay (less than 300fr is cheap). As you might expect, restaurants are more expensive in Paris and the Île de France than in most other parts of the country, and though back-street bistros can be good value, they can also be pretty basic, both in quality and service.

Restaurants in the suburbs tend to be less expensive than those in the centre, and there are some cheap and basic eating places in the student sector of the Latin Quarter, near the Sorbonne. A short selection of restaurants in various price ranges is given on page 91 with addresses. Note that many restaurants close in August, and that booking is advisable.

nineteenth-century school of landscape painters, led by Millet and Rousseau, used to gather in the Auberge du Père Ganne in the woodland village of **Barbizon**. They became known as the 'Barbizon School', and have put this pretty, peaceful village on the tourist map. It is now full of cafés, inns, and hôtels, but worth visiting for the famous auberge (now a museum), Rousseau's and Millet's studios, and their tombs at nearby Chailly.

Fontainebleau forest has been the hunting ground of the kings of France since the Middle Ages, but it was François I who turned his hunting lodge into a palace in the sixteenth-century. He imported Florentine artists to create a new style on Renaissance principles but reflecting his own personality. The **Château de Fontainebleau** became the prototype for the Fontainebleau style — ornate, richly decorated, grand and imposing. The château was later added to and modified by his successors, and now has examples of every decorative style from the Renaissance to the Empire. It is full of splendours. The court-yard with the famous horseshoe staircase, known as the 'Cour des Adieux' after Napoleon abdicated here in 1814; the François I gallery, with its rich decoration in the style of Michaelangelo; the Henry II ballroom; the apart-ments of the three queen mothers (Catherine and Marie de Medicis and Anne of Austria); the Louis XIII Throne Room; the Louis XV Council Chamber; Marie-Antoinette's boudoir; many salons redecorated by Napoleon and the Napoleon III theatre. The gardens are in two parts: to the west, formally French; to the east, like an English park.

The magnificent Fontainebleau château is a suitable place to end your tour. There are other attractions in the area: Fontainebleau town is smart and lively; Milly-la-Forêt, Courances and Moret-sur-Loing are attractive villages on the edge of the forest and, further afield, Étampes and St Sulpice-de-Favières have interesting churches. But if you do not wish to linger, the N7 leads south.

Additional Information

Places of Interest in Paris

Most national museums close on Tuesdays, and some are either cheaper or free on Sundays or Wednesdays. Paris municipality museums are gener-ally open Tuesday and closed Monday.

Conciergerie
Under Palais de Justice
Open: 10am-5pm daily.

Musée de Cluny
Latin Quarter: on old Roman baths
Open: 9.45am-12.30pm and 2-5pm, except Tuesday.

Musée d'Orsay
Open: 10.30am-6pm; Sunday 9am-6pm; closed Monday.

Musée Rodin
77 Rue de Varenne
Open: 10am-5.30pm, 4.30pm in winter; except Tuesday.

Musée de l'Armée
Hôtel des Invalides
Open: 10am-5pm or 6pm according to season.

Eiffel Tower
Open: 9.30am-11pm 1st and 2nd levels; 9.30am-8pm top level.

Palais de Chaillot
(Musée de L'Homme)
Open: 9.45am-5.15pm except Tuesday.
Also houses Naval Museum, Museum of French Monuments, Cinema Museum and Aquarium.

Modern Art Museum
11 Avenue du Pres.-Wilson
Open: 10am-5.30pm; 10am-8pm
Wednesday. Closed Monday.

Picasso Museum
Marais 5 Rue de Thorigny
Open: 9.45am-5.15pm, except Tuesday.

Hôtel Carnavalet
History of Paris
Marais
Open: 10am-5.40pm, closed Monday;
free Sunday.

Hôtel Soubise
National Archives
Marais
Open: 2-5pm daily except Tuesday.

Beaubourg
Open: 12noon-10pm daily; 10am-10pm
Saturday and Sunday, closed Tuesday.

Louvre
Open: 9am-6pm, 9am-9.45pm Monday
and Wednesday; closed Tuesday. Free
on Sunday.

Orangerie
In Tuileries Gardens
Open: 9.45am-5.15pm; closed Tuesday.

Grand Palais/Petit Palais
Champs-Elysées
Temporary exhibitions, modern science,
planetarium, fine arts.
Open: 10am-8pm daily, 10am-10pm
Wednesday; closed Tuesday.

Arc de Triomphe
Open: summit, 9am-5pm daily.

Useful Information: Paris

Breakdowns:
Two companies which offer 24-hour
breakdown service are Automobile Club
Secours ☎ 05 05 05 24 (toll-free number)
and SOS Dépannage ☎ 47 07 99 99
S.N.C.F. Trains ☎ 45 82 50 50
Change: Galeries Lafeyette C.C.F. ☎ 45
26 20 63. Monday to Saturday from
9.30am to 5.45pm.

Poste Centrale/Central Post Office.
☎ 40 28 20 00 24h, 52 rue du Louvre.
Pharmacie 24h, 84, av des Champs-
Elysées ☎ 45 62 02 41
S.O.S. Médecins/Medical Emergency,
☎ 47 07 77 77 or 43 37 77 77

Tourist Information Centre
Syndicat d'Initiative and Accueil de
France
127 Avenue des Champs-Elysées
☎ 47 23 61 72
Open: daily 9am-8pm.

Places of Interest in the Île de France

Versailles
*Palace, gardens, park, Grand and Petit
Trianon Châteaux*
Open: 9.45am-5.30pm except Monday
and national holidays; park daily
sunrise-sunset; occasional lecture-tours
(☎ 39 50 58 32)
Petit Trianon 3-5pm or 6pm except
Saturday, Monday and holidays.

St Germain-en-Laye
National Antiquities Museum
Open: 9.45am-12noon and 1.30-5pm,
except Tuesday.

Rambouillet
Bergerie Nationale
Open: 10am-12noon and 2-6pm or 5pm
out of season, except Tuesday and
Wednesday.

Maintenon
Château
Open: April to October 2-6pm; Sunday
and national holidays 10am-12noon and
2-6pm; off-season Saturday and Sunday
afternoons.

Chartres
International Stained Glass Centre
Exhibitions
Open: 10am-6pm, except Tuesday.

Giverny
Monet's House and Gardens
Open: 10am-6pm April to October.

Beauvais
National Gallery of Tapestry & Textile Arts
Open: 9.30-11.30am and 2-6pm; 10-11.30am and 2.30-4.30pm off-season, except Monday and national holidays.

Compiègne
Musée de la Voiture
In château
Open: 9.30-11.15am and 1.30-4.30pm; except Tuesday and national holidays.

Réthondes
1918 Armistice Railway Wagon
Compiègne Forest
Open: 8am-12noon and 1.30-6.30pm March to 11 November; 9am-12noon and 2-5.30pm except Tuesday, 12 November to February.

Pierrefonds
Château and grounds
Compiègne Forest
Open: 10am-1.45pm and 2-5.45pm April to October; 2-4pm October to March; closed Tuesday and Wednesday.

Abbaye de Châalis
Nr Senlis
Jacquemart-André collections
Open: 1.30-6pm Monday, Wednesday, Saturday, Sunday March to November, park daily except Tuesday.

Chantilly
Living Museum of the Horse
In eighteenth-century stables
Open: 10.30am-5.30pm; 2-4.30pm in winter, weekend 10.30am-5.30pm; closed Tuesday.

Écouen
National Renaissance Museum
Open: 9.45am-12.45pm and 2-5.15pm; closed Tuesday; free Wednesday.

Vaux-le-Vicomte
Château and Gardens
Open: March to 10 November 10am-1pm and 2-6pm; winter weekends only 2-5pm; closed January.

Fontainebleau
Château and Gardens
Open: 9.30am-12noon and 2-5pm except Tuesday; gardens and park, sunrise-sunset.

Barbizon
Auberge Museum
Fontainebleau forest
Open: April to October 10am-5.30pm, except Tuesday.

Euro-Disneyland
Off A4 motorway, 30km (19 miles) east of Paris.
Open: day and night.
Hotel accommodation on site; package arrangements via a number of travel agencies.

Tourist Information Centres in the Île de France

Beauvais
Office de Tourisme
Rue Beauregard
☎ 44 45 08 18

Chartres
Office de Tourisme
Place Cathédrale
☎ 37 21 50 00

Compiègne
Office de Tourisme and Accueil de
    France
Place Hôtel de Ville
☎ 44 40 01 00

Fontainebleau
Office de Tourisme
31 Place N. Bonaparte
☎ 64 22 25 68

Provins
Office de Tourisme
Place H. de Balzac
☎ 64 00 16 35

Vernon
Office de Tourisme
36 Rue Carnot
☎ 32 51 39 60

Versailles
Office de Tourisme
7 Rue Réservoirs
☎ 39 50 36 22

Restaurants in Paris

Higher-Priced — above 400fr.
Grand Vefour
17 Rue Beaujolais
☎ 42 96 56 27

Jacques Cagna
14 Rue des Grands-Augustins
☎ 43 26 49 39

Laurent
41 Avenue Gabriel
☎ 42 25 00 39

L'Ambroisie
9 Place des Vosges
☎ 42 78 51 45

Le Divellec
107 Rue de l'Université
☎ 45 51 91 96

Les Ambassadeurs
10 Place de la Concorde
☎ 42 65 24 24

Ritz-Espadon
15 Place Vendôme
☎ 42 60 38 30

Taillevent
15 Rue Lamennais
☎ 45 61 12 90

Tour d'Argent
15 Quai Tournelle
☎ 43 54 23 31

Vivarois
192 Avenue Victor Hugo
☎ 45 04 04 31

Medium-Priced — 300-400fr.
Beauvilliers
52 Rue Lamarck
☎ 42 54 54 42

Carré des Feuillants
14 Rue Castiglione
☎ 42 86 82 82

Charlot 1er 'Merveilles des Mers'
128 Boulevard de Clichy
☎ 45 22 47 08

Etoile d'Or
3 Place du Géneral-Koenig
☎ 40 68 51 28

La Cantine des Gourmets
113 Avenue de la Bourdonnais
☎ 47 05 47 96

Le Petit Bedon
38 Rue Pergolèse
☎ 45 00 23 66

Mercure Galant
15 Rue des Petits-Champs
☎ 42 97 53 85

Quai des Ormes
72 quai Hôtel de Ville
☎ 42 74 72 22

Relais Louis XIII
1 Rue du Pont-de-Lodi
☎ 43 26 75 96

Restaurant Opéra-Café de la Paix
Place de l'Opera
☎ 47 42 97 02

Lower-Priced — below 300fr.
Bistro 121
121 Rue de Convention
☎ 45 57 52 90

Bistrot de Paris
33 Rue de Lille
☎ 42 61 16 83

Chez Augusta
98 Rue de Tocqueville
☎ 47 63 39 97

Chez Pauline
5 Rue Villedo
☎ 42 96 20 70

Copenhague (Danish)
142 Avenue des Champs-Elysées
☎ 43 59 20 41

Jules Verne
2nd floor Eiffel Tower
☎ 45 55 61 44

La Boule d'Or
13 Boulevard de La-Tour-Maubourg
☎ 47 05 50 18

La Cagouille
10 Place Constantin Brancusi
☎ 43 22 09 01

La Petite Auberge
38 Rue Laugier
☎ 47 63 85 51

Pantagruel
20 Rue de l'Exposition
☎ 45 51 79 96

Petite Bretonnière
2 Rue Cadix
☎ 48 28 34 39

Pharamond
24 Rue Grand-Truanderie
☎ 42 33 06 72

Récamier
4 Rue Récamier
☎ 45 48 86 58

Tam Dinh (Vietnamese)
60 Rue Verneuil
☎ 45 44 04 84

Timgad (N.African)
21 Rue Brunel
☎ 45 74 23 70

Restaurants in the Île de France

R = With Accommodation
Barbizon (R)
Bas-Bréau
☎ 60 66 40 05

Chambray
Le Vol au Vent
☎ 32 36 70 05

Coignières
Auberge du Capucin Gourmand
☎ 34 61 46 06

Compiègne (at Réthondes)
Auberge du Pont
☎ 44 85 60 24

Cormeilles-en-Vexin
Relais Ste Jeanne
☎ 34 66 61 56

Enghien-les-Bains
Duc d'Enghien
☎ 34 12 90 00

Fleurines (Nr Senlis)
Vieux Logis
☎ 44 54 10 13

Fontainebleau
Aigle Noir Rest Le Beauharnais (R)
☎ 64 22 32 65

Houdan
La Poularde
☎ 30 59 60 50

La Ferté-sous-Jouarre
Auberge de Condé
☎ 60 22 00 07

Le Châtelet-en-Brie
Auberge Briarde
☎ 60 69 47 32

Les Mesnuls
Toque Blanche
☎ 34 86 05 55

Milly-la-Forêt
Le Moustier
☎ 64 98 92 52

Montfort l'Aumary
Auberge de l'Arrivée
☎ 34 86 00 28

Vernon
Les Fleurs
☎ 32 51 16 80

4

BRITTANY

B rittany is a lovely region for a holiday. It has fine sandy beaches which are never too crowded, the sea has real tides and is clean and warm in summer, the shellfish are marvellous and abundant, the coastal scenery is attractive and the weather can be kind. But there is more to Brittany than this. It has a strong and mysterious personality all its own, which is worthwhile getting to know. It has a variety of scenery, its own culture, language and customs, and a history that reaches back to the dawn of time.

The old name for Brittany was *Armorica*, or 'Land of the Sea' and the long coastline is the region's greatest asset. It is so deeply indented that no-one can really say how long it is. Its scenery varies from deep, shallow inlets (mainly on the south coast) to high, savage cliffs and boulder-strewn headlands, and, in the south-east corner, to the flat salt marshland of the Brière. Inland, the scenery is less varied — mainly agricultural land or bare low hills with heather and gorse. The forests are few and small as the great forest that once covered the whole of central Brittany was destroyed during her turbulent past.

Brittany's history is a long one, stretching back to those pre-Celtic tribes who littered the landscape with megalithic monuments at some period between 2000 and 4000BC. Who they were, and what their standing stones and burial mounds signified, are still matters of conjecture. Later, in Celtic times, the land was imbued with Arthurian legends and associated with the Holy Grail. These and other folk-tales were sung by minstrels in the Breton lays. They have always been seafaring people, and in times of poverty, some of them made their living (and an unsavoury reputation), from 'wrecking' and piracy. In the Middle Ages the Duchy was ravaged by war and repeatedly invaded by English and French, until it was finally united with France in 1547. The sufferings of the Bretons through their long history have made them a deeply religious people. This is shown in their veneration for old, obscure saints, and in their fondness for religious processions, or *pardons*.

Brittany is part of the European Celtic Fringe. Its traditions are linked to those of Scotland, Ireland, Wales, Cornwall, and Galicia in north-west Spain. They share a common geography and climate; their languages and customs are closely related, and older than most others in Europe, and their sense of their own identity is kept alive only by constant struggle. These links go back to earliest times, when Bretons and Cornishmen used to meet for annual competitive games, and it is being reborn today with pan-Celtic conferences and festivals. Today Bretons are proud of their Celtic language and traditional dress, music, dance and fine arts.

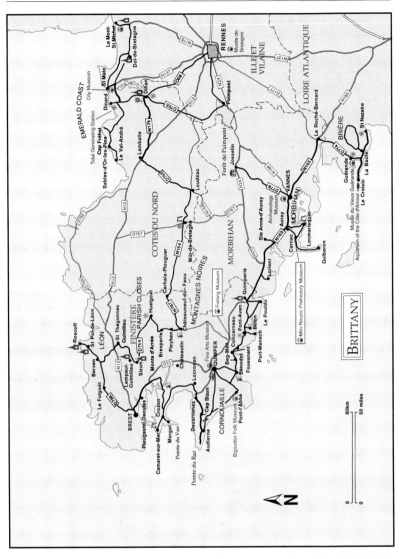

This tour begins on the western edge of Normandy, at Le-Mont-St-Michel, and ends at the mouth of the Loire, at St Nazaire.

The North East

❀ Although **Mont-St-Michel** is not quite in Brittany, it is an appropriate place to start a tour of the peninsula. It is one of the most popular tourist sites in France (it claims to be the most popular), and it has an affinity with the Celtic world, being a larger version of St Michael's Mount in Cornwall. Starting here gives you the chance for a last taste of that rich Normandy cuisine — try the spit-roast salt-meadow lamb or an omelette *Mère Poulard* in one of the excellent restaurants.

Perhaps your most indelible memory of this stupendous site will be your first view of it. As you approach it along the road bordering the Couesnon estuary, it rears up out of the sea like an island in some Arthurian legend, its harmonious pyramidal shape made more dramatic by the flatness of the surrounding salt-marshland. The discrete parts gradually become clearer: the surrounding walls at the bottom, with the village clustered around the rock behind them; the abbey buildings perched on rock outcrops higher up and, crowning the whole ensemble, the abbey church with its slender spire. Unfortunately, once inside the gates you may be less enchanted. The crowds in the steep, narrow streets and the souvenir shops are formidable in summer — press on beyond these to the abbey itself for your reward. Better still, stay overnight on the rock before starting your tour. You can then wander the lower streets at night, when they revert from the suffocating to the picturesque, and visit the abbey early before the crowds arrive.

The rock has a long history. It was a burial mound in Celtic times (called Mont-Tombe); the first abbey was founded in the eighth century, and the island renamed after the Archangel who had appeared to its founder. The abbey was enlarged and consolidated over the centuries, and a succession of magnificent churches built. It was fortified during the Hundred Years War, and though often threatened by the English was never taken. During the Middle Ages it became a high-place of pilgrimage. Later, monastic discipline became lax and the abbey declined. It was desecrated in the Revolution and converted into a prison in the nineteenth century, before being taken over and restored by the State in 1874. Today, a small monastic community is once again in residence.

The crowning glory of Mont-St-Michel is its abbey. Its construction was a

Dinan's enchanting medieval ambience makes it one of the most attractive towns in Brittany

considerable feat, requiring the summit to be strengthened with support buildings before the upper part could be added. The skill of the construction is most clearly seen in the incredible *merveille*, or 'marvel' (1203-28), which consists of three large Gothic halls one on top of the other, containing, respectively, an almshouse, a guests' hall and refectory. They seem to be hanging in mid-air on the side of the rock. The abbey church is magnificent (Romanesque, but with a late-Gothic choir) and the cloisters with their delicate colonnades are open on two sides to the sea. The earlier rooms below contain the original Carolingian crypt (Notre-Dame-sous-Terre). The views from the terrace, cloisters and lacework staircase are spectacular. The best parts of the abbey can only be visited on a guided tour (some in English). Down below, there is a parish church and three museums, and a fine rampart walk.

Before leaving Mont-St-Michel, you can walk round the base of the rock in about half an hour, but be careful of the tides — the sea comes in quickly, and there are dangerous quicksands. The site is spectacular during the spring and autumn high tides when the sea rushes in with great force. Colourful spring and autumn festivals are held in May and September.

Re-cross the *marais*, or marsh-flats, and turn right for St Malo. You can either take the inland road, via **Dol-de-Bretagne**, or the coast road, along the bay of Mont-St-Michel. Dol-de-Bretagne, whose name confirms that you are in Brittany, is a small, attractive town with a fine cathedral. Once an important bishopric and seaport, it is now capital of the *marais*. The bay is now unattractive, with long stretches of mud-flats, but has good distant views of Mont-St-Michel and good oysters and mussels at the fishing port of Cancale. At the western end of the bay is the **Pointe du Grouin**, the most easterly point of north Brittany's rocky coastline, which provides a spectacular view of the bay. At nearby Rothéneuf, a water-sports centre, 300 granite rocks have been sculpted into fascinating shapes by a local priest.

St Malo is a busy and popular channel port well-known to many English visitors who come across on the ferry. Though virtually destroyed in 1944, it has been rebuilt tastefully in the severe traditional style, using a rather forbidding grey granite. The town has four sectors: the two surrounding seaside suburbs of Paramé, with a fine beach, and St Servan, with rocky cliffs; the port, with its four wet docks and outer harbour; and the Ville Close or old walled city. The old town has an impressive site on a sandy island which was once connected to the mainland only at low tide. It is completely surrounded by medieval ramparts, strengthened by Vauban in the eighteenth century and preserved in the last war. The walk round these provides magnificent views of the sea and its islets, particularly at high tide when the waves beat upon the ramparts. Inside are the narrow streets of the old city, where the shipowners and mariners lived who contributed to St Malo's past prosperity. This is now a pedestrian area, with cafés and souvenir shops, and the much-restored cathedral in the centre. It is overlooked by the grim castle, once a prison and now housing the town hall and local history museum. The three islets of Grand Bé, Petit Bé and Fort National can be reached at low tide. Grand Bé was the solitary last home of St Malo's most illustrious son, the Romantic poet Chateaubriand. His tomb is on the island.

Opposite St Malo at the mouth of the Rance is **Dinard**. The Rance estuary is long and impressive, stretching inland 32km (20 miles) as far as Dinan, and

to harness its tidal power it has been dammed just below the mouth. You can ✳
drive across the dam from St Servan to Dinard, and visit the Tidal Generating
Station on the left bank. There is a lock nearby for boats to sail through. Boat
trips down the Rance estuary between St Malo and Dinan are popular and
very enjoyable. Dinard is a rather faded fashionable resort developed by the
British in late-Victorian times, with luxury hotels and mock-Gothic villas set
in exotic gardens. Today it is quiet and sedate, with pleasant promenades,
good beaches, a casino, a sea museum, sports facilities and boat trips to nearby ✦
islands. Beyond Dinard, the Emerald Coast continues as far as Le Val-André
in the west. It is a wild, broken, picturesque coastline with fine vantage points
from the rocky headlands, the most spectacular of which is Cap Fréhel. In
between the headlands are a succession of good sandy beaches, particularly
at Sable-d'Or-les-Pins.

Turn inland to **Dinan**, one of the most attractive towns in Brittany. It is an ✳
old walled town in a beautiful situation high above the River Rance, with a
little yacht marina and Gothic bridge on the river below. Its charm is its well-
preserved medieval atmosphere, with narrow cobbled streets overhung with
half-timbered houses, and a complete girdle of crenellated ramparts. Though
the houses are built of light grey granite, their window-boxes and pretty
gardens give them an air of gaiety reminiscent of more southerly climes. In the
centre is the picturesque Place des Merciers, while running down to the port
is the steep Rue du Jerzual with its sixteenth-century craftsmen's houses,
workshops and *crêperies*. A castle with a handsome oval keep houses a local
history museum; and the Basilica of St Sauveur holds a precious relic, the heart 🏛
of Bertrand du Guesclin. This swarthy Breton is the region's most illustrious
son and one of France's legendary heroes. A fourteenth-century Constable of
France and its ablest leader during the Hundred Years' War, he died in action
at Châteauneuf-de-Randon in the south and his body was led in state back to
his native town, parts of it being buried en route at Le Puy, Montferrand and
St Denis, and only the heart at Dinan. The church which holds it is a blend of 🛆
Romanesque, Gothic and Renaissance styles. Dinan has long had a sizeable
English community, whose presence is acknowledged in the attractive Jardin
Anglais, which has a fine view over the river.

Dinan makes a good base for a tour of the surrounding valleys of the Rance
and Arguenon. Further south, **Rennes**, the capital of Brittany, is a large
commercial and industrial town whose character is more French than Breton.
It has an interesting museum of Breton history and folklore. West of Rennes
is the **Forêt de Paimpont**, the largest forest in Brittany but only a remnant of
the great forest of Brocéliande mentioned in Arthurian folk-tales. It was the 🌲
home of the sorcerer Merlin and the fairy Viviane, and Arthur and his Knights
had some of their adventures here. The forest is heavily replanted with
conifers, but has a number of pleasant lakes.

Take the N176 from Dinan to Lamballe, the D768 to Loudeac and the N164
to **Mûr-de-Bretagne**, a lively little town prettily set in meadows and oak trees
(often painted by Corot), with a seventeenth-century chapel and a nearby
cromlech. It is a good base for exploring a picturesque area in central Brittany
where the waters of the Blavet river are dammed to form the winding reservoir called **Lac de Guerlédan**. This is quiet countryside of narrow steep-sided
gorges with crags and boulders, small forests of beech, spruce and pine,

scrubland, heath, field and pasture. Lac de Guerlédan is a splendid stretch of water, pleasantly wooded, providing fine views and lovely sailing.

Western Brittany
Continuing west on the N164, at Carhaix-Plouguer you enter the most westerly department of Brittany, **Finistère** (from the Latin *Finis Terrae* — 'The End of the World'). This is the land where Breton is widely spoken and Celtic traditions are strong, in dress, mythology, song and dance. To your left are the **Montagnes Noires**, a range of low hills once darkly-wooded (hence 'black'), now partly reforested, partly bare heathland with jagged rock outcrops. To your right, the more northerly range of the **Monts d'Arrée**, Brittany's highest mountains, rise to a height of 384m (1,260ft). They are slightly higher, wilder and more desolate than the Montagnes Noires, bare or covered in bracken and gorse. Both are old, eroded mountain ranges, and together they constitute the central spine of Brittany. Between them, on the northern slopes of the Montagnes Noires, is a little-known but peaceful area of delightful villages, with good fishing, walking and horse-riding.

A good centre for exploring this area is **Châteauneuf-du-Faou**, prettily sited on the slope of a hill overlooking the Aulne, with superb salmon and pike

Cobbled streets and half-timbered buildings in Dinan

The most elaborate calvary in the land, Guimiliau

Guimiliau's rival are carvings at St Thégonnec

fishing and a panoramic view of the Montagnes Noires. It has a festival of dance in mid-August and a colourful *pardon* on the last Sunday in August, starting with a candlelight procession from the chapel. A tour from here could include: **Cléden-Poher**, a typical Breton village with a fine parish close, a fifteenth-century church with good carving, and an interesting cemetery with an ossuary, elegant calvary, and two boat-shaped sacristies; **St Goazec**, a village of legends, with its dolmens, megaliths and stones, and a château housing an experimental farm; **Collorec**, with its old watermills and ancient bridge; Spézet and Gouézec with fine stained glass in their churches, and near Spézet, the charming **Notre-Dame-du-Crann** chapel, with its beautiful sixteenth-century stained-glass windows; and **Landelau**, with good canoeing, fishing and walks. Fine views can be obtained from the **Roc de Toullaëron** (the highest point in the Montagnes Noires at 326m, 1,069ft) and at the **Laz** viewpoint.

The area abounds in legends and folklore. One popular belief is that if Finistère is threatened by invaders you will see, ranged along the hill-crests of the Montagnes Noires at dawn, the *fantassins* (foot-soldiers) and knights in battle order of the army of King Arthur come to defend his land. That land is **Cornouaille**, the south-west part of Finistère named after the Celts who settled here from Cornwall in the sixth century. Bretons still venerate many obscure, long-deconsecrated saints, mainly early Celtic missionaries from Britain. Their memory is preserved in the names of villages, and they and their lives are depicted in painting and sculpture in parish closes.

Parish closes are common in this region, although the finest examples are a little further north, beyond the Monts d'Arrée. The parish close is unique to Brittany, the finest expression of Breton faith and artistic feeling. It grew out of their religious fervour and preoccupation with death (the skeletal figure of Death, or Ankou, is always present among the figures in the sculpted groups), coupled with rivalry between villages which caused them to try to outdo one another in rich ornamentation. It is popular art, born in the villages rather than the towns, and related to the Passion Plays which were popular here in the Middle Ages and beyond. The typical parish close has a gateway in the form of a triumphal arch, often richly ornamented with figures. Inside the graveyard, in front of the church, is a calvary, with a Crucifixion scene on a base decorated with groups of figures from Bible stories which are meant to illustrate the Scriptures for the majority who could not read. Beside the church is an ossuary, also richly decorated, holding the bones of the dead who could not be accommodated in the graveyard. The church porch is ornamented with statues, and the interior with animated wood carvings, often brightly painted, and with a carved and painted glory beam across the nave. In the best parish closes, church and churchyard form one unified ensemble. They were produced in the sixteenth to seventeenth century, and combine Renaissance decoration with local folk-art styles.

A selection of the best parish closes can be seen on a round tour. Take the N164 west from Châteauneuf-du-Faou to **Pleyben**, which has a magnificent calvary (the largest in Brittany) and a fine Gothic church with a remarkable Renaissance tower crowned with a dome and small lantern-turrets.

Turn north on the D785 to **Brasparts**, with a typical parish close whose calvary has a Pietà and its ossuary has two figures of Ankou at the corners.

Turn west on the D14 to **St Herbot**, whose desolately-sited small church has a finely-carved wooden screen, and outside a Renaissance ossuary and a fine Crucifix. Further on, **Huelgoat** is a good excursion centre in the Monts d'Arrée, beautifully sited between a small lake and a beautiful hilly forest with dense undergrowth, streams and picturesque granite rocks. Ascend the bare, heath-covered mountains by the D764 and turn left on the D785 to **Roc de Trévezel**, where a short walk brings you to a rocky escarpment with a fine panorama over the whole of Finistère. To the north lies the Léon plateau, bristling with church spires. On a fine day, the superb Kreisker spire at **St Pol-de-Léon** on the north coast can be seen. Nearby is the peat bog which locals call the Yeun Ellez, or 'Mouth of Hell'.

Continue westwards to **Sizun**, whose parish close has a magnificent sixteenth-century triumphal arch and a fine ossuary chapel, with decorated carved beams in the church. Floodlit guided tours are given on summer evenings. The road north leads to **Lampaul-Guimiliau**, with a splendid painted rood-beam and other carvings in the church and, to the north-east, to the two famous villages which rival each other in claiming the finest parish close in Brittany. Of the two, **Guimiliau** boasts the most elaborate calvary in the land, with over 200 sculpted figures. It dates from 1581 to 1588 and depicts scenes from the Passion and cautionary folk-tales, including the grim story of *Catell-Gollet* or 'Catherine the Lost', a servant girl who had a love-affair with the Devil. The poor girl is shown in the jaws of Hell, being torn limb from limb by demons. Guimiliau church is splendid, with a charming south porch adorned with statuettes and, inside, a wealth of ornament including a superb carved oak baptistry. Its rival, **St Thégonnec**, has perhaps the most elegant ensemble of any parish close. The beautiful ossuary and the church, with its rich carving, are the key elements in this magnificent sixteenth- to seventeenth-century Renaissance group. The elaborately-carved pulpit is one of the masterpieces of Breton art.

You are now in **Léon**, a fertile agricultural plateau of north-west Brittany known for its production of early vegetables such as artichokes, cauliflowers, onions and potatoes. The north coast has cliffs of pink granite, corniches and deep inlets, while the north-west area of the *abers*, or shallow estuaries, is a low, rocky coast dotted with islands and rich in seaweed. Continue north to **Berven**, whose parish close has a fine arch and a Renaissance church with an ornate screen. Nearby, on the coast, are the busy fishing and passenger port of **Roscoff** and the pleasant market town of **St Pol-de-Léon** with two of the finest buildings in Brittany, the beautifully-proportioned former cathedral, and the Kreisker Chapel, with a magnificent belfry. To the west on the D788, **Le Folgoët**, with its impressive Flamboyant Gothic church (fine carved granite rood-screen), is renowned as the home of one of Brittany's biggest *pardons*, or pilgrimages.

You should try to see a pardon while in the area. They are an important feature of Breton life, combining elements of pagan ritual with religious observance. A solemn procession of pilgrims, dressed in regional costume, makes its way to the local calvary or chapel where a religious ceremony is held, after which it turns into a more secular occasion, with food and drink, dancing, wrestling, stone-tossing and other trials of strength. The Great Pardon at Le Folgoët takes place on 7 and 8 September, or the Sunday before, with a cattle market the day after. Other pardons are held every Sunday in May, the fourth Sunday in July (to St Christopher, when they bless their cars), and 15 August. Other pardons take place regularly all over Brittany, though more frequently in Finistère. The biggest are at Ste Anne-d'Auray (throughout the summer), Tréguier, Perros-Guirec, Rumengol, St Jean-du-Doigt and Ste Anne-la-Palud. Dates vary, so consult the local Syndicat d'Initiative.

From Le Folgoët, take the D788 towards **Brest**, a large shipbuilding town and base of the French Navy. It was rebuilt after extensive war damage, and is unappealing to tourists, though from its superb roadstead you can see ships of many types and many nations. Skirt the town on the D205 and cross the estuary on the Pont A. Louppe, an impressive bridge with spectacular views over one of the finest natural harbours in the world. To your right on the strawberry-growing Plougastel peninsula is its chief town, **Plougastel-Daoulas**. The town and its church are unattractive, but it has a magnificent calvary, second only to Guimiliau for its population of carved figures (180). Built in 1602-4 after the plague of 1598, it was inspired by the Guimiliau Calvary and is perhaps better proportioned, though its figures are less lifelike.

The whole coast is wild and deeply indented, with the sea crashing in and constantly eroding the rocky, jutting shoreline. Much of it is bleak and wind-swept, but with bays and estuaries providing shelter from the cruel Atlantic. The central 'tongue' of this coast, between the 'jaws' of Léon and Cornouaille, is the Crozon peninsula, perhaps its most dramatic section. Take the N165 from Brest to Le Faou, then turn right on the D791 along a scenic corniche road to **Crozon**. This is a good base from which to explore the headlands and capes of the hammer-shaped peninsula: Dinan, Penhir and Espagnols points, and the capes of the Chèvre and Île Longue. The coast is harshly beautiful, with

This illustrative carving can be seen at Locronan

head-swimming views from the steep cliffs down to the angry breakers crashing on the multi-coloured rocks below. **Camaret-sur-Mer** is an important but dingy lobster port with an impressive array of menhirs nearby — the Lagatjar Lines. **Morgat** is a popular seaside resort with an excellent, sheltered sandy beach and caves to explore at low tide.

This peninsula is part of the Armorican Regional Park. At its base is the **Menez-Hom**, a rounded peak 330m (1,082ft) high, detached from the rest of the Montagnes Noires and commanding the best views in Brittany. On clear days it has a panorama on all sides — over the Crozon, Léon and Cornouaille peninsulas to the west, eastward to the mountain ranges, north and south to the coast (viewing table). Take the D887 from Crozon and branch off left onto the D83 (2km, 1 mile). Return and travel south on the D63 to **Locronan**, a very ✳ pretty and prosperous village beloved of tourists. Though it is popular it is not spoiled, as its fine Renaissance houses, church and chapel blend harmoniously round the charming village square with its old well in the centre. All the buildings are in grey granite, and with the open moors behind the place looks distinctly Gaelic. It was once famous for making sailcloth, and still keeps alive its weaving traditions, with plenty of craft shops to display its products. The Pénity Chapel, attached to the church, holds the black granite tomb of a local saint, St Ronan, and his life story is told in beautiful naive carvings on the church pulpit. The annual pardon in July, called a *Troménie*, retraces the path of his daily walk up the local hill; every sixth year they have a Grande Troménie, a huge, 10km (6 mile) long procession attracting pilgrims from all over Cornouaille.

Modern **Cornouaille** (though once it was larger) is the southern peninsula west of Quimper, centre of the old Kingdom of Brittany and its most unaffectedly Celtic part in appearance and traditions. Most of it apart from its northern rocky peninsula is flat and windswept, with hamlets of low whitewashed houses. Lining the coast are busy fishing villages specialising in sardines and crayfish, while the interior is densely cultivated for early vegetables. The southern part is the Bigouden, where the women wear a distinctive *coiffe* (headdress) called the *bigoudène*, with a tall, conical shape like a menhir. Breton, or Brezhoug, is widely spoken here.

Take the D7 west from Locronan to the busy fishing port of **Douarnenez**, once the capital of Cornouaille. North of here is the tiny village and church of Ste Anne-la-Palud, with its large, popular pardon. Follow the minor roads west along the north coast of the Cornouaille peninsula — there are many good viewpoints on the deserted rocky headlands, and a bird sanctuary at 🦆 **Cap Sizun**. At the end is the **Pointe du Van,** a wild headland with fine seascape views. The road left follows the graceful curve of the Baie des Trépassés. This is 'the Bay of the Dead', a place of legends where the souls of those drowned in shipwrecks appear at Halloween, and where the lost town of Is, the beautiful sixth-century capital of Cornouaille, was located. This fabulous place, said to be the model for Paris (Par-Is = like Is) was reputedly swallowed up by the sea as punishment for the behaviour of the king's dissolute daughter, who was in love with the Devil and let him into the city.

At the south end of the bay the road leads out to **Pointe du Raz**, the most famous cape in Brittany. The site is dramatic: a long narrow spur, cut away at the sides with 70m (250ft) drop into the crashing waves below, stretching a jagged finger out into the ocean in a chain of reefs towards the low, treeless island of Sein. Marked by the statue of Our Lady of the Shipwrecked at one end and the Vieille lighthouse at the other, it looks like the end of the world. In fact, it is not the most westerly point in France, as many think — that is Corsen point in Léon — and it is very commercial, with a tourist shopping centre, a museum with diorama, and a huge (paying) car park. To tour the point, you should hire a guide, wear non-slip shoes and hang on to the safety rope. If you can, go out of season, or in poor weather — the effect is more dramatic.

Take the D784 back to **Audierne**, a pleasant old fishing port. From here you can take a boat to Sein island, once the home of feared pagan 'wreckers'. To the south is the **Bigouden**, whose main attractions are the traditional dress worn by the women, the rocky but low-lying Penmarch peninsula, and the oldest calvary in Brittany, which stands alone and weather-beaten in the windswept dunes at Tronoën. Its capital is **Pont-l'Abbé**, which has an interesting Bigouden Folk Museum in its old castle. Continue on the D784 to **Quimper**, the capital of Cornouaille and a popular excursion centre for the region. It is an attractive market town which, though prosperous, has kept its old charm and Breton character. The old centre, with its cobbled streets, timber-framed houses and ladies in Breton costume selling local ware, is picturesque though often crowded by south-coast holiday-makers in wet weather. It has a splendid Gothic cathedral dedicated to its patron saint, St Corentin (fine fifteenth-century stained glass). Between its two elegant spires King Gradlon, on his granite steed, watches over the town he adopted as his capital after a tidal wave had engulfed the fabulous Is. There is a good Breton Museum in the old Bishop's palace and a Fine Arts Museum in the Town Hall. Boat trips down the pretty Odet estuary to Bénodet are popular.

Southern Brittany

From the Odet estuary eastwards, the Breton coastline is softer and more benign, with deep, shallow inlets, long sandy beaches and wooded estuaries and headlands. It is also the most popular part of Brittany for family holidays, and is thick with camp-sites and yacht marinas. The first resort, 15km (9 miles) south of Quimper on the D34, is **Bénodet**, perhaps the busiest and liveliest resort of them all. Beautifully situated at the mouth of the lush, wooded Odet estuary, it has a picture-book marina and splendid views from the lighthouse. It also has good sports facilities and nightlife, but over-development is in danger of destroying its character. Nearby **Beg-Meil** has good beaches with rocks, pines and dunes; inland is **Fouesnant**, famous for the best Breton cider and its girls' headdresses, displayed in all their glory at the Apple-Tree Festival (third Sunday in July), where you can see, and join in, folk-dancing in traditional costumes to wild Celtic music played on strange instruments. Fouesnant has an interesting twelfth-century church and good fish restaurants, and nearby **La Forêt-Fouesnant** a pretty little harbour at the head of a deep inlet surrounded by woods. There are pleasant walks, and good beaches with camp-sites in 2km (1 mile) at Kerleven.

Concarneau is a large fishing port (France's second biggest), but also something of a tourist trap. The activity down by the port is fascinating, especially when the long-distance fishing boats come in every 10 or 15 days, but the main tourist attraction is the old fortified walled town, or *ville close*, on an island in the middle of the port, linked to the mainland by two fortified bridges on one side and a small ferry at the other. There are good views from its ramparts (you pay for the sentry-tour), and the inner town has quaint narrow streets and old houses, most of which are either *crêperies*, cafés or souvenir shops. It is lit up and colourful at night, and has a lively fish auction starting at 10pm. There is a small Fishing Museum and a Marinarium.

Fourteen kilometres (9 miles) east, **Pont-Aven** is also a tourist mecca, but this time for its artistic associations. The picturesque village in its delightful landscape has long attracted artists wishing to escape into a rural idyll, and it became famous when Paul Gauguin and Émile Bernard established a new style of painting here in the 1880s, based on Breton folk-art. This became known as the 'Pont-Aven School', and established the town as a centre of artistic activity to this day, also providing paid employment for the locals as artists' models. The town lies in a lovely setting, where the River Aven opens out from a rocky stream between wooded hills to a tidal estuary. It once had more watermills than houses, but most of these have now been replaced by art galleries and souvenir shops. There are lovely walks in the romantically-named Bois de l'Amour above the town, and temporary art exhibitions by local painters in the museum-but beware of the crowds!

The countryside between Pont-Aven and the sea is pleasant, the estuary surrounded by fields between hedgerows, winding lanes, woods and inlets and thatched cottages dot the landscape. **Port-Manech** is a charming fishing village with a good beach at the mouth of the Aven and Bélon estuaries, the latter being the home of the famous flat Bélon oysters — you can see them exposed in the estuary at low tide. Further along the coast is **Le Pouldu**, at the mouth of the River Laita. This small port and seaside resort was Gauguin's home after he left Pont-Aven in 1889. Follow the Laita inland through the lovely Carnoët forest to **Quimperlé**. Like Quimper it derives its name from the Breton word *kemper*, or junction. Here the Ellé and Isolé rivers join to become the Laita. In the centre are attractive streets of ancient half-timbered houses, grouped round the beautiful Romanesque Church of St Croix. There is a colourful fish market.

Further down the coast is **Lorient**, a large port on the Blavet estuary created 300 years ago for the French East India Company (L'Orient means East). To the east, **Auray** is an older town with many historical associations. It is the site of a famous battle in 1364, where De Montfort and the English defeated the French and secured Breton independence. Later, in 1795, Breton Royalist rebels, called Chouans, defied the Revolutionary armies and were eventually defeated and slaughtered on the Champ des Martyrs, just outside the town. The nearby village of **Ste Anne d'Auray** is Brittany's Lourdes, its chief pilgrimage centre. It has a huge nineteenth-century Renaissance-style basilica, the focal point of many pardons. Auray is a centre of oyster production, with a pleasant river harbour and a picturesque old quarter, St Goustan, across the river from the main town.

Near the coast south-west of Auray, around the small town of **Carnac**, is one of the most extraordinary sites in Europe. Megaliths of various kinds abound in Brittany, but nowhere is there anything like the huge collection in this area, which has earned Carnac the title 'the Capital of Prehistory'. The words for the various types of megalith — menhir, dolmen, cromlech — are all Breton, and 'menhir' literally means 'standing stone'. In the area round the Morbihan gulf there are several thousand menhirs, the largest weighing over 350 tons. How they were carried here and aligned, for what purpose, and why here, are still mysteries, but the most commonly accepted theory is that they had religious significance, were connected with burial (skeletons have been found buried under dolmens, or stone tables) and this region was held sacred in some way. At Carnac are nearly 3,000 menhirs, most of them in three main alignments — in straight lines ending in semi-circles, like the foundations of gigantic cathedrals. The most impressive are the Ménec Lines just to the north of the town. Recent research leads to the belief that they were aligned towards the sun and moon at equinoxes and solstices and were therefore temples for sun-worship.

Carnac is proud of its monuments, and has an important Prehistory Museum in the town, founded 100 years ago by a Scotsman, J. Miln. There is also a large tumulus called St Michel, which is open to visitors — you can see passages and a burial chamber inside, and from the top there is a splendid view of the lines of menhirs. A tour of the other sites could include the Kermario and Kerlescan Lines and the Kercado and Moustoir tumuli. The town has other attractions than prehistory for the visitor: the seventeenth-

The port of Lorient situated on the Blavet estuary

century church of St Cornély, the patron saint of horned cattle, has an interesting porch and painted wooden vaults; the coastal suburb of **Carnac-Plage**
has a beautiful long sandy beach fringed by pines, with fine views of offshore
islands. The Quiberon peninsula is for once a literal translation of the French
presqu'ile — almost an island. It was once an island but is now joined to the
mainland by a strip of sand. The 'island' has a rocky western side called the
Côte Sauvage, while the eastern side has wide sandy beaches and the centre
is dull and flat. Quiberon itself is a busy fishing port and seaside resort.

Return to Carnac and continue west to **Locmariaquer** on the edge of the
Morbihan gulf. This is the second most important centre for prehistoric
remains after Carnac, and has some impressive stones. One is the Grand
Menhir or Witches' Stone at Men-er-Hroëc'h, the largest menhir ever found
— over 20m (66ft) high and 347 tons in weight. Sadly it was broken, probably
by lightning, and only four of the five pieces remain. Nearby is the **Table des
Marchands** (Merchant's Table) a magnificent dolmen consisting of three flat
tables with 17 pointed supports. On the stone are carvings of an animal, a
plough and ears of wheat. The dolmen of **Mané Lud** also has carved stones in
its underground chamber. Locmariaquer is a pleasant resort and convenient
centre for exploring the **Morbihan Gulf**, which is best done by boat, and at
high tide. This huge inland sea dotted with islands (forty of them inhabited)
is famed for its delicate light effects — its sunsets are said to be incredible.
However, at low tide great mud-banks appear and the scene is less attractive.
The lagoon has many oyster beds, and is popular for boating.

The drive round the gulf from Locmariaquer to Vannes is disappointing, as
views are restricted, but **Vannes** merits a visit. It has one of the most attractive
old town centres in Brittany, with narrow, twisting cobbled streets and overhanging timbered houses, enclosed in well-preserved ramparts with fortified
gateways. At the foot of the town walls are beautiful gardens leading down
to the river. The cathedral contains an interesting Renaissance rotunda chapel
and a former fifteenth-century House of Parliament holds an archaeological
museum rich in prehistoric specimens. From Vannes, an excursion inland can
be made to Brittany's most famous castle, the grandly imposing **Château de
Josselin**.

Take the fast N165 to La Roche Bernard and turn right on the D774 to
Guérande. This south-east corner of Brittany is a fascinating area of contrasts:
salt-pans, an extensive tract of inhabited marshland, a fashionable seaside
resort and a large shipbuilding centre. **Guérande** is handsomely sited on a
plateau overlooking a large expanse of salt-pans reclaimed from the sea. It is
a medieval walled town of almost perfectly circular shape, with four fortified
gateways at precisely north, south, east and west. The well-preserved ramparts, which you can walk round, are surrounded by a partly-filled moat and
a ring road. The east gateway houses a museum which tells the story of the
local salt industry, of which Guérande is the main centre. Inside the walls, the
streets are narrow and picturesque, but they can become crowded when poor
weather drives the holiday-makers off the beaches of nearby La Baule. In the
centre of the town is the church of St Aubin, with some lively Romanesque
capitals.

Continue on the D774 south to **Le Croisic**, at the end of a narrow peninsula.
Part fishing port (sardines and crustacea) and part yacht marina, it has a

pretty, lively harbour flanked by attractive-looking seventeenth-century houses. To the north, the town overlooks the Grand Traict lagoon and the salt-pans, while to the south the rocky sea coast, called the Côte Sauvage, has some good beaches and attracts many summer visitors. The Aquarium of the Côte d'Amour on the quay has a fine collection of shells and live sea creatures. Drive round the point and return to La Baule via **Batz-sur-Mer**, an old salt port and a seaside resort with three sandy beaches. Its church of St Guémolé has a fine 60m (197ft) high belfry giving a panoramic view of the area.

Drive round the Penchâteau Point for a sudden, breathtaking view of Brittany's major seaside resort, **La Baule**. Its magnificent beach, claimed to be the most beautiful in Europe, stretches before you for 5km (3 miles), from Le Pouliguen to Pornichet, in an uninterrupted arc of fine yellow sand. It is sheltered by headlands to east and west, and to the north by acres of pines set in the dunes. These factors, plus its mild climate and long season, make it one of France's most popular holiday resorts, on a par with Royan and Biarritz lower down the Atlantic coast. It has their international style and appeal, but lacks any real centre, being mainly a long succession of palatial hotels, apart-ment blocks and villas set among the pines behind its broad floral promenade. It is still fashionable with the younger set, and has every kind of facility imaginable for sport and entertainment.

Breton Cuisine

Though there are many fine restaurants in Brittany, it is not an area of *haute cuisine* but of good, fresh local produce, especially fish and vegetables.

The speciality of the region is its seafood, both fish and shellfish — probably the best in quality and variety in France, if not in Europe. The cold platter of raw (*cru*) shellfish is a good starter, if you like that sort of thing; otherwise mussels or clams *farcies/gratinées*, or garlic-buttered, breadcrumbed and grilled in half-shells; or *coquilles St Jacques* — scallops in white wine sauce with piped potato; or, of course, Bélon oysters. For the main course, there are lobsters, crayfish, crabs, spider-crabs or scampi for the shellfish lover. Otherwise salmon, trout or *côtriade* — Breton fish stew. In the Brière, the young marsh eels are superb.

The most famous meat dish is lamb *pré-salé*, or reared on salt pastures, often served with white beans. Pork is eaten mainly in highly-flavoured *charcuterie*. Game, particularly hare and partridge, is tasty. Breton vegetables are renowned, particularly globe artichokes, cauliflowers, peas, onions and potatoes. Plougastel strawberries and other fruits are good.

Brittany is famous for its pancakes, and there are more *crêperies* per square kilometre here than anywhere else in France. The brown ones (sometimes called *galettes*) are made with buckwheat flour and eaten salted, with savoury fillings (cheese, eggs, ham, sausage); the white ones, with ordinary flour, are sugared, with jam, honey or liqueurs. Quimper lace-pancakes are a speciality. In Breton, a cake is a *kouign*, and the best-known type is the *kouign-aman*, a sweet fried cake of wheat flour, eggs and honey. The *gâteau Breton* is a cake made with butter and usually fruit.

As in Normandy, cider is the main drink, though only Fouesnant cider can equal the Norman in quality. But dry white wines from the vineyards around Nantes — Muscadet and Gros Plant — are also widely drunk, especially with seafood. The best quality is *sur lie*, or 'on the lees'.

The coast from La Baule to St Nazaire becomes more rocky and indented, with small, quiet resorts like St Marc. Behind the coastal strip is the **Parc Regional de Brière**, a 200sq km (77sq miles) peat bog drained by a network of ditches. The Grande Brière has for centuries provided a living for the inhabitants of the 21 communes (who own the marshes collectively) by netting fish, fowling, stock-rearing and selling reeds and peat. They live in thatched cottages on islands in the marsh, and travel the canals in flat-bottomed boats called *blains*. The area became a Regional Park in 1970 in an attempt to preserve their unique way of life, and today canals are being cleared, villages restored and cottage industries established. A tour of the Brière should include the restored village of **Kerhinet** and the islands of **Fédrun**, **St Joachim**, **Ménac** and **Errand**. Boat trips on the canals are available, and there are frequent local fêtes on Sundays in summer. These are a unique experience: you can walk on floating paths of reeds, watch strange watersports on the lakes and eat local delicacies like barbecued marsh-eels.

Many of the marsh-dwellers work today in the shipyards and factories of nearby **St Nazaire**. This shipbuilding and commercial centre grew rapidly in the nineteenth century to accommodate ships too large for the shallow Loire estuary. It was naturally a target of aerial bombardment during World War II and in its latter stages the 'St Nazaire Pocket' was one of the last German strongholds, so it sustained severe war damage. Today it is completely rebuilt, with a smart new central area and a grand, very modern sports stadium. But its main interest is for lovers of the sea and ships. From a special viewing terrace you can see the shipyards and the deep-water basins of the port, including the German submarine base. The tour ends on the St Nazaire bridge, a toll bridge 60m (197ft) above the Loire, from where you have a fine panorama over the town and the estuary.

Additional Information

Places of Interest

Mont-St-Michel
Abbey
Open: daily, closed at 4pm in winter.

St Malo
City Museum and Wax Museum
In castle
Open: 10am-12noon and 2-6pm June to September.

Dinard
Tidal Generating Station
Open: 8.30am-8pm; entry on left bank downstream from lock.

Rennes
Musée de Bretagne and Musée des Beaux-Arts
In Palais des Musés
Open: daily except Tuesday 10am-12noon and 2-6pm.

Cap Sizun
Bird Sanctuary
Open: 10am-12noon and 2-6pm, 15 March to August; on Catel-ar-Roch promontory.

Pont-l'Abbé
Bigouden Folk Museum
In round fifteenth-century tower
Open: June to September daily 9am-12noon and 2-6.30pm except Sunday and national holidays.

Quimper
Brittany Museum
In former Bishop's Palace
Open: 10am-7pm except Tuesday.
Boat trips to Bénodet
Daily service May to September; 1hr
15min.

Fine Arts Museum
In Town Hall
Open: 9.30am-12noon and 2-6.30pm
(6pm in winter); closed Tuesday and
national holidays.

Concarneau
Rampart Walk round Walled Town
Open: Easter to September 9am-7pm.

Fishing Museum
Open: daily 9.30am-8.30pm July to
August; 10am-12.30pm and 2.30-6pm
out of season.

Carnac
Miln-le-Rouzic Prehistory Museum
Open: daily 10am-12noon and 2-5pm,
except Tuesday.

Vannes
Archaeology Museum
Open: daily 9.30am-12noon and 2-6pm,
except Sunday.

Josselin
Medieval Château
Open: 10am-12noon and 2-6pm July to
August; 2-6pm June and September; 2-6pm
Wednesday and Sunday March to May.

Guérande
Musée du Vieux Guérande
Open: Easter to September 9am-12noon
and 2-7pm.

Le Croisic
Aquarium of the Côte d'Amour
Open: 10am-8pm July to September;
10am-12noon and 2-7pm rest of year;
except Monday and 15 to 31 January.

St Nazaire
Viewing Terrace Over Old Submarine Pens
Open: 9.30am-7.30pm July to August;
9.30am-12noon and 2-6pm except
Monday in June and 1 to 15 September.

Tourist Information Centres

Carnac
Office de Tourisme
Avenue Druides
☎ 97 52 13 52

Concarneau
Office de Tourisme
Quai d'Aiguillon
☎ 98 97 01 44

Dinan
Office de Tourisme
6 Rue Horloge
☎ 96 39 75 40

Dinard
Office de Tourisme
2 Boulevard Féart
☎ 99 46 94 12

La Baule
Office de Tourisme & Accueil de France
8 Place Victoire
☎ 40 24 34 44

Mont-St-Michel
Office de Tourisme
Corps de Garde des Bourgeois
☎ 33 60 14 30

Mûr-de-Bretagne
Syndicat d'Initiative
Place Église
☎ 96 28 51 41
Open: 15 June to 15 September.

Quimper
Office de Tourisme & Accueil de France
Place Résistance
☎ 98 53 04 05

Rennes
Office de Tourisme & Accueil de France
Pont de Nemours
☎ 99 79 01 98

St Malo
Office de Tourisme
Esplanade St Vincent
☎ 99 56 64 48

Restaurants

R = With Accommodation
Haute-cuisine restaurants include:

Audierne
Le Goyen (R)
☎ 98 70 08 88

Bénodet
Ferme du Letty
☎ 98 57 01 27

Brest
Frère Jacques
☎ 98 44 38 65

Cancale
De Bricourt (R)
☎ 99 89 64 76

Concarneau
Le Galion (R)
☎ 98 97 30 16

Hennebont
Château de Locquénolé (R)
☎ 97 76 29 04

La Gouesnière
Hôtel Tirel-Guérin (R)
☎ 99 89 10 46

La Baule
Castel Marie-Louise (R)
☎ 40 60 20 60

La Roche-Bernard
Auberge Bretonne (R)
☎ 99 90 60 75

Les Ponts-Neufs
Lorand-Barre
☎ 96 32 78 71

Lorient
3km (2 miles) north-east
L'Amphitryon
☎ 97 83 34 04

Mûr-de-Bretagne
Auberge Grand'Maison (R)
☎ 96 28 51 10

Muzillac
Château de Rochevilaine (R)
☎ 97 41 69 27

Plancoët
Chez Crouzil (R)
☎ 96 84 10 42

Pléneuf-Val-André
Le Cotriade
☎ 96 72 20 26

Pont-Aven
Moulin de Rosmadec (R)
☎ 98 06 00 22

Questembert
Le Bretagne (R)
☎ 97 26 11 12

Quimper
Le Capucin Gourmand
☎ 98 95 43 12

St Brieuc
La Vieille Tour
☎ 96 33 10 30

St Malo
Duchesse Anne
☎ 99 40 85 33

St Avé
Near Vannes
Le Pressoir
☎ 97 60 87 63

Ste Anne-la-Palud
La Plage
☎ 98 92 50 12

Ste Marine
Le Jeanne d'Arc (R)
☎ 98 56 32 70

Vannes
Régis Mahé
☎ 97 42 61 41

Other restaurants, offering good value
for money, include:
Baden
Near Auray
Le Gavrinis (R)
☎ 97 57 00 82

Carantec
Near Roscoff
Pors Pol (R)
☎ 98 67 00 52

Guérande
Les Remparts (R)
☎ 40 24 90 69

La Grée-Penvins
Near Sarzeau
Espadon
☎ 97 67 34 26

Le Faou
Relais de la Place (R)
☎ 98 81 91 19

Pontivy
Gambetta
☎ 97 25 53 70

Port de Carhaix
Auberge du Poher
☎ 98 99 51 18

Quédillac
Relais de la Rance (R)
☎ 99 06 20 20

Quimper-Ty Sanquer
Auberge Ty Coz
☎ 98 94 50 02

Raguenès-Plage
Chez Pierre (R)
☎ 98 06 81 06

Sables-d'Or-Les-Pins
Voile d'Or (R)
☎ 96 41 42 49

Ste Anne-d'Auray
L'Auberge (R)
☎ 97 57 61 55

5

Alsace-Lorraine

A lsace-Lorraine is an area that has been tramped over by marching feet throughout the ages, and invading barbarians from the east (Holy Romans, Prussians and Nazi Germans) have been resisted by the French and their allies. From 1870, after France's humiliation in the Franco-Prussian war, the region was German until 1918, and during World War II part of it was once again declared German territory. The destinies of the two regions seem inextricably linked. Yet they could not be more different, in climate, appearance, culture and attitude. Divided by the considerable barrier of the Vosges mountains, they seem to be looking in different directions, one towards France, the other towards central Europe.

Lorraine is undisputedly French, in the appearance of its towns and villages, and in the fiercely patriotic attitude of its people. Although the northern part, around Metz and the Saar Valley, has a Germanic local dialect which is widely spoken, the whole region is proud of its two symbols of French national pride: Joan of Arc, the saviour of France against the medieval English invaders, was born at *Domrémy* (now 'La-Pucelle'), in Lorraine; and General de Gaulle who took as the symbol of the Free French Army in World War II the two-barred cross of Lorraine. The land is scarred with the marks of war, from the remains of the Maginot Line to the scene of World War I's bloodiest battle, Verdun. Parts of Lorraine are heavily industrialised, often with old and ailing industries. Yet it has pleasant farmland, woods and valleys, a peaceful Regional Park, some lovely scenery on the western slopes of the Vosges, and two cities with splendid old centres, Nancy and Metz.

Alsace is one of France's most delightful regions. The traveller's first reaction is surprise. It seems more like Germany than France, with its German architecture and place-names, its Alsatian patois, closely related to old High German, and its clean and orderly appearance. Yet it has a distinctly French air of informal elegance, and a quality of its own — a pride in its independence and its unique traditions, which it keenly preserves. It is a civilised place, conscious of its position at the hub of Europe and of the key role of its capital, Strasbourg, home of the European Parliament, in the future of the EEC.

In spite of having two of France's most handsome towns, Strasbourg and Colmar, within its borders, Alsace is a region of villages. The countryside is densely populated, with villages coming thick and fast on one another. They are invariably charming, sometimes even over-picturesque, with their half-timbered houses separated by narrow passages, their window-boxes and wrought-iron signs. The villages on the famous *wein-strasse*, surely France's

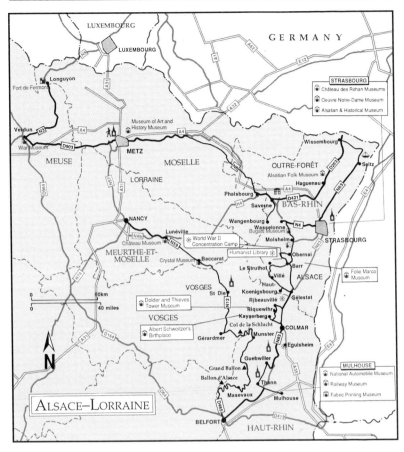

loveliest wine-route, are particularly attractive, and the climate is dry and sunny, sheltered by the densely-wooded Vosges mountains.

This tour starts and ends in Lorraine, but spends most of its time in Alsace and the Vosges. Alsace, on a narrow plain between the Vosges and the Rhine, is a compact area which can be easily visited from one or two bases, whereas the tourist sites in Lorraine are much more scattered.

Northern Lorraine

The tour begins in the north-west corner of Lorraine, near the Belgian border, at **Longuyon** where there is an excellent restaurant in the Hôtel Lorraine. The main interest of this area is war, particularly World War I. Near Longuyon is one of the forts of the Maginot Line, the Fort de Fermont, which gives an instructive and harrowing account of the sufferings of its occupants. An older memorial is the impressive Vauban citadel at **Montmédy**, on a ridge above the town. Forty eight kilometres (30 miles) south on the N18 is **Verdun**, scene of one of the blackest days in history, when over 800,000 men were killed in battle in 1916-17. In the town is a memorial to the battle, with books containing the names of all the participants, and the old Vauban citadel, whose underground vaults were used as refuges during the battle. There are organised tours of the many battle sites around the town, on which you can see monuments to destroyed villages, ossuaries, forts and a museum.

Take the D9803 east from Verdun to **Metz**, passing through the Lorraine Nature Park, scene of bitter fighting in World War I and now an area of forests, lakes and agricultural land. Metz is a commercial town at an important crossroads, surrounded by France's largest industrial belt, but its old town centre is surprisingly attractive and well preserved. Spaciously sited among several arms of the Moselle, it has a German solidity about it (the area is partly German-speaking) and a sense of prosperous well-being. It is well-blessed with spacious squares with pavement cafés (Cathédral, St-Jacques, République), and the Place St-Louis is particularly charming, ringed with tall old houses with ground floor arcades. It has the beautiful thirteenth to fourteenth-century Gothic St-Étienne Cathedral, rivalling any in northern France, built in golden sandstone, with superb east and south façades and a lofty nave. Its large expanse of stained glass is magnificent, richly glowing with colour, and in contrasting styles, fourteenth, fifteenth, sixteenth century and modern. The town has a well-organised and presented museum in a number of sections, housed in old buildings which include a medieval grain store and foundations of the Roman baths. The presentation of Gallo-Roman remains is especially fine. The esplanade, behind the Law Courts, is a pleasant walk offering views over the Moselle and its surrounding gardens.

Leave Metz by the eastern German Gate, stopping to admire this heavily-fortified surviving part of the thirteenth- to fifteenth-century ramparts. Take the A4 motorway through pleasant, undulating countryside (the alternative is the N3 to St Avold, the N56 to Sarralbe and the N61) to **Phalsbourg**. This pleasant little town is set at the foot of the easiest pass through the Vosges. It has an attractive wide, sixteenth-century paved square, the Place d'Armes. From here you can cross the Vosges either by the Col de Saverne (N4) or by the D132 to Lutzelbourg and **Haut-Barr**, a ruined twelfth-century castle known as the 'Eye of Alsace'. From the top you have a magnificent first view of the north Alsace plain.

Northern Alsace

Descend to **Saverne**, the gateway to Alsace. This town was for five centuries the property of the Rohan family, the prince/bishops of Strasbourg, who built an impressive red sandstone palace here in the eighteenth century (the poet Goethe admired its splendour when staying as a guest of the Cardinal, calling it the 'Alsatian Versailles'). It has two façades, an ornate one seen from the canal path, a more austere one flanking the central Place-du-Général-de-Gaulle. The town has an attractive pedestrian main street, the Grand'Rue, with old houses, and pleasant gardens on the river bank. There is an interesting Romanesque church at **St Jean-Saverne** nearby, and a larger, more beautiful one at **Marmoutier**, further south.

The **Forêt de Saverne**, an attractive area south of the town with a maze of forest roads and GR footpaths, is part of the region known as the Little Vosges. A good base for exploring this region is **Wangenbourg**, a small mountain resort with an alpine air. It is overlooked by a ruined thirteenth-century castle, destroyed by Swedish troops in 1663. There is accommodation for walkers here, and skiers in winter (if they get the snow), and a good restaurant at the Parc Hôtel. Nearby, the Schneeberg (960m, 3,149ft) has excellent views, and the ruined fortress of **Nideck**, hidden away in dense forest, has a pretty waterfall. There are other ruined castles, too — Hohenstein, Birkenwald, Freudeneck — standing romantically on eroded outcrops of the soft sandstone that characterises the region.

From Wangenbourg, the D224 winds down through the forest to Wasselonne, at the northern end of the Alsace wine-road. Take the D25 to Hochfelden, and the D421/D44 to **Haguenau**, the gateway to northern Alsace. This little-known area north of Strasbourg is different from the rest of the region. Bordered on two sides by Germany, it is flatter and wider; it produces beer rather than wine (except for one small pocket round Cleebourg), and is devoutly Protestant. The old villages, though just as picturesque as further south, are neater, more ordered and spacious and, in fact, more Germanic. Local costume is still worn occasionally, and not just for the tourists. Haguenau is the Alsatian capital of beer production, surrounded by a sea of hop fields. The town has a pleasant, pedestrianised centre with handsome old houses, one of which holds the tourist office and a small but prettily-staged Alsatian Folk Museum. St George's Church, in pink and yellow sandstone with pitched roofs of multi-coloured tiles, houses a beautiful fifteenth-century altarpiece in the right transept.

On the northern edge of the town is the Haguenau forest, the largest in Alsace, and beyond that the quiet, charming region called, for obvious reasons, the **Outre-Forêt**. Here life is peaceful, orderly and traditional, with Protestant values clearly displayed. The villages are stunningly pretty, with their neat rows of spotless black and white half-timbered houses, their orderly gardens and clean streets. **Betschdorf**, on the northern edge of the forest, is known for its pottery; **Hoffen**, **Hunspach** and **Seebach** are perhaps the prettiest villages while **Cleebourg**, the only wine-producing village, has a good and friendly co-operative that dispenses generous tastings. To the west of the Outre-Forêt is the Parc Regional des Vosges, a peaceful wooded region ideal for activity holidays. The road along the border, overlooking the German Pfalzerwald, is hilly and wooded, with dramatically-perched castles at **Fleckenstein** and **Falkenstein**.

To tour the region, take the D263 from Haguenau, and in 12km (7 miles) turn right for Betschdorf. Continue to Hatten, then left on the D104 to Buhl, and left again for Stundwiller and Hoffen. Cross the D263 to Hunspach, Ingolsheim and Cleebourg, then over the Col du Pfaffenschlick to the pretty village of **Lembach**, a good base for exploring the Nature Park and the border area. Then take the D3 east via Climbach to **Wissembourg**. This border town is charming and colourful, with flower-lined quays, old houses with colour-washed walls, and gardens on the ramparts. It is usually full of Germans, coming across the border to shop or eat the north-Alsatian speciality, *tarte flambée* or *flammkuchen*, an egg, bacon and onion flan which is baked like a pizza. Stroll through the Bruch district, where small bridges cross the several branches of the River Lauter, to **Anselmann Quay**, with Renaissance houses, and the picturesque Salt House, dated 1450, with its irregular, steeply-pitched roof.

The Church of St Peter and St Paul, in Vosges sandstone, is Gothic with a Romanesque tower, and has fourteenth-century frescoes.

Take the D263 out of Wissembourg and in 3km (2 miles) bear left on the D34 to Seebach, another village with lovely old houses. Continue to Niederroeden, then left on the D28 to **Seltz**, a town of Roman origin on the Rhine. Seltz is a small tourist centre, with a beach along the river, sailing facilities, and a ferry across to Germany. There are two roads from here along the Rhine Valley to Strasbourg: the N63/D468 is slow and winding and goes through all the villages; the D300 is fast, straight and avoids them. Whichever you choose, prepare for heavy traffic as you approach the capital of Alsace and seat of the Council of Europe, **Strasbourg**. The city that was once the capital of the most war-torn province in Europe is now one of its leading cities: prosperous, cosmopolitan, an industrial and commercial centre, a busy inland port, and a university town with a lively student population. It has a picturesque old centre and an even more picturesque old artisan's quarter, but around these are the appurtenances of any big city — shopping malls, apartment stores, office blocks, and car-parks.

Parking in Strasbourg is difficult and expensive and accommodation is often scarce. Yet it is an exciting place to be in, with plenty of activity at all times of the day or night and even though it has a large international community, it retains its Alsatian provincial charm. Its wine-taverns still dispense their glasses of Edelzwicker and plates of baked ham and pork knuckles, and welcome visitors to join the locals at the *stammtisch* (regulars' table). Its handsome old half-timbered houses, cobbled streets and pavement cafés still have their distinctive style.

Of the many sights in Strasbourg, the magnificent Cathedral of Notre-Dame is the crowd-puller — the mecca of so many visitors that you may have to queue to get in, especially on a German bank holiday! The first sight of its pink sandstone façade, from the Place Gutenberg looking down the Rue Mercière, is compelling. It is a Gothic lacework of stone, with beautiful statuary around the doorways, and topped by an elegant, though slightly askew, 142m (466ft) spire, for several centuries the tallest in Christendom. The sculpture of the Tempter and the Foolish Virgins over the right doorway is particularly fine, as is the Tympanum of the Virgin on the south side door. Inside, among many treasures, is the superb Pillar of the Last Judgement (thirteenth century) in the transept, and nearby is the most popular exhibit, the elaborate Astronomical Clock. The foundations and crypt are Romanesque, the rest Gothic. There is a wonderful view from the top of the tower.

The old pedestrian town centre round the cathedral is very attractive. The cathedral square has two finely-carved timber-framed houses, the Kammerzell House and the Pharmacie du Cerf. The Rue Mercière is lined with half-timbered houses and pavement cafés and the Place Gutenberg has a statue of the inventor of printing and a superb Renaissance Chamber of Commerce, housing the tourist office. The area comes alive at night, with *son et lumière* in French and German, and street artists entertaining at the café tables. The Château des Rohan, the palace of the Prince-Archbishops who ruled Strasbourg, has a beautiful façade over the River Ill, and contains three museums (fine arts, decorative arts and archaeology) and the sumptuous State Apartments. The Historical Museum tells the story well of Alsace's turbulent past; the Alsatian Museum explains and illustrates her unique arts, crafts and folklore; and the Oeuvre Notre-Dame Museum has priceless art and documents relating to the cathedral. The Petite France district, the old fishing, tanning and milling quarter at the junction of the two arms of the river Ill that encircle the old town, is the most picturesque part of the city. It has half-timbered houses with galleries overhanging the river, and covered bridges over the canals with towers and old watermills. Its narrow alleys are traffic-free. For those sated with history and culture, the Kronenbourg brewery and Seita cigarette factory may be visited. The Palais de l'Europe, the ultra-modern European Parliament building set in a lovely park, may be visited by appointment.

Provinces capable of growing grapes are vying with one another to produce the finest wines in France

The Northern Wine Road

Following a wine-route has its built-in problems. The obvious one is the drink-drive dilemma — it rather defeats the object if you cannot sample any of the products en route. The only answer to this for car-users is to travel in a party and do the route in stages, over several days; but this does not solve the problem for cyclists! Another problem is that, however good the wines you are tasting, you can become sated with them after a while and fail to distinguish their qualities. Though wine-roads are a good thing in theory, in practice they are best done either in short sections or with the aim of enjoying their scenery and ambience rather than their products.

The Alsace wine road fits the bill admirably in this regard. It is a delightfully pretty route, winding among vineyards through a quick succession of enchanting villages, each one crying out to be photographed. The route is well signposted, and follows mainly minor roads in the foothills of the Vosges, occasionally descending to the plain or shooting up into the wooded mountains. There is plenty to see en route and there are the villages themselves, the jewels of Alsace. Set amid the neat rows of vines that grow right up to the village walls, their pink Vosges stone contrasts tastefully with the greenery around them. The houses are a bewitching blend of carved, patterned dark timbers, white or coloured plaster walls and deeply-pitched orange-tiled roofs, with balconies bursting with colour from the petunias and geraniums in their window-boxes. The village squares are decorous with ornate fountains (often flowing with wine on festival days) and wrought-iron signs for shops or taverns.

The wine road has its attendant symbol, or mascot — the famous storks which stand one-legged in nests perched either on poles, chimneys or steeples along the route. The stork is the emblem of Alsace, and they are treasured for the good luck they bring to the house on which they perch. The pairs of storks returning in summer have declined in numbers in recent years, and the Alsatians are trying to rebuild their population by mating them with those reared in 'stork parks' (baby storks do migrate). If you are lucky you may see a stork or two along the wine road, and if not you can certainly see some in one of the stork parks.

The vast majority of viticulturists in Alsace are small private producers, who live in the village and are only too happy to tell you about their wines and let you taste and buy, should you wish to do so. Before you undertake a wine tour, you should learn about the wines of the region. Alsatian wines differ from most other French wines in that they are sold under the name of their grape variety and there is only one AOC for the whole region (see the Fact File under the Food and Drink section). There are seven permitted grape varieties, plus an eighth blended from the others. Seven of the eight are white wines, and all are dry, high quality and good value. They are in distinctive long and slender bottles and all, including the red, are drunk young and cool. The eight types are: Riesling (very dry, fruity, delicate); Gewürztraminer (distinctive, perfumed and spicy); Tokay or Pinot Gris (dry, rich and full); Pinot Blanc (dry, rounded and balanced); Sylvaner (dry, light and fresh); Muscat d'Alsace (dry, raisin-flavoured, a good aperitif); and Pinot Noir (dry, elegant light red or rosé) and Edelzwicker (a non-AOC wine blended from several varieties, for everyday drinking). The words *Grand* or *Réserve* mean they are stronger than normal, and *Vendange Tardive* means the wine is made from late-picked grapes, and so is stronger and sweeter.

Leave Strasbourg by the N4 (SP Saverne/Metz) for **Marlenheim**, at the northern end of the Alsace wine-road. Of the cluster of villages in this area, Marlenheim is known for its rosé wine and its oddly-named festival in August, 'Friend Fritz's Wedding'. Wangen has a festival in July where the wine flows freely from the attractive fountain in the square and Avolsheim has one of the oldest chapels in Alsace (eleventh to twelfth century). **Molsheim** is a larger town than most on the wine-road, and has some industry. The Bugatti factory no longer makes cars here, but the town museum has a collection of old Bugatti cars. The central square, with its fountain and Renaissance *Metzig* (Butchers' Guild building), is attractive. There are old streets and remains of the town walls, and a stork park. Nearby **Mutzig** offers a change from wine-tasting — it is the home of some of France's biggest breweries. **Rosheim** is a pleasant town, though its buildings are not typical of the region, being built mainly in yellow sandstone. It has two important Romanesque monuments: a quaint town house (twelfth century), reputedly the oldest secular building in Alsace, and the superb twelfth-century church of St Peter and St Paul. Some of the old town gates remain, with their turreted towers. Boersch also has town gates and a pretty square. Nearby is Mont Ste Odile, a pilgrimage site to the shrine of Alsace's patron saint.

Sheltering under the mountain, and guarded by the two ruined fortresses of Rathsamhausen and Lutzelbourg at Ottrott, **Obernai** is both a prosperous and a strongly picturesque town, exuding an air of opulence. It was the birthplace of Ste Odile in the seventh century and, in the fourteenth century, a member of the Decapolis, an alliance of ten free cities of Alsace. Obernai has a wealth of beautiful half-timbered buildings in typical Alsatian style, and a lovely market square, with a Renaissance town hall, belfry, decorated fountain and old corn market. There are pleasant signed walks in the forest above the town, leading to the massive Pagan Wall, a Bronze Age 10km (6 mile) wall completely enclosing Mont Ste Odile. From the Convent terrace on the summit you have a magnificent view over the Alsatian plain and the Rhine. Descend to **Barr**, another town with a handsome seventeenth-century town hall, in an attractive square with an elegant fountain and enclosed by old houses, one of which was thought so luxurious when built in the eighteenth century that it was nicknamed the Folie Marco. This now houses a small museum, with wine-tasting in the cellar. Barr has a Protestant church with a twelfth-century bell-tower, and a splendid wine fair in July and October. The Klipfel wine-house on the edge of town gives excellent tastings and, by arrangement, provides a traditional Alsatian meal which includes *baeckaoffe*, a rich and fortifying dish of three meats (beef, pork and mutton) marinaded in wine and baked with potatoes in a bakery oven.

If your mood is too euphoric after these Epicurean delights, an excursion into the Vosges from Barr can bring back the grim realities. Take the D854 towards Mont Ste Odile, then bear left onto the D426 towards Le Hohwald. Before reaching the village, turn right onto the D130 for La Rothlach, and continue for 8km (5 miles) to **Struthof**. This is the site of the only World War

II concentration camp on French soil, where 10,000 of its 40,000 prisoners were killed between 1941 and 1944. Unlike the rest of France, Alsace was declared part of Germany after the occupation, and its population subjected to a harsh process of 'Germanisation', where names were changed, the French language and habits were forbidden, and able-bodied men were drafted into the German army (this resulted only in increasing pro-French feeling). The camp was therefore technically on German soil, and it became the destination of many of Alsace's large Jewish community, amongst others. Much of the camp's accoutrements remain. You can see huts, a barbed-wire enclosure, watch-towers, a gas-chamber, a cemetery and a museum. The visit is a moving and chastening experience. There are guided tours.

Return via **Le Hohwald**, which is a good centre for exploring this section of the Vosges. If your spirits need reviving, the **Villé** Valley just south of Le Hohwald via the Col du Kreuzweg is just the place. It is the production centre of Alsace's famous cherry-flavoured spirit, kirsch. There is a 'kirsch route' (the D39), and you can visit distilleries at Bassemberg and Steige. From Villé, return to the wine-road by the D253.

From here the well-marked wine road winds south through a succession of pretty villages overlooked by ruined castles. **Andlau**, just south of Barr, is just such a one. Its Romanesque abbey church has a lovely carved doorway and frieze, and a tenth-century crypt containing a statue of the bear that inspired the abbey's founder, Ste Richarde. The fifteenth-century village well displays another statue of the saint and her bear. Two ruined perched castles overlook the village. **Dambach-la-Ville** has a medieval appearance, enclosed within ramparts, with three town gates and lovely old galleried houses. Dieffenthal, Scherwiller and Albe are also picturesque.

Another short excursion can be made into the mountains from Kintzheim. Turn right on the D159 for the château of **Haut-Koenigsbourg**; on a hill 650m (2,132ft) above the plain (good views from the terrace). The château is a piece of pure *kitsch*, but popular with tourists. An old ruined castle was rebuilt in gruesome mock-Gothic to the orders of Kaiser Wilhelm II in the early twentieth-century, with the full paraphernalia of weapons and armour, animal and bird skulls and paintings of eagles in the vaults. There is a souvenir shop and a 'traditional' Alsatian tavern. On the way from Kintzheim, you can visit a monkey park, a stork park and displays of falconry at the Château de Kintzheim. Return to the wine-road at St Hippolyte, a pretty village with a stork tower. The nearby old town of **Sélestat** has a Humanist Library founded in 1542, containing manuscripts from the seventh century on, early printed books and important works of Renaissance scholarship. It has two pink-sandstone churches, the Gothic St George and the Romanesque Ste Foy.

The section of the wine-road from Sélestat to Colmar is the most popular and 'picturesque', so beware of crowds and high prices. **Ribeauvillé**, over-looked by no less than three castles, is relatively quiet and sedate, though very attractive, with its flower-bedecked fountains and narrow, shaded Grand'Rue straddled by the thirteenth-century Butchers' Tower and over-looked by beautifully restored houses. It was once the headquarters of the Minstrels' Guild (see the Minstrel House). Today it is a busy wine-centre, and offers many good tastings. There is a colourful wine festival in September, and a restaurant specialising in *baeckeoffe*. Ribeauvillé is a good place to spot

A picturesque place to visit on the Alsace Wine Road is Ribeauvillé

nesting storks, and there is a stork rehabilitation centre at nearby **Hunawihr.**
Riquewihr is less tranquil. This is the best-known and most popular town on
the whole wine road, and is often thronged with visitors. In spite of its
abundant charms, it has become overly commercial, with souvenir shops,
créperies and boutiques, and wineries that charge you for tastings. If you can
catch it on a quiet day, it has much to offer: the best *riesling* in Alsace; well-
preserved buildings built by sixteenth-to seventeenth-century wine-growers;
a pedestrian centre enclosed in rectangular fortifications; oriel windows,
sculpted galleries and doorways; elaborate shop-signs; fountains and wells,
yards and passages; a thirteenth-century gate, the Dolder, and a Thieves'
Tower, both with museums; a torture chamber and an old Jewish ghetto.

Sigolsheim was badly damaged at the Liberation in 1945, and has a moving
National War Cemetery on the Blutberg (Hill of Blood) above the village,
where the thousands killed in the fighting are buried. **Kaysersberg** has all the
charm of Riquewihr and less of the crowds. It is a delightful small town, with
banners flying from the ruined castle overlooking its fortified bridge over the
River Weiss. It has a beautiful gilt wood altarpiece in its Gothic church, and a
Renaissance town hall surrounded by fine sixteenth-to seventeenth-century
houses. Kaysersberg is proud to be the birthplace of Albert Schweitzer, and
has a small museum devoted to him and his work.

The Southern Wine Road

Kaysersberg is a good point to break your wine-road tour to visit the cultural
and wine capital of Alsace, and its loveliest town, **Colmar.** Twelve kilometres
(7 miles) away on the N415, Colmar is a busy commercial city, the capital of
the Haut-Rhine department, and though its suburbs are sprawling and un-
sightly, it has preserved in its centre an unparalleled collection of fine old
buildings that make it almost a museum of old Alsace. Because of its central
position at a crossroads of Europe, it is much visited and not the place for a
quiet holiday, especially during the annual Alsace Wine Fair in the 15 August
holiday week. Its prosperity and reputation as a cultural centre date from the
Middle Ages, when it was the chief town of the Decapolis and attracted artists
from as far afield as Italy and Flanders. Most of its elegant town houses, richly
decorated with fine carving, date from the fifteenth to sixteenth century, when
its burghers prospered in the wine trade and became patrons of the arts. Its
greatest master was the painter, draughtsman and engraver Martin
Schongauer, who was the teacher of Albrecht Dürer.

Leave your car in the Rapp Square car park near the Champ de Mars, and
visit the old town on foot. Most of the old buildings lie between the tourist
office in the north-east and the tanners' quarter in the south-west. The Old
Customs House is a delightful building, with a passage through to the
Grand'Rue, and a wide square leading to the Rue des Tanneurs, lined with tall
old buildings. The Pfister House, in the Rue des Marchands, is finely decorated with medallions and religious paintings, and the Maison des Têtes, in
the Rue des Têtes, has a loggia covered with carvings of grotesque heads. The
Cathedral of St Martin has fine sculptures round the south and west doorways, and finely carved choir stalls and the Dominican Church houses the
superb *Virgin and the Rose Bush* by Schongauer (1473), a stunningly beautiful
painting with a richly symbolic background (you must pay to see it). The

Unterlinden Museum, one of the richest and most beautifully housed in France outside Paris, holds the treasure which everyone comes to Colmar to see, the Issenheim Altarpiece by Matthias Grünewald (1515). The effect of this multi-panelled masterpiece is hypnotic. Its scenes of the religious seasons, including a Crucifixion and Resurrection, are both graphically realistic and strongly symbolic, giving it a compelling power (it was thought to have a therapeutic effect). The Unterlinden is not just a one-masterpiece museum. There are fine paintings by Schongauer, and good sections on folk arts and crafts, all housed in old convent buildings round a verdant, shady cloister.

There are many other treasures in Colmar, but before leaving you must visit the Little Venice quarter, or the Krutenau district. This picturesque area of weeping willows, flowered balconies and little bridges over the River Lauch looks ravishing when lit up at night. You might also look into the fine town library, housed in a Dominican monastery, and the wine information centre in the Maison du Vin. Leave Colmar by the D417 to **Wintzenheim** (great Tokay wines here), where you rejoin the wine-road, and turn right for **Turckheim**. This charming small town should really be a suburb of Colmar, but shows no sign of losing its identity as an ancient free town. It has remnants of its old walls, three gates, a fine bell-tower, a pleasant square, an elegant town hall and lovely Renaissance houses, including a beautiful old inn, the Hôtel des Deux Clefs. It also boasts the only remaining town crier in France, who still turns out at dusk in full regalia (summer only). Its 'Brand' vineyards are celebrated.

The wine road south of Colmar is not as clearly defined as it is further north, and at times requires either following a stretch along the fast N83 or a winding detour up into the hills. The next of the typically pretty wine villages, Eguisheim, is really the last — after this, they are more workaday, although some of them possess fine churches. **Eguisheim** is delightful, a small town in a circular shape, with narrow streets running in concentric circles round the remains of an eighth-century feudal castle. It has a long, distinguished history from prehistoric times to the Middle Ages, when its powerful counts were a force in the Holy Roman Empire. Now it lives on past glory and wine: a web of cobbled streets lined with quaint old half-timbered houses, including a tithe house; a Renaissance fountain with a statue of Pope Leo IX (Saint Leo), who was born here in 1002; a Romanesque church with a remarkable twelfth-century porch, a fine bell tower, and a polychrome statue of the Virgin; an ancient town hall built in 1364; remains of its old ramparts, which you can walk round; and an archaeological museum. Its church belfry, statue of the Virgin, fountain and castle wall are classified as Historic Monuments. There are plenty of tastings of its fine wines.

From Eguisheim you can make a short tour on the 'Road of the Five Castles' where, in the space of 18km (11 miles), you can see five ruined fortresses, one of them reputedly haunted by a White Lady (Pflixbourg). Continue south via Hattstatt and Gueberschwihr (fine Romanesque bell-tower) to **Rouffach**, which has a splendid Cathedral Square with a twelfth to fourteenth-century church and fine medieval and Renaissance houses, and a 'Witch's Tower' crowned with a stork's nest. **Orschwihr** has a good wine co-operative and **Guebwiller**, an industrial town at the gateway to the beautiful, flowery Lauch Valley (known locally as Florival), has three remarkable churches, all in different styles: St Léger is Romanesque, with a fine façade; the Dominican church is fourteenth-century Gothic, and contains the Florival Museum; and Notre-Dame, now a Protestant church, is eighteenth-century neo-Classical, with a superbly lavish Baroque choir. Nearby **Soultz** has an attractive square town hall with an external double staircase, and narrow, twisting old streets with some fine Renaissance houses. There are two pretty Romanesque churches at Murbach and Lautenbach in the Florival.

The wine road ends inauspiciously at the two small industrial towns of **Cernay**, at the starting point of the Route des Crêtes of the Vosges, and **Thann**. Cernay, badly damaged in both World Wars, has preserved an old town gate, and has a stork park and a tourist steam railway. Thann has one proud possession, the superb fifteenth-century Gothic Collegiate Church of St Thiébaut with its famous steeple. Alsatians have a saying: 'Strasbourg's steeple is the highest, Fribourg-en-Brisgau's is the widest, Thann's is the finest'. Not only the steeple but the whole church is beautiful, with sculpted doorways, lovely stained-glass windows and comic carved choir stalls.

From Cernay, take the N66 to **Mulhouse**, the second largest city in Alsace and an important industrial and commercial centre. It has little of the charm of other Alsatian towns, and was long affiliated to the Swiss federation. It has one building of interest, the unusual town hall, whose walls are brightly painted with eye-catching designs and which contains a historical museum. But the main reason for a visit is its three superb museums: the Fabric Printing Museum is the best of its type in the world, with over ten million samples of the industry that gave Mulhouse its wealth; the Railway Museum is the largest in Europe, a fascinating display of all aspects of railways and rail travel; and the National Automobile Museum is a 'must' for car lovers — the famous Schlumpf brothers' collection of 440 cars of all periods, all in working order.

The Vosges Mountains

The journey back to Lorraine from this south-eastern corner of Alsace takes a tortuous route over some of the crests of the Vosges. If you want to short-circuit this route, or avoid it altogether, you can easily do so. The A36 motor-way runs below the southern end of the mountains, and there are several good road passes through at points higher up. The scenery en route is spectacular at times, with too many fine views along the way to mention each one and the roads are normally well surfaced, though they can be narrow and twisting at times. Leave Mulhouse by the N468 or by the 'La Comtoise' A36 motorway to **Belfort**. This town is not in Alsace, but has its own administrative department in the broad valley between the Vosges and the Jura. It is a fortress town (fortifications by Vauban) with a reputation for bravery in withstanding past invading hordes, and is well-known to the French for its lion, a symbol of its contribution to the preservation of France. You can see the oddly-shaped pink-sandstone Belfort Lion standing proudly beside the citadel walls.

From Belfort take the D465 north to the **Ballon d'Alsace** (1,250m, 4,100ft), the peak at the southern end of the Vosges (a *ballon* is an open, rounded mountain-top). The last part is a steep and spectacular climb, with many hairpin bends. From the pass at the top, where three roads meet, there is a dramatic memorial to the World War II bomb disposal experts who cleared the mountains after the war, and a small exhibition of bombs and other war

The Place Stanislas, at Nancy, is a master-piece of design and stunningly beautiful

The abundant charm of Riquewihr and its well-preserved build-ings make it a popular place to visit

debris in the restaurant. A 20 minute walk from here takes you to the summit. Descend by the D466, past the attractive lakes of Alfeld and Sewen, to **Masevaux**, a sleepy little town with a pleasant pedestrianised centre and a pretty main square and fountain (good food at the Golden Eagle in the square). Turn left here onto the D14B and follow the scenic Route Joffre to Thann. Turn left into the Thur valley and in 1km ($^1/_2$ mile) at Willer-sur-Thur, turn right for the **Grand Ballon** or **Ballon de Guebwiller** (1,424m, 4,671ft), the highest peak in the Vosges. From the restaurant it is a 15 minute walk to the top, where there is a Blue Devils' monument to the Hunters' Battalions, and a view down over the Moselle Valley in Lorraine. Continue to Le Markstein, a small ski resort. From here the Route des Crêtes follows the long ridge of the peaks, with the best view in the Vosges from **Mount Honeck** (1,362m, 4,467ft). Turn off right in 3km (2 miles) on the D27 over the oddly-named Col du Platzerwasel to Sondernach. From here a side road leads to the summit of the **Petit Ballon** (1,267m, 4,156ft). Further on, at Metzerel, a footpath (GR5) leads to the lakes of Fischboedle and Schlessrothried, and there is an interesting Log Transport Museum at nearby **Muhlbach**.

A good base for exploring the area is **Munster**, the chief town in the valley and the home of one of France's finest, and smelliest, cheeses (if you want to see it made and taste it, there is a cheese route). Munster has a covered market, a weaving factory and a small spa. From here, take the D417 and turn left onto the D5B to **Hohrodberg**, a quiet mountain resort, and continue until you join the Route des Crêtes at the Col du Calvaire, doubling back along the ridge to the Col de la Schlucht (1,339m 4,392ft). Here you leave Alsace for Lorraine and descend sharply to the leading Vosges resort of **Gérardmer**, a textile town reputed for the production of fine linens. Like many towns in Lorraine, Gérardmer suffered heavy war damage and is now plain and unappealing, though it has an interesting Forestry Museum and Vosges Craftshop. But its long-time appeal as a holiday resort (it boasts the oldest tourist office in France, founded in 1875) lies in its setting, with lakes (including the largest lake in the Vosges), forests, meadows, mountains, gorges, waterfalls and rocks, including mossy boulders known as 'Gérardmer sheep'. It is a delight for the walker, with over 300km (186 miles) of marked trails, and Lake Gérardmer has a full range of tourist amenities.

Gérardmer is an ideal base for exploring the gentler slopes of the western Vosges, including the areas round Celles and Donon further north. **St Dié**, north on the D8 and N415, has two attractive churches, the cathedral and Notre-Dame, linked by a beautiful cloister and it is surrounded by beautiful Vosges countryside. Continuing north-west on the N59, **Baccarat**, with a name made famous by the card game, lies on the western edge of the Vosges. It is renowned for its crystal, and the crystalworks and Crystal Museum next door can be visited. Further north is **Lunéville**, the town that Voltaire called 'the Versailles of Lorraine' on account of its magnificent château with equally magnificent gardens. Built by Duke Leopold in the early eighteenth century and restored after World War II, it houses a ceramics museum and an interesting audio-visual display of the work of the local artist Georges de la Tour. It has *son et lumière* in the park in summer. The town, like Versailles, has an eighteenth-century elegance, and possesses an unusual Rococo church of St Jacques.

Cuisine of Alsace-Lorraine

Alsatian cuisine is renowned throughout France, and Alsatian restaurants can be found in Paris and other large cities. It is attractive partly because it is different — its heavy, rich Germanic flavours provide a contrast with normal French fare. Its best-known dish, but not its finest, is *choucroute garnie*, a plate of *sauerkraut* (pickled cabbage) garnished with Strasbourg sausage, smoked pork and boiled potatoes. Pork products are widely used (sausage, liver sausage, saveloy, black pudding, bacon) and *foie gras* is eaten *en croute* or in a pâté, with bacon. *Baeckeoffe*, the rich meat hotpot, is popular on special occasions. The bacon and onion tart *flammenkuche* is popular in the north. Meat, game and poultry may be braised in wine (usually Riesling) and served with noodles. River fish such as pike-perch (*sandre*) may be poached in Riesling.

Fruit tarts and pies, and the *kugelhopf*, a yeasty raisin cake, are popular desserts. *Brioches*, or sponge cakes, can be savoury, with a sausage inside.

Lorraine's contributions to French cuisine are the *quiche Lorraine* (bacon and egg flan — from the German *kuche* or cake) the *potage Lorraine* (leek and potato soup), the *potée Lorraine* (cabbage and bacon stew), and the *rhum baba*. Mirabelle plums are popular in sweets. Beer and fruit-flavoured *eaux-de-vie* are widely drunk in both regions.

❋   The tour ends 30km (19 miles) west on the N4 at **Nancy**, the capital of Lorraine. Nancy is a large industrial and university town, with some interesting museums (fine arts, local history, art nouveau) but it is built uninspiredly on a grid pattern and, apart from one feature in the centre, is rather characterless. It has a proud history as the seat of the Dukes of Lorraine, and owes its central masterpiece to the dethroned King of Poland, Stanislas Leszczynski, who was appointed Duke by his father-in-law Louis XV in 1738 and proved a benefactor to the town. The Place Stanislas and the adjacent Place de la Carrière, linked together by a triumphal arch in honour of Louis XV, are a magnificent architectural ensemble unrivalled in France. The Place Stanislas in particular, an elegant spacious square flanked by exquisite Baroque fountains and gilt wrought-iron gates, grilles, balusters and lanterns, with a statue of King Stanislas in the centre, is a triumph of design and a delight to the eye. To end your tour, feast your eyes on the sight as you sip your aperitif at one of the surrounding pavement cafés.

Additional Information

Places of Interest

Longuyon
Fort de Fermont (Part of the Maginot Line)
Open: April to September daily 1.30-5pm; Saturday and Sunday in October; Sunday, November to March.

Verdun
Citadel and War Museum
In underground tunnels
Open: 8am-12noon and 2-5pm or 7pm

according to season; closed 15 December to 28 February.

Metz
Museum of Art and History
Open: daily except Tuesday, 9am-12noon and 2-5pm or 6pm.

Haguenau
Alsatian Museum
In Tourist Office
Open: 8am-12noon and 2-6pm; Saturday and Sunday 2-5pm; closed Tuesday.

Strasbourg
Château des Rohan Museums
State Apartments, Fine Arts, Archaeology
Oeuvre Notre-Dame Museum,
Alsatian and Historical Museums
All the above open: 10am-12noon and 2-6pm April to September; Sunday, weekdays in afternoon rest of year; closed Tuesday.

Molsheim
Bugatti Museum
Open: 8-10am and 2-6pm summer, in Cour du Chartreux.

Barr
Folie Marco Museum
Open: daily except Tuesday 10am-12noon and 2.30-6pm July to September; June and October, Saturday and Sunday; rest of year by appointment.

Struthof
World War II Concentration Camp
Open: May to September, 8-11.30am and 2-4.30pm; rest of year 9-11.30am and 2-4.30pm.

Haut-Koenigsbourg
Kaiser Wilhelm II's Castle
Open: 9am-12noon and 1-6pm; closes 4.30pm off season.

Sélestat
Humanist Library
Open: 9am-12noon and 2-5pm, closed Saturday afternoon and Sunday.

Hunawihr
Stork Preservation Centre
Open: 10am-12noon and 2-6pm April to October, except Sunday morning; Wednesday, Saturday and Sunday in autumn if fine.

Riquewihr
Dolder and Thieves' Tower Museums
Open: 9am-12noon and 1.30-6pm Saturday and Sunday, Easter to 1 November; daily July and August.

Kaysersberg
Albert Schweitzer's Birthplace Museum
Open: 10am-12noon and 2-6pm daily Easter and 2 May to 31 October.

Colmar
Unterlinden Museum
Open: 9am-12noon and 2-6pm April to October; until 5pm rest of year; closed Tuesday and holidays.

Cernay
Doller Valley Tourist Steam Train
☎ 89 82 88 48
Open: Sunday and national holidays May to October; daily except Monday and Tuesday in July and August.

Mulhouse
National Automobile Museum
192 Avenue de Colmar
Open: 11am-6pm except Tuesday.

Railway Museum
Open: 9am-6pm April to September; 10am-5pm October to March; closed holidays.

Fabric Printing Museum
Open: 10am-12noon and 2-6pm except Tuesday and holidays; demonstrations Monday and Wednesday in July and August.

Muhlbach
Near Munster
Log Transport Museum
Open: 3-6pm, 7 July to 1 September.

Baccarat
Crystal Museum
Open: 10am-12noon and 2-6.30pm 16 July to 15 September; 2-6.30pm 16 June to 15 July; weekends 2-6pm and occasionally in winter.

Lunéville
Château Museum.
Open: 9am-12noon and 2-5pm or 6pm daily except Tuesday.

Tourist Information Centres

Colmar
Office de Tourisme and Accueil de France
4 Rue Unterlinden
☎ 89 41 02 29

Gérardmer
Office de Tourisme
Place Déportés
☎ 29 63 08 74

Metz
Office de Tourisme and Accueil de
    France
Place d'Armes
☎ 87 75 65 21

Mulhouse
Office de Tourisme
9 Avenue Maréchal Foch
☎ 89 45 68 31

Nancy
Office de Tourisme and Accueil de
    France
14 Place Stanislas
☎ 88 35 22 41

Obernai
Office de Tourisme
Chapelle du Beffroi
☎ 88 95 64 13

Riquewihr
Office de Tourisme
Rue lère Armée
Open: 15 March to 11 November
☎ 89 47 80 80

Strasbourg
Office de Tourisme and Accueil de
    France
Palais des Congrès
Avenue Schutzenberger
☎ 88 37 67 68

10 Place Gutenberg
☎ 88 32 57 07

Restaurants

R = With Accommodation
Haute-cuisine restaurants include:
Ammerschwihr
Aux Armes de France (R)
☎ 89 47 10 12

Blaesheim
Au Boeuf
☎ 88 68 81 31

Belfort
Château Servin
☎ 84 21 41 85

Le Sabot d'Annie
☎ 84 26 01 71

Colmar
Schillinger
☎ 89 41 43 17

Fer Rouge
☎ 89 41 37 24

Rendez-Vous de Chasse
☎ 89 41 10 10

Da Alberto
☎ 89 23 37 89

Eguisheim
Le Caveau
☎ 89 41 08 89

Gérardmer
La Réserve (R)
☎ 29 63 21 60

Host. Bas-Rupts (R)
☎ 29 63 09 25

Illhaeusern
Auberge de l'Ill
☎ 89 71 83 23

Kaysersberg
Chambard
☎ 89 47 10 17

Landersheim
Auberge du Kochersberg
☎ 88 69 91 58

Lembach
Auberge Cheval Blanc
☎ 88 94 41 86

Longuyon
Hôtel de Lorraine et Rest. Le Mas (R)
☎ 82 26 50 07

Lunéville
Château d'Adomenil (R)
☎ 83 74 04 81

Marlenheim
Hostellerie du Cerf (R)
☎ 88 87 73 73

Metz
3km (2 miles) dir. Bellecroix
Crinouc (R)
☎ 87 74 12 46

Belle Vue
At Borny
☎ 87 37 10 27

Mulhouse
Auberge de la Tonnelle
☎ 89 54 25 77

La Poste
☎ 89 44 07 71

Nancy
Le Goéland
☎ 83 35 17 25

Capucin Gourmand
☎ 83 35 26 98

Obersteinbach
Anthon (R)
☎ 88 09 55 01

Phalsbourg
Au Soldat de l'An II
☎ 87 24 16 16

Ribeauvillé
Vosges (R)
☎ 89 73 61 39

Riquewihr
Auberge Schoenenbourg
☎ 89 47 92 28

Sélestat
Edel
☎ 88 92 86 55

La Couronne
(Baldenheim)
☎ 88 85 32 22

Strasbourg
Le Crocodile
☎ 88 32 13 02

Buerehiesel
☎ 88 61 62 24

Verdun
Hostellerie Coq Hardi (R)
☎ 29 86 36 36
Other restaurants, offering good value
for money, include:
Ammerschwihr
Near Colmar
A l'Arbre Vert (R)
☎ 89 47 12 23

Haguenau
Barberousse
☎ 88 73 31 09

Lapoutroie
Host. A la Bonne Truite (R)
☎ 89 47 50 07

Lièpvre
Near Sélestat
A la Vieille Forge
☎ 89 58 92 54

Masevaux
l'Aigle d'Or (R)
☎ 89 82 40 66

Mutzig
Auberge Alsacienne au Nid de Cigogne
☎ 88 38 11 97

Niedersteinbach
Cheval Blanc
☎ 88 09 55 31

Ottrott
Near Obernai
A l'Ami Fritz
☎ 88 95 80 81

Wangenbourg
Le Parc (R)
☎ 88 87 31 72

6

BURGUNDY

The very word 'Burgundy' has a rich sound. To most people it suggests either velvety red wine or the deep, warm colour associated with it. To the gourmet it again suggests wine, as a basic ingredient of the rich *boeuf bourguignonne* or *coq au vin* regional dishes. To the historian it suggests a rich and powerful dukedom that was for many years a rival to France, and in the fifteenth century held at its capital, Dijon, the wealthiest and most powerful court in Europe. To the art-lover it suggests Romanesque churches and abbeys endowed with a wealth of decoration and to the traveller it evokes a smiling land of plenty, with a rich diversity of scenery.

Most Burgundians would agree that their land is blessed, in climate, scenery and the good things of life. The fields are lush and green, rearing the world-renowned white Charollais cattle that are a feature of the landscape. The region is extensive, corresponding roughly to the pre-1789 province, although in earlier centuries it had been much bigger. It stretches from the border of the Île de France in the north to the outskirts of Lyon in the south, and from the Loire in the west to Lorraine in the east. It has the rugged wooded hills of the Morvan, gorges, river valleys, the sunny, south-facing wine slopes of the Côte d'Or, and the broad pastures of its agricultural heartland. It is crossed by canals, and dotted with châteaux and villages of warm yellow stone and red or multi-coloured roofs.

Like Normans, Burgundians are solid, down-to-earth and practical people. The two areas have similarities: large solidly-built houses, fertile farmlands, a rich and heavy cuisine, and Germanic origins. The original Burgondes were vandals from northern Germany, on the Baltic, and seem to have shared some of the characteristics of modern nordic youth. They were rivals to the Franks (though they allied with them to defeat Attila and the Huns) and continued this rivalry through the ages, allying with the English to defeat France in the Hundred Years' War. Their wealth and power reached its height in the fifteenth century, when their ruler, Philip the Good, wore a sash worth a hundred thousand pounds, and their dominions stretched from the Low Countries to Provence. The region lost its independence and was attached to the French crown in the sixteenth century.

Burgundy was the birth-place of medieval monasticism, from the time when the Benedictine abbey was founded at Cluny in AD910. This became the leading abbey in Europe, controlling and ordering monastic life in the early Middle Ages. Many splendid churches were built, the finest at Cluny itself — 'the greatest Romanesque church in Christendom' (it was largely destroyed in the Revolution). Later, in revolt against its opulence, the new, severe Cistercian order introduced a new style of church building, stripped of all ornament. Fine examples of both styles can be seen in the region.

Above all, Burgundy is synonymous with good food and wine. It produces some of the finest, and most expensive, wines in the world, not only the *Grand Cru* reds of the Côte d'Or, but the fine whites of Chablis, Meursault, Montrachet and Pouilly-Fuissé, and its cuisine has created some of France's best-known dishes including snails and frogs' legs!

Burgundy is a large area for a single tour, so a selection of its more interesting sites will be made, with brief reference to others en route. The region is a crossroads at the heart of France, and can be visited many times in passing. This tour starts in the north, at Sens, and takes a winding route through the region (north, centre and south) ending in the south at Mâcon.

Northern Burgundy

Your starting-point, **Sens**, is not yet Burgundian in style as it still has the look of the Île de France about it. Its dominant feature is its splendid Cathedral of St Étienne, the earliest in date of the great French Gothic cathedrals (1140). This church has played its part in history. Pope Alexander III confirmed Thomas à Becket's primacy here in 1164, and met him here while he was in exile at nearby Pontigny (the story of Becket's murder is told in one of the twelfth-century stained glass windows) and Louis IX (St Louis) married Blanche of Castille here in 1234. The west façade doorway has a fine statue of St Étienne, and inside, the medieval stained glass windows and Flamboyant Gothic transepts are superb. The treasury is one of the richest in France. In the town are some old buildings, including the thirteenth-century Synod Palace, and pleasant garden walks on the site of the old ramparts.

Sens stands on the main route to the south, the N6. Leave by this road, following the course of the River Yonne, to **Villeneuve-sur-Yonne**, a small medieval town built as a residence for Louis VIII. It has two handsome town gates, and a church with a superb Renaissance façade. Further on, **Joigny**, a pleasant town standing on both sides of the river, is more distinctly Burgundian than Sens with some lovely old half-timbered houses and attractive bell-towers. It has a prosperous air, with some good shops and fine *haute-cuisine* restaurants, and good views from the quay.

Continue on the N6 to **Auxerre**, a charming town on a beautiful site (best seen from the bridge over the Yonne to the south). It has a lovely old centre, with narrow cobbled streets and timbered houses, and a Gothic clock tower. Of its three churches, the Cathedral of St Étienne is impressive, though less richly endowed and well preserved than Sens. Its doorway sculptures, though fine, are badly damaged. The interior has good stained glass, an eleventh-century crypt, and ancient frescos. The ancient St Germain abbey church has a fascinating Carolingian crypt, with AD850 frescos depicting the martyrdom

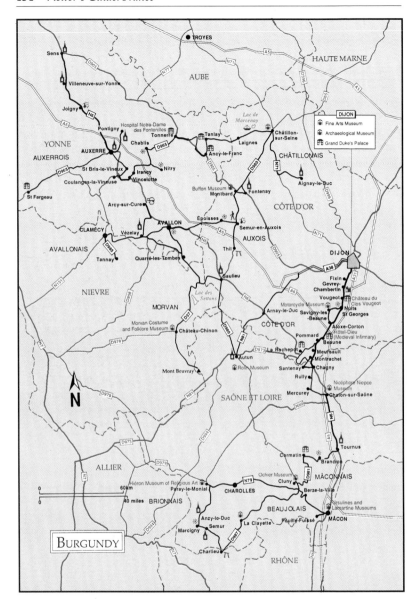

of St Stephen. There are pleasant gardens by the river. To the south and east of Auxerre are two vine-growing regions producing the reputed wines of north (or lower) Burgundy. Turn left off the N6 after 4km (2 miles) to the sleepy village of **St Bris-le-Vineux**. This village, along with Coulanges-la-Vineuse, Vincelotte and Irancy, is in the south-Auxerre region, producing good *appellation régionale* wines, mainly white although there is some fruity though rather astringent red at Irancy. The Sauvignon de St Bris is an excellent crisp, dry white, and the Bourgogne Aligoté from this region is of high quality.

Visit Nitry with its old Burgundian half-timbered buildings

Auxerre is best viewed from the bridge spanning the River Yonne

The wines here are good value, cheaper than in the neighbouring east-Auxerre wine region of **Chablis**, where the world-famous *appellation communale* Chardonnay wines can command high prices. Whether overpriced or not, Chablis is a delicious wine, crisp, bone-dry and fruity, and the Grands Crus are among the world's finest white wines.

ADDITIONAL TOURS IN THE AUXERROIS: Pontigny, 21km (13 miles) north-east — Romanesque church; **Appoigny**, 10km (6 miles) north — thirteenth to sixteenth-century church with Renaissance choir-screen; **Seignelay**, 11km (7 miles) north — wooden covered market; **Chablis**, 19km (12 miles) east — wine-cellar in old infirmary, and churches of St Martin and St Pierre; **Chitry**, 13km (8 miles) south-east — fortified church; **Nitry**, 34km (21miles) south-east — old Burgundian half-timbered houses and town gate with clock-tower; **Irancy**, 18km (11 miles) south — old houses and narrow streets; **St Fargeau** 45km (28 miles) west — château; views over Yonne Valley from surrounding hills.

Take the D965 east from Auxerre to **Tonnerre**, an attractive small market town thriving on commerce from the Burgundy canal. Its outstanding monument is the Hospital Notre-Dame des Fontenilles, founded in 1293. This has an 80m (262ft) long great hall with a superb carved oak roof, the tomb of the founder, Marguerite of Burgundy, and a beautiful fifteenth-century sculpture, the *Entombment of Christ*. The Hôtel d'Uzès, now the savings bank, has a fine Renaissance façade. A lovely and unusual Roman pool, the Fosse Dionne, lies on a plateau above the town. This God-given spring ('Dionne' is a corruption of 'Divine') was the only source of water for the town in Gallo-Roman times, and appears as a 15m (49ft) diameter pool of blue-green water enclosed by a wall and encircled by a covered gallery decked with flowers.

Not far from Tonnerre are the two finest châteaux in Burgundy, at Tanlay and Ancy-le-Franc. In 10km (6 miles) on the D965, the **Château de Tanlay** is a beautiful sight when approached down a mile-long double avenue of limes. First you reach a decorous moat flanked by elegant pavilions, then the Court of Honour and the round towers and bell-shaped domes of the château itself. Inside are some fine frescoes, trompe-l'oeil paintings and furniture. In 19km (12 miles) on the D905 is the **Château d'Ancy-le-Franc**, a charming example of Italian Renaissance architecture. Its front is sober and Classical, its inner closed courtyard richly decorated with pilasters, alcoves and dormer windows. The furniture and decoration inside are magnificent, particularly the murals in the Sacrifice and Pharsala galleries, and the hall of the Roman Emperors with its odd acoustic effect. The contrast with Tanlay is marked — the setting and exterior are less charming, the interior more sumptuous. Sadly, unlike Tanlay, the Ancy-le-Franc château is uninhabited, and is in need of restoration.

Rejoin the D965 and continue east to **Laignes**, a quiet, pretty village with a pool graced by elegant swans at the side of the main square. A deviation to the left on the D102 leads to the **Lac de Marcenay**, an attractive tree-lined lake that has been developed for water sports, with a good restaurant, Le Santenoy, nearby. Return to the D965 and continue to **Châtillon-sur-Seine**. The Seine here is a pretty stream, running through the town in surroundings of lawns, grottoes, flower-beds and trees (its source is 50km, 31 miles south, just off the N71). Châtillon's main interest to the visitor is its museum, attractively housed in a Renaissance mansion. Amongst other Gallo-Roman local finds is the magnificent Vase of Vix, a huge sixth-century BC Greek bronze vase found with other treasures in a Gallic princess's burial mound at the nearby village of Vix. It is 1.64m (5.37ft) high, 208kg in weight, and has a superb frieze. There is a good restaurant at the Côte d'Or hotel.

ADDITIONAL TOURS IN THE CHÂTILLONAIS: Vix, 7km (4 miles) north — the treasure village under Mont Lassois, Romanesque church; south west — the Fôret de Châtillon; south — the Seine and Coquille valleys and sources; **Aignay-le-Duc**, 33km (20 miles) south — Gothic church; **Duesme**, 33km (20 miles) south — ruined château, waterfall; **Molesmes**, 23km (14 miles) northwest — ruined abbey.

At Châtillon take the D980 for Montbard, and after 28km (17 miles) turn left through the forest to **Fontenay Abbey**. This elegant but severely plain Cistercian monastery, beautifully set in a wooded valley, surrounded by a trim, flowery garden with a carp-pool, is the finest of its type still standing. It was founded in the twelfth century by St Bernard of Clairvaux, who had rebelled against the luxury and secular ornamentation of the Benedictine order, and urged a return to fasting and prayer. Here the beauty of the buildings lies in their design and materials, not in their decoration. The abbey was used as a paper mill from the Revolution to 1906 by the Mongolfier family of balloon fame. The church, cloister and statue of the Virgin of Fontenay are particularly fine. Nearby **Montbard** was the former home of the Dukes of Burgundy (John the Bold spent his youth here), and later was the birthplace of the famous eighteenth-century naturalist Buffon. There are pleasant walks in the Buffon Park, which he designed, and where you can visit the Aubepin and St Louis towers and the great man's study. Six kilometres (4 miles) from Montbard are the Buffon Forges, an eighteenth-century industrial centre with steel-making exhibits.

Continue south on the D980, and in 18km (11 miles) you will be confronted with a sight out of a fairy story — a medieval town with a profile of conical towers, spires and multi-coloured roofs perched on a pink-granite spur over the River Armançon. This is **Semur-en-Auxois**, one of the most attractive towns in Burgundy. Once inside the fourteenth-century Sauvigny gate, you are into a maze of narrow streets lined with old houses, leading to the Church of Notre-Dame, a fine thirteenth-century Gothic church with Burgundian snails carved on the façade. It has an unusually narrow nave, and some good stained-glass. There is an interesting museum in a former Dominican convent, and a pleasant walk among shady trees, with splendid views, around the old ramparts, dominated by the four circular fourteenth-century towers with their pointed red-tiled roofs. You will eat well at Les Gourmets, or at the Hôtel du Lac de Pont 3km (2 miles) south.

Flowers are reflected in the blue-green waters of the Fosse Dionne pool at Tonnerre

The attractive Renaissance mansion at Châtillon-sur-Seine houses a museum of local interest

ADDITIONAL TOURS IN THE AUXOIS: Lac de Pont, 4km (2 miles) south– a bathing and sailing centre; **Thil,** 13km (8 miles) south–the site of a ruined castle and collegiate church; **Bourbilly,** 9km (6 miles) south-west–fourteenth-century château; **Époisses,** 12km (7 miles–ruined church; **Châteauneuf,** 44km (27 miles) south-east–picturesque village and château; **Commarin,** 39km (24 miles) south-east–beautiful château; **Posanges,** 23km (14 miles) south-east — château; **Flavigny-sur-Ozerain,** 16km (10 miles) east–picturesque village with abbey; **Bussy-Rabutin,** 19km (12 miles) north-east-beautiful château.

The Morvan

Take the D954 west from Semur, turning right onto the N6 at Cussy-les-Forges. In 5km (3 miles) at La Cerce, the Relais Fleurie has a good restaurant. Five kilometres (3 miles) further on is **Avallon,** on the edge of the Morvan Regional Nature Park. This is a town that most people speed through on the N6, but it has an attractive old centre enclosed by ancient ivy-covered ramparts and guarded by weathered watchtowers. In the Middle Ages Avallon was a strongly fortified gate to Burgundy and now its ramparts provide a pleasant promenade round the town. The church has an ancient crypt, and beautiful, though damaged, carved twelfth-century doorways. In the centre is a pretty fifteenth-century clock tower.

Thirteen kilometres (8 miles) west from Avallon on the D957 is one of the high spots of the tour, **Vézelay.** This picturesque hilltop village overlooking the rich Burgundy plain is crowned by one of the jewels of Christendom, the Basilica of Ste Madeleine, a Romanesque masterpiece that has been designated as an international treasure by UNESCO. When it was founded in AD878, the abbey was believed to hold the remains of St Mary Magdalene, and in the Middle Ages the church became a popular pilgrimage centre, both for itself and as a starting point for the pilgrim roads to Jerusalem and Compostela. Its power and influence were destroyed, first by the Huguenots, who massacred the inhabitants in 1569, and later when the Revolutionaries razed the abbey in 1796. The derelict church was restored by Viollet-le-Duc in the nineteenth century.

Start your visit at the car park and follow the pilgrim trail up through the winding village streets to the basilica on top of the hill (the site is popular — go early or late to avoid coach parties). The façade is impressive, but its relief sculptures are surpassed by those above the inner doorways. These are magnificent in their detail and vivid realism, showing Christ in glory with his apostles on the tympanum, surrounded by fabulous creatures, signs of the Zodiac and labours of the months. Inside, the nave is high and luminous, its arches attractively striped with bands of light and dark stone. But its greatest treasures are the capitals above the pillars of the nave: one hundred in all, in different styles and with a variety of subjects, they are a source of endless fascination, as they must have been to the medieval pilgrims whose instruction and entertainment they were designed to provide. You would be advised to obtain a detailed guide to explain them.

ADDITIONAL TOURS IN THE AVALLONAIS: **Arcy-sur-Cure**, 19km (12 miles) north — grottoes; the **Cousin** valley; **St Père-sous-Vézelay** 13km (8 miles) west — Gothic church; **Clamecy**, 36km (22 miles) west-old houses; **Tannay**, 37km (23 miles) south-west — white wines; **Châtel-Censoir**, 28km (17 miles) west — site and church.

South of Avallon and Vézelay is the **Morvan Massif**, a wild, underpopulated region of lakes, hills and forests that is being developed as a holiday centre. It offers water-sports on its many lakes and reservoirs, with canoeing on the Cure and Cousin, walking (the GR13 runs through it from north to south) and horse-riding, with marked rides and equestrian centres. It is an attractive area, though rather sombre with its dense pinewoods (it provides France with most of its Christmas trees), and it can be wet. The area is extensive (80km, {31 miles], north-south by 50km, [31 miles], east-west), and its main income is from timber, paper-mills and hydro-electric power.

There are few resorts of any size in the region. **Château-Chinon** is the largest: though not very attractive as a town, it has good views over the area from the Calvary ridge above it, and an interesting Morvan Costume and Folklore Museum. The prettiest and most popular lake is the Lac des Settons, with swimming, boating and fishing facilities and some small resorts; and the highest hill is **Mont Beuvray** (821m, 2,693ft) in the extreme south, with fine views from the chapel at the top. **Quarré-les-Tombes** is named after the hundred or more mysterious sarcophagi that surround the church, the work of primitive stone-masons. The Saut de Gouloux is an attractive waterfall, and nearby St Brisson has the office of the Regional Nature Park.

Saulieu, the eastern gateway to the Morvan, is an attractive town with a fine Romanesque church and an enviable reputation for gastronomy. It has been popular with travellers and pilgrims through the ages for its fine restaurants (Rabelais and Mademoiselle de Sévigné both praised the quality of its food and wine). Its twelfth-century Basilica of St Andoche stands on a lovely square with a fountain and museum next door. However the real treasure of the church is its figured capitals, a charming mixture of sacred and secular themes (*Flight into Egypt, Hanging of Judas, Christ and the Holy Women*). Around the church are pleasant old streets with good food shops selling local delicacies. Saulieu would be a convenient base for exploring the Morvan, with a good camp-site and a choice of pleasant hotels. It is 39km (24 miles) from Avallon on the N6.

From Saulieu, take the D980 south, through a pretty corner of the Regional Park. At the south-eastern end of the Morvan is the old Roman capital of Burgundy, **Autun**. This was one of the most important cities in Gallo-Roman times, its name deriving from the Emperor Augustus, who reduced and then rebuilt the old Gallic stronghold. The Arroux and St André gates remain of the four original Roman city gates, and fragments of the old Roman theatre, once the largest in Gaul. Remains of the medieval ramparts still enclose the town. Autun's two important possessions are its cathedral and its Rolin Museum.

The Romanesque Cathedral of St Lazare is famed for its amazing tympanum of the Last Judgement in the doorway, signed by one of the few medieval sculptors known by name, Gislebertus (twelfth century), who was renowned throughout Europe. One of the most dramatic representations of the medieval world-view ever drawn, with grimacing devils waiting eagerly to receive the damned souls howling for mercy, and the elect piously making their way to heaven escorted by trumpeting angels, this compares with the Vézelay tympanum as one of the masterpieces of Romanesque art. Inside the church are some fine carved capitals, most of them grouped together in the chapterhouse. Another Gislebertus masterpiece (a recumbent Eve) can be found in the Rolin Museum across the square, with a fifteenth-century *Virgin of Autun* in polychrome stone and the *Nativity* by the Master of Moulins.

The Côte d' Or

Take the N81 north-east out of Autun to **Arnay-le-Duc**, which has an old almshouse staging an exhibition of regional crafts and a good restaurant, Chez Camille, in an old Burgundian home. Sixteen kilometres (10 miles) further on, the N81 becomes the A38 motorway, taking you quickly along the Ouche Valley to **Dijon**, the capital of Burgundy. Dijon is really three towns: a busy commercial and industrial centre with a large railway junction and sprawling and unattractive suburbs; an elegant regional capital reflecting in its public buildings the power and grandeur of the ancient Duchy; and a gastronomic centre famous for mustard and blackcurrant liqueur, or *cassis*. The blackcurrant is the regional fruit of Burgundy (the colour, at least, is appropriate!) — blackcurrant ice-cream and sweets are popular, and the favourite aperitif is *vin blanc cassis*, or white wine with a dash of *cassis*. The locals call this *Kir*, after the popular ex-mayor of Dijon, Chanoine Kir, who invented the drink. *Kir Royale* is a variant with sparkling wine.

The old centre of Dijon is a delight to explore, a world away from the bustle outside the encircling boulevards. At its heart is the Place de la Libération, an elegant semicircular space in front of the Grand Duke's Palace, with its Courtyard of Honour leading via a splendid staircase to a series of sumptuous rooms. The grandest of these is the Guards' Hall, which contains the beautiful fifteenth-century tombs of Philip the Bold and John the Fearless, the two greatest Dukes of Burgundy. The groups of mourners that hold up their recumbent statues are wonderfully vivid, each with his own expression or gesture — one picking his ear another wiping his nose. The Guards' Hall forms a section of the Fine Arts Museum, one of the richest art collections in France, with Flemish Primitives, Dutch Masters, great French and Italian painters, and many others. The Flemish influences are marked, both in the seventeenth-to eighteenth-century buildings and in the works of art they contain. The palace has some remaining older parts, including the fourteenth-century Bar Tower and the fifteenth-century Tower of Philip the Good, from which there is a fine view of the town (316 steps). There are some exquisite old houses in the medieval streets behind and around the palace, including the Aubriot, Lantenay, Lantin and Liégard Mansions. There are also three splendid churches: Notre-Dame, early Gothic, with gaping gargoyles and a Jacquemart clock; the St Bénigne Cathedral, with a glazed-tile roof and a Romanesque crypt with pre-Romanesque capitals; and St Michel, a Flamboyant Gothic building behind a Renaissance façade. A fine Archaeological Museum, with Gallo-Roman votive statues, is housed in the twelfth-century dormitory of the former abbey.

Outside the city centre on the western side is the Champmol Charterhouse, built by Philip the Bold to house the bodies of the Dukes of Burgundy and destroyed in the Revolution. The site is now a psychiatric hospital, but two treasures remain which you can see on request: a group of statues round a chapel doorway (1390), and Moses' Well, the base of a Calvary surrounded by six superb statues of prophets. Just beyond is the Kir lake, a popular recreation spot for city-dwellers, with a beach, leisure centre, sailing club and restaurant. Like the aperitif, it was named after the much-loved mayor. As befits its reputation as a gastronomic centre, Dijon has some excellent restaurants.

Three parallel roads lead south from Dijon — the A31 motorway, the N74 trunk road and the D122. They run along the edge of the best-known vine-slopes in the world, the Côte d'Or or 'Golden Coast', known to the French simply as La Côte. Superlatives abound: this is France's most expensive agricultural land, producing the world's most expensive wines, sold in the world's most famous and influential wine sale at Beaune, and so on. Although Burgundy wines have a very old pedigree dating back to Roman times or beyond, it was medieval monks who were responsible for developing and improving them (some modern vineyards were once dependencies of abbeys) and gradually established an international reputation. Today three-quarters of the vineyards are entitled to their AOC status, or controlled place-name of origin. Within an AOC there may be many small growers, some with tiny but extremely valuable plots of land containing as little as a single row of vines, contributing to the *appellation communale*, which is the status applied to the finest wines. Lesser quality wines are graded *appellation regionale*, with a less specific origin. Some of these are defined by the grape variety rather than the place of origin, such as Bourgogne Aligoté, a white wine made from that grape, or Bourgogne Passetoutgrains, which is a red made from a mixture of Pinot Noir and Gamay grapes. Other lesser quality wines may be labelled Bourgogne Grand Ordinaire, or simply Bourgogne.

Take the N74 out of Dijon until you are past the long string of garish hypermarkets and commercial centres, then turn right for Chenôve and the D122, onto the **Route des Grands Crus**. This is where the great vineyards start. The Côte is divided into two sections: the first running from just south of Dijon to Corgoloin, south of Nuits St Georges, is known as the Côte de Nuits and produces almost exclusively *Grand Cru* red wines; the second section runs from just north of Aloxe-Corton to Santenay — this is known as the Côte de Beaune, and produces both excellent red and superb white wines, including some of the world's top *Grand Cru* whites. The best quality wines are usually produced on the middle and lower slopes; the upper slopes produce wine that is often labelled Hautes-Côtes, and sold to co-operatives for blending. It can

The beautiful Hôtel-Dieu at Beaune

Religious scenes are depicted around the Basilica of St Andoche, Saulieu

still be excellent wine, but will lack the depth and finesse of the *Grands Crus*. All the great red Burgundies are made from one single grape variety, the Pinot Noir, while the great whites are made from the Chardonnay.

Before leaving **Chenôve**, you will notice that some of the serried ranks of vines are protected in walled enclosures, the *clos* that feature in many vineyard names. The two chief ones here are the Clos du Roi, belonging at one time to the Dukes of Burgundy, and the Clos du Chapitre, once the property of the canons of Autun. In the *cuverie* (fermenting room) of the former are two huge ancient wine presses, the Pressoirs des Ducs, dating from 1228. Continue through Marsannay-la-Côte (rosé wines), Couchey and Fixey (Romanesque church with glazed tile belfry) to **Fixin**, the first *Grand Cru* red wine village. It has a statue of Napoleon *Awakening to Immortality* by a local artist, François Rude, with a small museum of Bonaparte souvenirs close by. After Brochon, the next village is the famous **Gevrey-Chambertin**, which has a tenth-century castle. Its wine production, by a commune of 139 small proprietors holding about 150 acres, is typical of the region. Although the village AOC wine, Gevrey-Chambertin, is superb, it is surpassed by the nearby *cru* Le Chambertin, Napoleon's favourite tipple — he called it 'the king of wines'. The next village, **Morey St Denis**, has the magnificent Clos de Tart as its most precious appellation and in **Chambolle-Musigny** the excellent commune wine is again surpassed by Le Musigny. At the next village, **Vougeot**, the D122 rejoins the busy N74 and the Route des Grands Crus ends.

 Before leaving Vougeot, you must visit the Château du Clos-Vougeot, one of the most picturesque châteaux on the Côte. Built by Cistercian monks in 1551, it stands proudly within its walled *clos*, its rust-coloured tiles gleaming among the sea of surrounding vines. It is now the headquarters of the brotherhood of the Chevaliers du Tastevin, the famous confraternity of Burgundy wine-producers which has existed since 1934 partly to celebrate the region's long and glorious past, partly to promote their product, and partly as an excuse for a good annual beano amid much colourful pomp and ceremony. This happens in November, when three sumptuous banquets, known as the Trois Glorieuses, are held at Clos de Vougeot, Meursault and Beaune, the last one in the town's splendid medieval market building after the famous annual wine sale. The brother *vignerons* dress up in traditional costume for the feast, the walls are draped in tapestries, much complicated ceremony takes place, and old Burgundian songs are sung. Honoured guests are treated to a gourmet meal with superb wines, and if deemed worthy are initiated into the Confrérie. Fourteen other similar banquets, or *disnées*, are held in the château's cellars each year, so becoming a Chevalier could be an onerous task as well as an honour! You can visit the vast twelfth-century cellars, and the thirteenth-century *cuverie* with its four huge wine presses.

For the next village, **Vosne-Romanée**, rejoin the N74 and then turn off right. This commune represents the apex of the Côte de Nuits, producing not only Vosne-Romanée itself but the four rarest and most expensive wines in the world: Romanée-Conti, Richebourg, La Tache and the almost unpronounceable Grands Echézeaux. Do not expect to taste these wines; in fact, tastings along the Côte de Nuits are few and far between, and those you do find will be of lesser wines than the great growths, which take at least 10 years to mature. Côte de Nuits wines are richer and more full-bodied (*corsé*) than Côte de Beaune, and take longer to reach their peak, so there is not too much point in tasting them young. The best place for sampling Burgundy is Beaune, where the headquarters of the big wine merchants are found. You may have to pay for a tasting, but it will be worth it as you will be given a greater selection of better-quality wines and allowed to sample at your own pace.

The last wine-producing places on the Côte de Nuit are **Nuits St Georges** and its neighbouring commune of **Prémeaux**. Nuits St Georges, somewhere in size between a large village and a small town, is an old Gallo-Roman settlement with an archaeological museum in the seventeenth-century clock tower. Today it is prosperous, smiling and welcoming, the commercial centre of its area. Continue on the N74 to **Aloxe-Corton**, the first wine-producing village on the Côte de Beaune. This and its neighbouring village of **Pernand-Vergelesses** produce great red wines, the nearest in style to Côte de Nuits. This whole area used to belong to Charlemagne, and the great white wine of the commune, Corton-Charlemagne, bears his name. Off the N74 to the west is **Savigny-lès-Beaune**, a prosperous wine village with a Romanesque bell-tower, a fifteenth-century church, and a château with a Motorcycle Museum. A pleasant round tour can be made from here to Nuits St Georges by the Combe Pertuis.

Beaune lies at the heart of the Côte d'Or and is the commercial capital of the Burgundy wine trade. It lives and breathes wine, and is a mecca for the oenophile (wine-lover), and yet it is a lovely town with many art treasures to attract the visitor. The old town is circular in shape, surrounded by old ramparts and tree-lined boulevards, with narrow cobbled streets leading to a cluster of buildings at the centre, dominated by the Hôtel-Dieu. This beauitful and much-visited building, an emblem of Burgundy, is a medieval infirmary, founded in 1443 by Rolin, chancellor of Burgundy, whose statue stands in the garden. It was in continuous use as a hospital until 1971, and part of it is still used as a home for the aged. The exterior is sombre, with a roof of shiny grey tiles, but the inside is a staggering contrast. Across the cobbled courtyard with its wrought-iron well is a display of turrets and dormer windows above pillared wooden galleries and, above it, the ultimate in multi-coloured glazed-tile roofs. The guided tour reveals a long medieval ward with a chapel at one end, and curtained-off beds (meant to hold two people each), medieval kitchens and pharmacy, and a museum containing, the magnificent polyptych of the *Last Supper* by Roger Van der Weyden (1443). This Flemish masterpiece can be examined in detail with a mobile magnifying glass.

Other interesting buildings in Beaune include the Collegiate Church of Notre-Dame, mainly Romanesque, with fifteenth-century tapestries depicting the *Life of the Virgin* (behind the altar); the old covered market, which houses the famous wine auction and Tastevin banquet; the mansion of the Dukes of Burgundy, a handsome old hotel housing an attractive and informative Burgundy Wine Museum; and many other fine mansions of the four-

Churches and cathedrals throughout Burgundy are endowed with a wealth of decoration

Charollais cattle are a common feature of Burgundy's farmland

teenth to seventeenth centuries, some now used as offices of the wine trade. Tastings can be made at several establishments in the town, such as Patriarche, or you can help yourself, for a small fee, at the Marché aux Vins. There is a liberal free tasting just outside Beaune on the Meursault road, at the Coopérative des Hautes-Côtes de Beaune, although these are less prestigious wines.

The Côte de Beaune continues through **Pommard**, **Volnay** and **Monthélie**, three villages making superb red wines (guided tour with tasting at the Château de Pommard), to the first of the great white-wine-producing villages, **Meursault**. This pleasant little town has a Town Hall and château with glazed-tile roofs, and good wine-tastings at the château (cellars, modern art display in the Orangery) and at the Hôpital de Meursault, just outside the town on the N74. Here they charge by the glass for the Meursault, but you can try other good local wines free. Meursault holds the third of the Tastevin banquets, which it calls the Paulée, in the château every year on the Monday after the Beaune auction. It is also a good base for exploring the southern Côte, with camping around the municipal swimming-pool above the town. Nearby is **Auxey-Duresses** (excellent red and white wines, good restaurant); and above, on the Haute Côte, the charming village of **St Romain**, producing good red and rosé, and offering fine views of the Côte from beyond the village. Nearby Orches produces a pleasant rosé, and just beyond, in a natural amphitheatre of the Côte, is the handsome and dramatically-sited **Château de La Rochepot** (guided visits).

The D113 connects Meursault with the twin villages of **Puligny-Montrachet** and **Chassagne-Montrachet**, one on each side of the N6. Each of them produces superb white wines, but the wine known simply as Le Montrachet, shared by the two communes, is widely acknowledged to be the best white wine in the world. It is rare, highly-prized and very expensive. Red wines have the last word, however. Three kilometres (2 miles) from Chassagne is **Santenay** (Les Bains), at the southern end of the Côte, whose reds can compare with most of the more northerly *crus*. It also has a small spa with a hot spring, on the site of a Roman bath. Nearby **Chagny** has some good restaurants.

Southern Burgundy

Beyond Chagny there are villages producing fine wines, though they are more scattered than on the Côte and they do not reach the heights of the *Grands Crus*. This area is known as the Côte Chalonnaise, and the villages with their own appellations are: **Rully** (white wines); **Mercurey** (red wines, including five *Premiers Crus*); **Givry** (reds); **Montagny** (whites); and **Bouzeron** (Bourgogne Aligotés). Other than these, the Côte Chalonnaise produces a lot of drinkable wine under the Bourgogne Rouge label, and is a good area for liberal tastings and for buying wine *en vrac* (loose in containers). There is a large Cave Coopérative at **Buxy**. The chief town of the area is the industrial and commercial river-port of **Chalon-sur-Saône**, largely sprawling and unattractive but with a pleasant old quarter by the river. Chalon was the home of Nicéphore Niepce, the inventor of photography. A museum in an eighteenth-century mansion explains his life and work.

Take the N6 from Chagny to Chalon, and continue south to **Tournus**. A small town squeezed between road and river on a busy highway, Tournus is often by-passed without a second glance by travellers rushing south. Yet in an area with an unparalleled wealth of Romanesque churches, it has one of the finest and most unusual, the Basilica of St Philibert. Monks from the island of Noirmoutier in the north-west, fugitives from the Normans, arrived here in AD875 with relics of St Philibert and rebuilt the 300-year-old abbey, parts of which remain today. The church is built like a fortress, in massive and uncomplicated style, giving a remarkable impression of simplicity and power. Its nave is remarkable, with tall, sturdy pillars and unusual transverse barrel vaulting, its stark effect softened by the delicate pinkish colour of the stone. The choir and chapels, and an eleventh-century chapel of St Michel on the first floor of the narthex, are all fine examples of Romanesque style. The abbey buildings, grouped round the cloister at the side of the church, house exhibitions in summer.

At Tournus, turn right onto the D14 for a tour of the most attractive part of south Burgundy. This is an area dominated by the influence of Cluny, whose legacy is a huge number of Romanesque churches and some ruined abbeys. It also has lovely scenery of rolling hills and rich pasturelands, dotted with pretty villages and châteaux. To the south is the hilly, wooded and vine-covered **Mâconnais**, to the west the gentler, undulating farmland of the **Brionnais**. The road takes you over the Col de Beaufer and past the castles of Ozenay and Martailly-lès-Brancion to **Brancion**, a highly picturesque medieval village encased in ramparts, perched on a rocky spur beneath a tenth- to fourteenth-century castle. To visit the village on the spur, pass through the once-portcullised entrance gate into the Middle Ages. Here is a fifteenth-century market, a communal bakehouse, a gibbet, a sanctuary stone (which guaranteed asylum for 24 hours), a cluster of fifteenth-century houses overgrown with vegetation, earth streets, a well-restored castle, and a beautifully restored twelfth-century Romanesque church containing splendid fourteenth-century frescoes. **La Chapelle**, in the valley below, has another Romanesque church, and a fresco repair workshop.

Continue on the D14 to **Chapaize**. As you approach on the straight road through the forest, you will see the splendid 35m (115ft) high Lombard bell-tower of its eleventh-century church dominating the valley, all that remains of a Benedictine priory. Nearby, at **Lanchaire**, are the ruins of an eleventh-century convent. At **Cormatin**, in 5km (3 miles), is a charming Renaissance château (1600), sumptuously furnished and decorated inside. There are Romanesque churches at nearby **Ameugny** and **Taizé**, and at the latter an ecumenical religious community, founded in 1940, made up of Christians of many denominations from all over the world. Visitors are welcome, and invited to join their services and meetings. From Cormatin, take the D187 to **Chissey-lès-Mâcon**, whose thirteenth-century church has interesting capitals. From here you can drive to the top of **Mont St Romain** (579m, 1,899ft), which gives fine views over the Mâconnais and the Saône Valley. On the slopes below, vines are grown which produce the fine white wines of **Mâcon-Lugny**. Descend to **Blanot**, with its twelfth-century church and ruined fourteenth-century priory. Just outside the village is an extensive series of grottoes. Further on, **Donzy-le-Pertuis** has an eleventh-century church with a fine tower, and nearby **Azé** has a grotto with an underground river flowing through it, and a prehistory museum in the village.

At the heart of the Mâconnais is **Cluny**, reflecting quietly on its past glory as home of the greatest, most famous and powerful abbey in Christendom. The first impression is disappointing: only one transept tower, with two transepts and five naves, remains of the huge Romanesque church, nearly 200m (656ft) long, that once dominated monastic life throughout Europe. The Benedictine monastery was founded in AD910, and demolished after the Revolution in 1798. Some of its original area has been built over, but you can get an idea of its original massive beauty from what remains. In the surviving buildings are displays, models and unearthed fragments, including a fine set of figured capitals in the thirteenth-century flour store. There is a small museum in the town, and a Romanesque church (1159) with a fine bell-tower.

South of Cluny, the D980 joins the N79. Turn right onto this, and in 1km ($^1/_2$ mile) bear right onto the D17 for a pleasant scenic run through the Brionnais (the 592m, [1,942ft] high Butte de Suin, on your right in 13km [8 miles], gives superb views) to **Charolles**. This town, which gives its name to the Charollais region and its famous white cattle, has an important cattle market. Thirteen kilometres (8 miles) further on the N79 is **Paray-le-Monial**, a pleasant market town on the Bourbince and the Canal du Centre that has in part taken over the role of Cluny. Since the seventeenth century it has been an important Roman Catholic religious centre, with annual pilgrimages to holy relics held in its magnificent Basilica of Sacré-Coeur. This church, built on a plan that resembles Cluny, has three pointed towers and a beautiful eastern end with an array of fine chapels. Its sober elegance is particularly striking when the church is illuminated at night. Paray has a fine town hall, a museum of religious art, and good restaurants.

AN ADDITIONAL TOUR OF THE BRIONNAIS FROM PARAY-LE-MONIAL TO CHAROLLES COULD INCLUDE: Montceaux-l'Étoile — church with fine carved tympanum; **Anzy-le-Duc** — fine bell-tower, beautiful church, perhaps the model for Vézelay, with superb carvings on the tympanum and capitals; **Marcigny** — fifteenth-century houses, Mill Tower Museum; **Semur-en-Brionnais** — ruined château and twelfth-century church with carved doorway; **St Julien-de-Jonzy** — church with fine bell-tower, tympanum and doorway; **Fleury-la-Montagne** — tympanum on church; **Charlieu** — ruins of Romanesque Benedictine abbey with superb portal, Gothic houses in town; **La Clayette** — moated château by road, with Automobile Museum in outbuildings; **Dree** — seventeenth-century château; **Bois Ste Marie** — eleventh-century church, oldest in Brionnais.

Return from Charolles to Mâcon by the N79. Turn off left after 34km (21 miles) for **Berzé-le-Châtel**, whose triple-walled feudal château is set among superb Mâcon-Viré vineyards, and **Berzé-la-Ville**, with a small chapel that was a summer retreat of Cluniac monks. This chapel is one of the jewels of Burgundy, and indeed France, for its superb twelfth-century frescoes, miraculously preserved behind whitewash until uncovered in 1887. Byzantine frescoes are rare in France, but the magnificent *Christ in Majesty* in the apse rivals the best of Italy or Greece for its brilliance of colour and virtuosity of design. Across the valley, under the road and railway, is the village of **Milly-Lamartine**, the childhood home of the Romantic poet.

This region, on the southern edge of Burgundy, is famous for its white Chardonnay wines, rivals to those of the Côte d'Or (and considerably cheaper). The best-known of these is produced by five communes (Pouilly, Fuissé, Solutré, Vergisson and Chaintré) with the collective name of Pouilly-Fuissé. This dry, fruity wine is now in great demand, and its price is rising accordingly. Other wines of the region (St Véran, Mâcon-Viré, Mâcon-Lugny, or plain Mâcon) remain more affordable. A tour of the region should afford some good tastings, though you can no longer get Pouilly-Fuissé *en vrac*. If you stray over the border into the attractive hilly region of the **Beaujolais**, you can taste some of its famous Gamay red wines. One of the villages, **Solutré**, is

---

Burgundy Cuisine

Burgundy is paradise for the gourmet. This is one of the great French cuisines, full-flavoured and hearty, with red wine, bacon and mushrooms as common ingredients. The snail is almost an emblem of Burgundy, and in French restaurants, *escargots bourguignonnes* is a classic dish — a dozen or half-dozen, cooked and served in their shells on a special dish, with garlic and parsley butter (they are especially good with a dash of Chablis). Frogs' legs are also renowned. Another starter is *oeufs meurettes*, eggs poached in red wine with bacon, mushrooms and baby onions.

Apart from terrines and galantines of game, pork or rabbit, a favourite cold starter is *jambon persillé*, or jellied ham with parsley. Morvan mountain ham is often served with a cream and white wine sauce known as a *saupiquet*, from an old word meaning 'to spice with salt'. Tripe sausages, or *andouillettes*, are popular, grilled and served with Dijon mustard. River fish are common, particularly trout. A *pochouse* is a fish stew with white wine. *Quenelles de brochet* are dumplings of pike, usually served with a white wine and mushroom sauce.

The classic meat dish is *boeuf bourguignonne*, best made with Charollais beef and a good red Burgundy wine. *Coq au vin* is traditionally made with Chambertin — it should be an old farmhouse cock, stewed slowly with bacon, mushrooms, button onions and plenty of wine. Corn-fed chickens from Bresse are highly rated, and usually cooked in a half-cream, half-wine sauce.

Local cheeses are Chaource, St Florentin, Époisses (a strong cheese often matured in *marc*), and Soumaintrain. Goat cheeses are small and sharp. A favourite pudding is the *clafoutis*, a doughy tart made with blackcurrants or cherries. A *gougère* is a baked dough ring with a glazed cheese crust.

The blackcurrant is Burgundy's favourite fruit, served in a sorbet, in sweets, or used to make the famous *cassis de dijon*. A favourite aperitif is *kir*, and after the meal a *marc de bourgogne* (brandy) aged in oak barrels.

famed for more than its wine. Under the distinctive silhouette of its rock were found 100,000 skeletons of prehistoric animals, driven over the cliff by hunters, together with some human skeletons and Bronze Age artefacts. Solutré has become a centre of prehistory, and has given its name to the Solutrean Era (15,000-12,000BC).

Return to **Mâcon**, your tour destination, by the D54, passing the suburb of Charnay with its good Cave Co-operative. Mâcon is a busy commercial town and important wine centre on the Saône. Though not a tourist centre, it is colourful and lively, with floral displays and pleasant parks, and it has a distinct air of the south about it. There are two good museums: the Ursulines Museum has archaeology, including the Solutré excavations, and fine art, and the Lamartine Museum tells you all you want to know about Mâcon's famous son. It has good restaurants, camping and hotels and its Maison des Vins is an informative and refreshing place to end your tour.

Additional Information

Places of Interest

St Fargeau
Puisaye
Château
Open: 10am-12noon and 2-7pm, Easter to 11 November; *son et lumière.*

Tonnerre
Hospital Notre-Dame des Fontenilles
Open: 10-11.30am and 2-5.30pm except Tuesday, June to 15 September.

Tanlay
Château
Open: 9.15-11.30am and 2.15-5.15pm except Tuesday, Palm Sunday to 1 November.

Ancy-le-Franc
Château
Open: 9.30am-6.30pm April to November.

Châtillon-sur-Seine
Museum
In Renaissance Philandrier mansion
Open: 9am-12noon and 2-6pm except Monday; November to February weekends only 10am-12noon and 2-5pm.

Fontenay
Abbey
Open: 9am-12noon and 2 or 2.30-6.30pm; guided tours every hour, or half-hour July and August.
Montbard
Buffon Museum
In Château Park
Open: 8.30am-12noon and 2-5pm April to October, except Tuesday. Buffon Forges 2.30-6pm except Tuesday, June to September.

Bussy-Rabutin
Château
Open: 9am-12noon and 2-6pm April to November; 10-11am and 2-3pm December to March; closed Tuesday and Wednesday.

Arcy-sur-Cure
Caves
Open: 9am-12noon and 2-6pm, March to November.

Château-Chinon
Morvan Costume and Folklore Museum
Rue St Christophe
Open: 2.30-6pm Wednesday, Saturday and Sunday. 1 June to 30 September only.

Autun

Rolin Museum
Open: 9.30am-12noon and 2-6.30pm 15
March to September; 10am-12noon and
2-4pm October to 14 March; except
Sunday mornings and Tuesday.

Dijon

Fine Arts Museum
In Grand Duke's Palace
Open: 10am-6pm except Tuesday.

Archaeological Museum
Open: 9.30am-6pm except Tuesday;
9am-12noon and 2-6pm in winter.

Vougeot

Château du Clos-Vougeot
Open: 9-11.30am and 2.30-5.30pm;
closed 20 December to 5 January.

Savigny-lès-Beaune

Château with Motorcycle Museum
Open: 9am-12noon and 2-6.30pm; closed
15 to 31 December.

Beaune

Hôtel-Dieu Medieval Infirmary
Open: 9am-6.45pm, 5.30pm in winter.

Burgundy Wine Museum
Open: 10am-12.30pm and 2-6.15pm.

La Rochepot

Château
Open: 9.30-11.30am and 2.30-5.30pm,
except Tuesday.

Chalon-sur-Saône

Nicéphore Niepce Museum
Open: 9.30-11.30am and 2.30-5.30pm,
except Tuesday and national holidays.

Cormatin

Château
Open: 10am-12noon and 2.30-6.30pm.

Cluny

Ochier Museum
Open: 10am-12noon and 2-4pm, 6.30pm
in summer; closed 20 December to 15
January.

Paray-le-Monial

Hiéron Museum of Religious Art
Open: 15 May to 8 September, 9am-7pm.

Charlieu

Romanesque Benedictine Abbey Ruins
Open: June to September 9am-12noon
and 2-7pm; April to May except Tues-
day; October and November and
February to March except Tuesday and
Wednesday.

Berzé-la-Ville

Monk's Chapel and Priory Church
Open: 9.30am-12noon and 2-6pm, Palm
Sunday to 1 November.

Mâcon

Ursulines Museum
Open: 10am-12noon and 2-6pm except
Tuesday and Sunday mornings.

Lamartine Museum
Open: 2-5pm except Tuesday, May to
October.

Tourist Information Centres

Auxerre

Office de Tourisme
1 & 2 quai République
☎ 86 52 06 19

Beaune

Office de Tourisme
Facing Hôtel-Dieu
☎ 80 22 24 51

Château-Chinon

Office de Tourisme
Rue Champlain
☎ 86 85 06 58

Dijon

Office de Tourisme and Accueil de
    France
Place Darcy
☎ 80 43 42 12

Mâcon

Office de Tourisme
187 Rue Carnot
☎ 85 39 71 37

Restaurants

R = With Accommodation
Haute-cuisine restaurants include:

Arnay-le-Duc
Chez Camille (R)
☎ 80 90 01 38

Auxerre
Barnabet
☎ 86 51 68 88

Beaune
Jacques Lainé
☎ 80 24 76 10

Bernard Morillon
☎ 80 24 12 06

L'Écusson
☎ 80 24 03 82

Relais de Saulx
☎ 80 22 01 35

Ermitage de Corton (R)
4km (2 miles) north
☎ 80 22 05 28

Hostellerie de Levernois (R)
5km (3 miles) south-east at Levernois
☎ 80 24 73 58

Bouilland
Host du Vieux Moulin (R)
☎ 80 21 51 16

Chablis
Hostellerie des Clos (R)
☎ 86 42 10 63

Chagny
Lameloise (R)
☎ 85 87 08 85

Chalon-sur-Saône
St Georges (R)
☎ 85 48 27 05

Chevannes
Near Auxerre
La Chamaille
☎ 86 41 24 80

Cluny
Bourgogne (R)
☎ 85 59 00 58

Dijon
Jean-Pierre Billoux
☎ 80 30 11 00

Chapeau Rouge (R)
☎ 80 30 28 10

Thibert
☎ 80 67 74 64

La Chouette
☎ 80 30 18 10

Le Petit Vatel
☎ 80 65 80 64

(at Marsannay-la-Côte)
Gourmets
☎ 80 52 16 32

Gevrey-Chambertin
La Rôtisserie du Chambertin
☎ 80 34 33 20

Les Millésimes
☎ 80 51 84 24

Joigny
A la Côte St Jacques (R)
☎ 86 62 09 70

Modern'H Frères Godard (R)
☎ 86 62 16 28

Mercurey
Hôtellerie du Val d'Or (R)
☎ 85 45 14 70

Nuits St Georges
Le Côte d'Or (R)
☎ 80 61 06 10

Puligny-Montrachet
Le Montrachet (R)
☎ 80 21 30 06

Saulieu
Le Côte d'Or (R)
☎ 80 64 07 66

St Rémy
Near Chalon-sur-Saône
Moulin de Martorey
☎ 85 48 12 98

Tonnerre
Abbaye St Michel (R)
☎ 86 55 05 99

Tournus
Le Rempart (R)
☎ 85 51 10 56

Restaurant Greuze
☎ 85 51 13 52

Velars-sur-Ouche
Near Dijon
Auberge Gourmand
☎ 80 33 62 51

Vézelay
(at St Père)
L'Espérance (R)
☎ 86 33 26 15

Other restaurants, offering good value
for money, include:
Autun
Le Chalet Bleu
☎ 85 86 27 30

Auxey-Duresses
La Crémaillère
☎ 80 21 22 60

Avallon
Relais Fleuri (R)
☎ 86 34 02 85

Chalon-sur-Saône
La Réale
☎ 85 48 07 21

Châtillon-sur-Seine
Le Côte d'Or (R)
☎ 80 91 13 29

Cluny
La Moderne (R)
☎ 85 59 05 65

Fuissé
Pouilly Fuissé
☎ 85 35 60 68

La Croix-Blanche
Relais du Mâconnais (R)
☎ 85 36 60 72

Mâcon
Rocher de Cancale
☎ 85 38 07 50

Auberge Bressane
☎ 85 38 07 42

Marcenay
Le Santenoy (R)
☎ 80 81 40 08

Meursault
Relais de la Diligence
☎ 80 21 21 32

Migennes
Paris (R)
☎ 86 80 23 22

Paray-le-Monial
Les Vendanges de Bourgogne (R)
☎ 85 81 13 43

Les Trois Pigeons (R)
☎ 85 81 03 77

Saulieu
Poste (R)
☎ 80 64 05 67

Tour d'Auxois (R)
☎ 80 64 13 30

Auberge du Relais (R)
☎ 80 64 13 16

Le Lion d'Or (R)
☎ 80 64 16 33

Semur-en-Auxois
Le Lac (R)
☎ 80 97 11 11

Gourmets (R)
☎ 80 97 09 41

Tournus
Les Terrasses (R)
☎ 85 51 01 74

Villeneuve-sur-Yonne
Le Dauphin (R)
☎ 86 87 18 55

7

PROVENCE

Provence conjures up an image of a Mediterranean landscape with pantiled villas and cypress trees, hot sun and strong wine, and *boules* in the dusty village square. The yearning for escape impels many people down the Rhône Valley to holiday, or to settle. It has attracted people for different reasons: artists like Van Gogh, who was entranced by the light; gourmets looking for a cuisine based on different ingredients; the ailing, looking for a miracle cure in a friendlier climate; the lovers of the arts, attracted by the summer festivals and schools; or simply the sun-worshippers.

The modern region of Provence-Côte d'Azur corresponds fairly closely to the old province, lying between the lower Rhône and Italy. It has six *départements*, three of them Alpine (Upper Provence), and three generally low-lying (Lower Provence). The main population centres are in Lower Provence — the Vaucluse, Bouches-du-Rhône and the Var — where the fertile plains and good climate produce much of France's *primeurs*, or early fruit and vegetables, and a lot of its wine; while the upper areas, gradually ascending to the High Alps, are mainly barren and sparsely populated, with medieval villages perched on hilltops and an agriculture not far removed from subsistence level. In the Rhône Valley and delta, oil refineries and power stations contrast oddly with the wild cowboy country of the Camargue.

Like most Mediterranean lands, it was civilised early. Greek settlement was followed by Roman colonisation, and the *Provincia Romana* became the civilised part of Roman Gaul, as its many relics testify today. The Middle Ages saw this Provence become a kingdom in its own right, with its own language and vibrant culture, providing Europe with its troubadours. The Popes established their alternative Vatican here for a while, at Avignon, but the region long had an uneasy relationship with the north and eventually saw its independence destroyed after bitter struggles. Today it is recovering its identity and reviving its old language and customs.

This tour begins and ends on the Rhône. It starts where the 'south' begins, at Montélimar, and takes a winding, even tortuous route through Lower Provence, ending on the edge of the Rhône delta at Arles. Two areas not included in the tour are the Alps and the Côte d'Azur.

The Northern Vaucluse

Montélimar is actually in the Dauphiné but it is a good place to branch off the Rhône on your way south, as the river is lined for some distance after here with hydro-electric and nuclear power stations. This is the gateway to the south. The valley opens out, at least on the eastern side, the sky looks bluer, the air clearer, the sun hotter and olive trees begin to dot the fields. Before leaving, take a *pastis* (see Food and Drink section in the Fact File) at a pavement café in the spacious main square, or a *dégustation* at one of the many nougat establishments in the area. Nougat is the main product of Montélimar, and has made its name world-famous. It is a modern variant of an old Provençal delicacy which was black and made with caramelised honey. Now it is white and has egg-whites, almonds, pistachios and flavourings.

 Take the D4 through the Fonbrenoux woods to **Grignan**. This pretty little town is built round its imposing château, on a rocky hillock overlooking the Tricastin plain. It is a place of pilgrimage for lovers of literature for its associations with Madame de Sévigné, who wrote a series of delightful letters to her daughter, the Countess of Grignan, in the late seventeenth century, telling of Paris society and life at the court of Louis XIV. Madame de Sévigné made long stays here on several occasions. You can see her and her daughter's bedrooms in the château, beautifully furnished in period style. From the terrace is a splendid panorama of Mont Ventoux and the Massif Central.

While in the area you can visit the Wine University at **Suze-la-Rousse**, to study oenology or simply to taste the local *Côteaux de Tricastin* wine. Then continue east on the D941 to **Valréas**, oddly sited in an enclave of the Vaucluse surrounded by the Drôme. The reasons for this anomaly date back to complex medieval land transactions between church and state, but today Valréas is proud to be Provençal and makes good Côtes-du-Rhône wine to prove it — sample it at the local co-operative. Tree-lined boulevards encircle this quiet old town where its walls once stood. In the centre is a fine fifteenth- to eighteenth-century town hall, an eleventh- to twelfth-century Romanesque church and a seventeenth-century chapel of the White Penitents. Nearby **Richerenches**, still within the enclave, is a former commandery founded in the twelfth century by the Knights Templars. Rectangular in shape, it still has most of its walls and its four round corner towers.

Continuing east, the D941 takes you back into the Drôme to **Nyons**. This busy little town is an agricultural centre famous for its fine-quality olives and olive oil, and also known for its jam, its truffle market and its mild climate. It is attractively set at the end of a gorge where the River Eygues emerges from the mountains into the Tricastin plain. At the upper end of the town is a fine old single-span bridge over the gorge. Narrow streets, overlooked by a fortified old quarter on a hill, lead down to the wide boulevards of the lower town. There are two old oil mills, an olive museum, and an excellent oil and wine co-operative on the edge of town. Nearby are two pretty wine villages producing excellent Côtes-du-Rhône: **Vinsobres**, on a hill overlooking the plain, and

Mirabel-aux-Baronnies.

Take the D538 towards Vaison-la-Romaine, but branch off left onto the D46 for Buis-les-Baronnies, to begin a circular tour (including an ascent) of Provence's most famous landmark and its favourite mountain, **Mont Ventoux**. It is isolated, symmetrical, and striking in appearance, as its bare rock summit makes it look snow-capped all the year round. It dominates the landscape (1,909m, 6,262ft high) and can be clearly seen from every direction throughout northern Provence — it is virtually a symbol of the region. The road to Buis runs along the border of Provence and the Drôme, first in one, then the other. On your left is the Baronnies massif, and on your right the attractive valley of the Ouvèze, with rocky outcrops topped by ruined castles and surrounded by sleepy old villages, and with the indented ridge of the Dentelles de Montmirail in the background. Three such villages are **Faucon** (excellent Côtes-du-Rhône), **Entrechaux** (quite good Côtes de Ventoux), and **Mollans-sur-Ouvèze** (pretty, with an old well and bridge). At Mollans, you have a choice of two routes: the D5, in the Drôme, follows the Ouvèze Valley towards Buis; while the D40 follows the quiet Toulourenc Valley, in Provence, hugging the northern skirts of Mont Ventoux.

The D5 takes you past **Pierrelongue**, with its church perched dramatically on a needle-rock, to **Buis-les-Baronnies**. This picturesque old market town is attractively set at the gateway to the pre-Alpine Baronnies massif, and has tree-shaded boulevards and an arcaded square where a famous herb market is held every July. The weekly market is large and colourful, selling local olives, herbs and Côteaux-des-Baronnies wines. From here you have a further choice of route. The longer road, along the upper Ouvèze Valley on the D546, takes you via the pleasantly-sited village of **Séderon** and the Macuègne pass. The shorter route on the D72 climbs over the Col des Aires to **Brantes**, an old, restored Provençal village clinging dramatically to a cliff face. The three routes reunite just before the small town of **Sault**, prettily set amid lavender beds on the wide Vaucluse plateau, with a terrace commanding a fine westerly view of Mont Ventoux.

From here, begin your ascent of the mountain on the D164. Though winding, the road is good right to the summit and down the other side. The scenery is spectacular, particularly on the upper slopes, and as you climb the vegetation changes from deciduous trees, vines and olives to conifers, scrubland and finally tufts of Alpine grass among white shingle scree. At the summit are a few souvenir shops, a radar station and television mast, and a viewing platform from which, when visibility is good, you have a stupendous view over the whole of south-eastern France, from the Alps to the Pyrénées and from the Auvergne to the sea. The summit earns the peak its name of 'Windy Mountain', as there is nearly always a strong wind blowing, though it is not usually cold in summer. In winter the higher slopes are snow-covered, there is good skiing and the air is clearer. Unfortunately in summer it is often hazy. The best time for long views is at dawn or sunset, and the view at night is said to be magical.

For those with weak stomachs there is a road that avoids the summit and

skirts the southern edge of the mountain. Turn left at Le Chalet-Reynard and follow the D974 via the picturesque village of Bédoin. Otherwise, take the more gradual western descent past Mount Serein to Malaucène, passing near the bottom the Vauclusian spring of **La Groseau**. The spring issues from several fissures in a sheer rock-face and forms a pool of clear water, prettily set among trees at the side of the road. Nearby is an attractive little square, domed twelfth-century chapel, all that remains of a Benedictine abbey. **Malaucène** has a wide, shaded main avenue and an interesting old sector with narrow streets, old houses, oratories, fountains and wash-houses and, in the centre, an old belfry. It has a fine fourteenth-century church, fortified on the façade with battlements as it was once part of the town's ramparts.

Malaucène is a good starting point for a tour of the **Dentelles de Montmirail**, a lozenge-shaped area of wild pine and oak forest at the foot of the Ventoux with, in the centre, a ridge of sharp, white limestone peaks of delicate, lacy appearance (*dentelle* means lace). Malaucène is at its eastern point of the lozenge; at the southern point is **Carpentras**, a busy market town known for its caramel sweets, its late-Gothic cathedral and its old Jewish quarter containing the oldest synagogue in France. It is the chief town of the Comtat, an area owned by the Papacy in the Middle Ages, when Carpentras benefited from the munificence of the Avignon Popes. At the north point of the Dentelles is Vaison-la-Romaine, while on the western side are a string of charming villages producing some of Provence's finest wines.

Take the narrow D90 from Malaucène to Suzette through the vertically-walled **Cirque de St Amand**. At the head of the pass are fine views of the Dentelles, Mont Ventoux and the Baronnies. At Suzette, branch left for Le Barroux, whose restored Renaissance château stands high on a rock overlooking the Carpentras plain (good views from the terrace). Join the Carpentras road, then turn right for **Beaumes-de-Venise**, a terraced village at the foot of the Dentelles world-famous for its Muscat, a delicious sweet fortified wine. Join the D8 to **Vacqueyras**, passing the charming little Romanesque chapel of Notre-Dame d'Aubine with its elegant bell-tower. Vacqueyras makes a good red wine with a Côtes-du-Rhône-Villages appellation, while its neighbouring village of **Gigondas** has its own appellation for a red wine which many think rivals Châteauneuf-du-Pape. From Gigondas a small road leads to the **Cayron Pass**, at the centre of the main peaks of the Dentelles. This is a mecca for rock-climbers, who practise their skills on the 100m (328ft) high complex rock faces. The road through the pass is unsurfaced, and is best travelled on foot, with splendid views of the Rhône plain. Continue from Gigondas to **Sablet**, another village with its own excellent red wine appellation, and then on to **Séguret**. This village is picturesque in the extreme, built against the side of a steep hill. In its narrow pedestrian main street, entered from the road through a covered passage, is a twelfth-century church with fourteenth-century belfry and sundial, and a fifteenth-century covered fountain. It also has a ruined castle and steep streets with old houses, and a small museum and shop selling *santons*.

Santons, from the Provençal *santoun*, or little saint, are a tradition in Provence. They are small figures, modelled in clay, fired and brightly painted, and dressed in local or traditional costume. Originally they were figures of Biblical characters, made to populate the Christmas cribs which families vied with each other to produce. But later, secular figures were added. At their best they are charming and original, and made with great skill, a far remove from the usual tourist dolls in regional costume. There is an annual *santons* fair in the last week of November at Marseilles.

✳   From Séguret, join the D977 to **Vaison-la-Romaine**, a town of great charm and many facets. As its name suggests, it has Roman origins. It was a large and prosperous Roman town and has revealed the greatest expanse of remains from that period of any town in France. But it has other features than the Roman to interest the visitor: a prehistoric site, a medieval fortified town, a ruined castle on a rock, a fine Romanesque cathedral, a lively and attractive modern town in a beautiful setting, a number of summer festivals, and a range of excellent wines, fruits and other local products. It stands on both sides of the Ouvèze, with a single-arched Roman bridge spanning the river at its narrowest and deepest point. It has a long and chequered history. It started as the capital of a Celtic tribe, became a federated city in the *Provincia Romana*, declined and was partially destroyed in the Dark Ages, moved to a new fortified site in the Middle Ages, returned to the old site and uncovered its Roman foundations in the nineteenth to twentieth centuries. Today it has three distinct centres — Roman, medieval and modern.

ⵜ   The impressive feature of Vaison's Roman ruins is their extent. They are found in two large sites (the Puymin and La Villasse quarters), covering a total area of 32 acres, the layout of a substantial part of a large town. You can visit both on one ticket and see streets, houses, gardens, courtyards, colonnades, fountains, baths and a theatre. In the Puymin quarter is an attractive museum showing the best fragments found at Vaison. The former cathedral is a splendid building, a fine example of Provençal Romanesque built on the foundations of a Roman temple and incorporating parts of the previous Roman and Merovingian churches, including a sixth to seventh century apse. The eleventh-century cloisters display fragments of previous buildings. St Quenin's Chapel, to the north of the town, is an unusual old building (probably twelfth century but with earlier elements) with a triangular apse and antique decoration. Across the river, opposite the old bridge, is the sharply sloping road to the medieval fortified upper town, a quiet haven of old cobbled streets and attractively restored buildings on the side of a steep hill. You can climb beyond the town to the ruined twelfth-century castle on the cliff-top, with a fine view over the Ouvèze Valley and Mont Ventoux.

Modern Vaison has some pedestrian streets, with pleasant shops and cafés. The Maison de Vin, under the tourist office, has a good selection of the fine wines of the area for you to taste, attractively displayed and well explained. Other delicacies of the area (truffles, honey, lavender) are available there and in nearby shops. Just outside the town, off the Malaucène road, is the typical Vauclusian village of **Crestet**, clinging to the side of a cliff. Its tiny central square with a fourteenth-century church, a fountain and arcades, its Renaissance houses and medieval castle, are all being restored.

Return to Vaison by the D938 and turn right over the new bridge onto the D975. This road takes you through vineyards and wine villages — **Roaix** (the Roaix-Séguret red Côtes-du-Rhône Villages is excellent); **Rasteau** (a sweet fortified Muscat to rival Beaumes-de-Venise); and **Cairanne** (another excellent Côtes-du-Rhône) — to **Orange**. This famous old town stands at an important crossroads in the Rhône Valley, on the N7 trunk road and at a motorway junction — it seems beset by traffic jams! Nevertheless, it is a must for the visitor to Provence, as it holds two of the most important of her Roman monuments, the theatre and the Triumphal Arch. The Roman theatre is one of ⼂ France's architectural treasures and is classified the ninth monument in the world. It is the world's best-preserved Roman theatre, its most impressive feature being its stage wall (Louis XIV called it the 'finest wall in the Kingdom'), 103m (338ft) by 36m (118ft) and decorated with columns and niches for statues. The central one is occupied by a bust of the Emperor Augustus. The body of the theatre is the usual tiered semicircle, with perfect acoustics from the central orchestra. It is widely used for concerts, and in summer houses the Chorégies, a famous festival of opera and other music. In one of its side rooms you can taste local wines, including Châteauneuf-du-Pape and Gigondas.

Orange has been called the 'Gateway to the South', partly because of its magnificent Triumphal Arch, which greets you as you approach from the ⼂ north on the N7. It is the third largest in the world, and richly decorated with sculptures commemorating the campaigns of the II Legion in the time of Augustus. The city's other Roman remains include a large temple and gymnasium, and there is a good Municipal Museum which explains them. Orange ⬛ is also proud of its long history and its famous name. This does not derive from the fruit, but from the ancient Celtic settlement of *Arausio*, which later became an important Roman city. In the Middle Ages it was a separate principality which eventually became a fief of the German Nassau dynasty, passing to the Dutch prince William the Silent and then to the Dutch royal family. From them come the Orangemen of Ulster, the Orange Free State and river in South Africa, a cape in Brazil, and towns in Australia and the USA. Today the French town is a thriving industrial centre and market for truffles, honey, herbs and fruit.

Ten kilometres (6 miles) south on the D68 is the charming small town that makes the most highly-prized wine in the southern Rhône, **Châteauneuf-du-** ✳ **Pape**. The wine is gutsy, strong, deep red, and with a burnt taste that comes from the hot alluvial soil with its carpet of *genêts*, or smooth flat stones, that retain the heat and give the wine its special character. There are many places to taste it in and around the old town, especially at the annual medieval fair, called the Véraison, or 'Reddening of the Grapes', on the first weekend in August. (Be careful — the combination of strong wine and hot sun can be dangerous!) The 'Pope's New Castle' from which the town derives its name was built as a summer palace by the Avignon popes in the fourteenth century, on a hill above the town (they were also supposed to have planted the first vines). It is now a ruin, but the walk up to it is worthwhile for its fine view over ⛰ the Rhône Valley and the Cévennes beyond. The wine and its secrets are explained in a small wine museum above Père Anselme's wine cellars. ⬛

The Southern Vaucluse
Take the D17 from Châteauneuf-du-Pape and join the N7 south to **Avignon**. This resplendent city, capital of the Vaucluse and metropolis of the southern Rhône, is a hive of activity in summer, its normal heavy complement of

The huge and impressive Gothic Papal Palace at Avignon

The Old Mint in Avignon's Palace Square

tourists being overlaid with students, artists and culture-lovers attending the prestigious July Dramatic Arts Festival. Even then, it is still a dream city, with its intact circle of high, battlemented ramparts broken only by imposing gateways, its towers and belfries, its severely beautiful Papal Palace, its wide boulevards and spacious squares, its narrow back streets and old houses pressed against the town walls. It is an exciting, vibrant place, mixing the casual elegance of the wealthy with the bohemian scruffiness of the poor student. There is much to see and many byways to explore; and when you are sated with Avignon's treasures, you can relax and watch the street entertainers, refugees from the festival's fringe, over a beer or *pastis* at a café in the Place de l'Horloge.

Avignon owes its reputation and its wealth of art and architecture to a group of renegade popes in the Middle Ages. The first to make his court here was Clement V, in 1308, fleeing from the strife of war-torn Italy, and his successors continued the exile, in ever-increasing opulence, for nearly 100 years. Towards the end, at the shameful period of the Great Schism, there were two popes, one in Rome and the other in Avignon, vying with each other for wealth and power. Avignon was condemned by the poet Petrarch and many others for the arrogant display of wealth of its 'anti-popes' and the luxury and corruption of the town, which had become an asylum for refugees and criminals from all over Europe. Eventually the popes returned to Rome, leaving the city they had rebuilt for later generations to enjoy. Today Avignon is busy and prosperous, extending far beyond its walls, but the old town retains its style.

The main attraction is the Papal Palace, a huge and impressive Gothic building that was both fortress and palace. Inside it is a maze of galleries, passages, chambers and chapels, only a few of which you see on your guided tour (some in English). Now empty and deserted, it is difficult to imagine the splendour of its past, in spite of the elegant chambers with their beautiful frescoes. Opposite the palace, across the spacious Palace Square, is the Old Mint, with its ornate Baroque façade and crowning balustrade decked with statues. Also in the square is the cathedral, a restored building containing the damaged tomb of Pope John XXII, and behind it the beautiful Doms Rock Gardens, with a terrace overlooking the river and the famous St Bénézet Bridge. The old bridge is now simply a few arches jutting out into the Rhône. Alongside the gardens at the end of the square is the Petit Palais Museum, the old archbishop's palace housing a large and sumptuous collection of medieval and Renaissance paintings. On the west side of town, near the river, are some elegant eighteenth-century hotels, including the beautiful Hôtel Calvet (lovely gardens with peacocks), housing a museum of wrought iron and other collections. There are many other attractive old streets with fine buildings, including the Rue Joseph-Vernet, the Rue des Teinturiers and the Rue du Roi-René, and other interesting museums and churches.

Before leaving the area, it is worth while to cross the Rhône to **Villeneuve-lès-Avignon**, partly for the splendid view of Avignon across the river, and partly for the interest of the town itself. It is not in Provence, but in the Gard, and in the Middle Ages belonged to the Crown. When the popes established their power base at Avignon, the kings replied by building a large fort on a hill opposite, to keep an eye on them and to remind them of the presence of royal power. This is the St André Fort, a massive defensive structure now in ruins but with a fine fortified gate with two cylindrical towers, a twelfth-century Romanesque chapel, and fine views of Avignon from the Italian gardens of the old ruined abbey. Nearby is the Val de Bénédiction Charterhouse, a monastery founded by Pope Innocent VI in 1356 and now a cultural centre. It has attractive cloisters with elegant classical doorways, and Innocent VI's decorated tomb in the church.

When the popes ruled Avignon, some cardinals chose to build their luxury villas in Villeneuve, turning it into an elegant residential suburb which it remains today, pleasantly set among woods on the west bank of the Rhône, sheltered from the river mists and the *mistral*. Its Municipal Museum, housed in a seventeenth-century mansion, has a masterpiece by Engerrand Charonton, the *Coronation of the Virgin* (1453); and the church has a superb polychrome ivory Virgin, carved from an elephant's tusk. At the entrance to the town, by the Daladier bridge, stands the tower of Philip the Fair, a surviving relic of the medieval town defences. It once stood at the end of the old St Bénézet's bridge but now it is isolated on the bank. There are lovely views of Avignon, the river and Mont Ventoux from the upper terrace.

Return to Avignon, encircle the town walls, and leave by the N100 to **L'Isle-sur-la-Sorgue**. This little town is attractively sited at the foot of the Vaucluse Plâteau, and its centre is enclosed by two arms of the River Sorgue, with tree-lined avenues along the river bank. It was once industrial, with silk, paper and oil mills powered by the river. Now all that remains are a number of old water-wheels. The church and hospital are attractive buildings, with ornate decoration. From here, take the D938 and the D25 to **Fontaine de Vaucluse**, on the plateau above the town. The village is of interest only for its famous fountain, hence its name, and for the fact that the fourteenth-century Italian poet Petrarch, the inventor of the sonnet, lived here for 16 years from 1337 to 1353, pouring out his unrequited love for a beautiful but virtuous married lady named Laura. He first met her in an Avignon church when he was attached to the pontifical court there, and fell madly in love with her. But the love remained ideal and he retired to the peaceful Vaucluse to transmute it into poetry, while Laura died of the plague in Avignon in 1348. There is a small museum in the village in what is claimed to be Petrarch's house, with some rare editions of his works.

The Vaucluse fountain is misnamed. It is an underground stream that emerges from the ground inside a large cavern, forming the source of the River Sorgue. In summer it is a curious rather than an impressive sight, but in winter it rises dramatically and is a magnificent spectacle when in flood. The fascination of the spring is its unknown origin. Though it is known to be fed by the rainwater falling on the limestone Vaucluse plateau and seeping down to one of the vast underground caverns, or *avens*, no-one has yet traced its source or been able to tell how deep it goes. It has given its name to all such phenomena, which are known as Vauclusian springs. The cavern is dramatically sited at the foot of high cliffs, and the short walk from the village to the source alongside the shady river-bed is enchanting (though it can be crowded in summer). There is a small underground speleological museum on the way to the cave, and regular *son et lumière* shows in summer.

From Fontaine de Vaucluse take the D100 and the D2 for Gordes. Before reaching the town, take a turn to your left for the picturesque **Village des Bories**. These curious dry-stone beehive-shaped huts are a common feature of the Vaucluse plateau and the Luberon. *Bories* are usually dotted about the landscape in ones and twos, but here is a whole village of about twenty of them grouped round a communal bread oven. Some of the larger ones have a small upstairs room, and were obviously used by human beings, while smaller ones were probably for animals and tools. They were mainly temporary dwellings for shepherds and other workers on the land, but some were permanently inhabited from the Iron Age until the eighteenth century. The *bories* on this site have been restored and now form a museum of rural life.

Return to the D2 and just afterwards bear left on the D15 for **Gordes**. About 1km ($^{1}/_{2}$ mile) before the town is a rock platform giving a superb and much photographed view of its impressive site, perched on a rocky hill above the Imergue Valley. On top of the hill is a château, toward which the narrow paved alleys or *calades* climb, sometimes in vaulted stairways. The town is picturesque, with its tall arcaded houses, rampart ruins, craft shops, boutiques and market, but very popular with tourists. The Renaissance château, which has a splendid chimneypiece (1541), houses a small collection of the works of the modern painter of geometrical shapes, Vasarély. Just outside the town to the south, at the Moulin des Bouillons, are two interesting museums: a Museum of Stained Glass and a Museum of Oil Mills; and 4km (2 miles) north on the D177, nestling in a hollow in the Vaucluse plateau, is one of the jewels of Cistercian monastic architecture; **Sénanque Abbey**. The view is beautiful as you approach from Gordes — a harmonious group of abbey buildings serenely set in the austere Sénancole Valley, surrounded by a blue sea of lavender. Sénanque Abbey was founded in 1148, and all its buildings except one are original, with simple, elegant lines and little decoration. The church, cloisters and chapterhouse are particularly fine. Exhibitions of Cistercian life and Romanesque symbolism can be seen in the refectory and kitchens. The abbey is now a cultural centre and holds regular concerts and exhibitions.

Return to Gordes, rejoin the D2 and turn right on the D102 for **Roussillon**. This village earns its name as the home of the red and yellow ochre pigments used in painting. The low range of hills between the Vaucluse plateau and the Calavon Valley are worn by erosion and quarrying into sharp, jagged shapes made more dramatic by their bright ochre colouring — at least fifteen different shades have been identified. The village itself stands on the highest of these hills, with spectacular views of the surrounding cliffs. The houses are built in the surrounding stone, and are very attractive with their varying shades of red, orange and yellow (Roussillon is popular with artists, some of whom live

and have their studios here). The main street, the Rue de l'Arcade, is prettily stepped and partly covered, and there are viewpoints all round the village (the best being the castrum on the cliff top) from where you can see the Fairies' Valley Needles and the Giants' Causeway, two weird cliff formations. Around the village there are pleasant walks among the cliffs.

Continue on the D104, the D4 and the N100 to **Apt**. This typical small Provençal town, the centre of ochre production, lavender essence and crystallised fruit, is not particularly appealing to tourists, though it might make a good base for exploring the Luberon. It has a pleasant main square ringed by tree-lined boulevards, traces of the old town walls, some old houses, an eleventh-century cathedral with a rich treasury, and an archaeological museum. But in general it has a busy, workaday air, particularly animated on market day (Saturday morning), when it presents a colourful display of local produce. To the north-east are more ochre quarries, the most scenic being the aptly-named Rustrel Colorado, which really does look like a miniature Grand Canyon. Apt lies at the foot of the **Luberon**, a long, round-topped mountain range which is now a regional nature park, hoping thus to preserve its flora, fauna and traditional way of life. It is not as high or striking as Mont Ventoux, but it is worth exploring for its rich variety of vegetation, its numerous *bories*, its romantic deserted villages (mainly on the northern slope), and its towns dramatically perched on rocky spurs.

The northern side of the Luberon is more scenically rewarding than the south, and a sharp contrast in appearance. The southern face is gently-sloping, sunny and Mediterranean, with fields of southern crops, herbs, olive and cypress trees. The north is cooler and more humid, steeper and more ravined, and more heavily forested. The northern side has a high road that links a number of attractive 'perched' villages, worth a detour. Take the D943 from Apt, over the Col Pointou, and right on the D232 to **Bonnieux**. This large terraced village stands imposingly on a promontory over the Apt Valley. It has four fine primitive German paintings on wood in the new church, a small Bakery Museum in the tourist office, and a splendid view from a terrace by the old church. Continue west on the D109 to **Lacoste**, dominated by the imposing ruins of the château where the notorious writer the Marquis de Sade was lord of the manor. Further on is **Ménerbes**, which has a thirteenth-century citadel on a sheer rock, and fine views towards the Vaucluse plateau and Mont Ventoux. **Oppède-le-Vieux** has a lovely terrace site on a picturesque rocky spur. It was once virtually abandoned, but has been restored and is now an artists' and writers' colony, with good craft shops.

Return by the D109 to rejoin the D943 (you can take an even higher road, the D3, for part of the way). Ahead of you is the picturesque ruin of Buoux fort, on a rocky spur-it can be visited on foot. Turn right to pass through the Combe de Lourmarin, which is the only way across the Luberon by road. At its southern end, the village of **Lourmarin** is dominated by its castle on a rock,

(Opposite) The spectacular site of Les Baux gives the impression of being hewn out of rock

and its cemetery holds the body of the writer Albert Camus, who died in 1960 when his car hit a tree near here. Turn left onto the D56 to the village of **Cucuron** where there is a small Luberon Museum and continue to **Ansouis**. This village has a charming seventeenth-century castle, whose exterior looks like a forbidding fortress but which is pleasantly decorative inside, with lovely gardens and a fine view from the terrace of Mont St Victoire and the Durance Valley. There is also a curious museum, called the Musée Extraordinaire, devoted to underwater life.

Bouches-du-Rhône

Continue to Pertuis, in the Durance Valley (nearby is the twelfth-century Cistercian abbey of **Silvacane**), and on by the D556 and N96 to **Aix-en-Provence**, the old capital of Provence and perhaps its loveliest town. It is easy to fall in love with Aix, for it appears all that a town should be — elegant, charming, noble, civilised, relaxed. The French call it a *bourgeois* town, but not in a derogatory sense: they mean it has style and 'class'. It seems to distill the essence of the south of France. In summer it is vibrant with activity, when students of all nationalities, studying at its highly-reputed university, mingle with visitors attending its famous International Music Festival.

Aix was an old Roman spa (*Aquae Sextiae*), and remains one today. In addition to its eighteenth-century spa complex on the site of the old Roman baths, it has water with curative properties pouring from many of its lovely fountains (there is a hot one in the Cours Mirabeau). In the Middle Ages the counts of Provence held their refined and literate court here from the twelfth century, but it reached its apex in the fifteenth century when Good King René, one of the most intelligent, highly-educated and cultured of rulers, turned it into an intellectual and artistic centre of world repute. In the sixteenth century it became a seat of Parliament, and from then on earned a reputation as an opponent of monarchical power and a centre of the law. In the seventeenth to eighteenth centuries it was transformed into a dignified and elegant city of Classical proportions, with wide avenues and squares, fountains and new buildings, which it remains to this day. Though it lost power and influence to nearby Marseilles in the nineteenth century, it has had an increase of industry and population in modern times, and now has extensive suburbs (not its most attractive feature). It is the centre for the production of almonds, and is famed for its local delicacy, the *calisson*, a small marzipan cake.

Start your tour of Aix at the Place du Général de Gaulle, a large, bustling square where the crowds gather in the evenings, and stroll down the world-famous Cours Mirabeau. This broad, elegant avenue, the hub of the town, is completely shaded by four rows of plane trees and lined with attractive cafés, brasseries, bookshops and confectioners, interspersed with fine seventeenth- to eighteenth-century hotels (mansions), many in the Baroque style, with fine doorways, balconies and caryatids. To the south is the elegantly-Classical Mazarin quarter, containing two museums: the Paul Arbaud (books and archaeology) and the Granet (fine arts and archaeology); and the delightful Four Dolphins Fountain. To the north is the old town, with many fine hotels and fountains, elegant squares (Town Hall, Albertas, Verdun, Précheurs, Martyrs), several good museums (Natural History, Old Aix, Tapestry), and the St Sauveur Cathedral. This curious building is in a medley of styles, from Romanesque to Classical, with a Merovingian baptistry, some superb six-teenth-century carved wooden door panels, and a masterpiece of fifteenth-century art, the Triptych of the Burning Bush by Nicolas Froment, showing King René as donor. The small Romanesque cloisters are delightful. Out of the town centre, art lovers should not miss Cézanne's Studio, left just as it was when he died in 1906, and the Vasarély Foundation, a striking building holding the geometrical abstractions of the modern Hungarian artist.

Before leaving Aix-en-Provence, you should make a tour of the Cézanne country east of the town, encircling the spectacular **Mont-St Victoire**. The scenery will be familiar to lovers of his painting — a white limestone ridge with bright red clay at the foot, sheer on the south side, gently sloping to the north. This was the site of a famous Roman battle, when Marius slew 100,000 Teutons to prevent a march on Rome in 102BC. Take the D17 to **Le Tholonet** (eighteenth-century château and avenues of plane trees), **Le Bouquet** (best view of the mountain), **Puyloubier** (ruined castle and military pensioners' hospital), the D57 to Les Puits-de-Rians, and the D10 to **Vauvenargues**. Here is a seventeenth-century château on a rock spur and, in the park in front, the grave of Picasso, who spent his last years here (died 1973). For the energetic, a footpath just beyond the village leads to the peak of Mont St Victoire, where stands the 17m (56ft) high Cross of Provence, giving a marvellous panorama over the Aix plain and mountains beyond. Continue to the Bimont Dam and reservoir (short road left) for a fine view of the woods and gorges below, then return to Aix. There are opportunities en route to taste Côteaux d'Aix-en-Provence and Côtes de Provence wines.

Leave Aix by the N7 to St Cannat, then bear left to **Salon-de-Provence**, centre of the olive-growing country and seat of the flying school of the French Air Force. It was the home of the astrologer Nostradamus, whose house in the old town contains a small museum. The town is dominated by its massive Château de l'Empéri on a rock, which houses a large and well-presented museum of the French army. Salon is well-known today for its summer Jazz Festival, held in late July. Leave by the D17 for **Eyguières**, at the foot of the Chaîne des Alpilles. This jagged ridge of white limestone peaks is a landmark of the Bouches-du-Rhône, visible for miles around — there is a good view from the twelfth-century church at the top of the village. Take the D659 and turn left onto the D25 at the ruined Roquemartine Castle. The road passes to the left the tower on a hillock of Les Opiés, then rises to a low pass at Mas de Montfort, with a good view of the Alpilles' highest peak, La Caume (387m, 1,269ft). Turn left onto the D24 to Le Destet, then right on the D78, passing on your right the dark red Entreconque rocks (former bauxite quarries), to **Maussane-les-Alpilles**, a good base for exploring the region.

Five kilometres (3 miles) north of Maussane by the D5 and D27 is the most spectacular site in Provence, **Les Baux**. The word, which means 'rocks' in

The Triumphal Arch (above) and Cenotaph (below) are well-preserved Roman monuments which can be found at Les Antiques

Provençal, gives its name to the mineral bauxite (the source of aluminium), first discovered on this land. Les Baux-de-Provence has a fascinating history, being the home of a powerful and lawless family of warrior lords in the Middle Ages, who claimed descent from the Biblical Wise Man Balthazar, and wore a Star of Bethlehem on their shields to prove it! One of their practices was to throw those of their prisoners who failed to attract a ransom off the cliffs of their rocky stronghold. It developed as a Court of Love in the thirteenth century, where beautiful, educated women of noble birth discussed questions of gallantry and chivalry with visiting troubadours, the romantic poets of the day, thus defining the medieval courtly love tradition. The troubadours would dedicate their ballads to these ladies, and prizewinners would get a kiss and a crown of peacock feathers. They would then, while worshipping their fair ladies from afar, carry their songs around the world in the language of love, Provençal. The power of Les Baux was destroyed in 1632 by Richelieu, Louis XIII's chief minister, who demolished the ramparts, fined the inhabitants and charged them for its demolition!

Today Les Baux is an almost-deserted ruin, except for the hordes of tourists who invade it in summer. It stands over 1km ($^1/_2$ mile) long by 200m (656ft) wide on a plateau with sheer cliff faces all round it, with a single entrance on the north side. Part of the upper town is now reinhabited, with craft shops, artists' studios and small museums occupying some of the ruins of the elegant Renaissance town houses. The houses higher up are mostly still in ruins. Down below in the valley is a new village with some good hotels and restaurants. The site is highly picturesque and evocative, particularly at sunset or at night when most of the tourists have departed. In the vicinity are **Hell Valley**, a jagged gorge with once-inhabited caves, and the bauxite quarries housing a giant three-dimensional open-air picture palace.

Four kilometres (2 miles) north of Les Baux, at the northern door of the only gap through the Alpilles, are two important Roman sites, **Les Antiques** and *Glanum*. Les Antiques, on the left, consists of two elegant, ornate, Roman monuments in superb condition: a triumphal arch, the oldest in Gaul, and a Cenotaph, dedicated to Caius and Lucius, the grandsons of the emperor Augustus. They both have beautiful carved decoration showing Greek influence, and they stand isolated in a pleasant rural spot among trees and scrub. The triumphal arch was probably the entrance to the city of *Glanum*, whose ruins are to the right of the road. These are not well preserved but tell enough for us to know that there were settlements here from the sixth century BC to the third century AD, when the city was sacked by Germanic tribes.

Just to the north is the delightful small town of **St Rémy-de-Provence**, which grew up after the fall of *Glanum* and captures today the essence of Provence: its colourful fruit, flower and herb market, its traditional fairs, its plane-tree-shaded avenues, lovely fountains and charming alleyways. It is a place to linger with a coffee or *pastis* in the lively Place de la République, opposite the imposing St Martin's Church. There are two good museums nearby, the Alpilles Folklore Museum and an archaeological collection of finds from *Glanum* in the Hôtel de Sade. But it is for its associations rather than its monuments that St Rémy is known. It was the birthplace of Nostradamus and Provence's leading poet, Frédéric Mistral (who wrote in Provençal) and it shares with Arles the memory of Van Gogh. It was in the fields near here that he dashed off many of his finest paintings and after the incident of the severed ear he lived in the convalescent home here, where he was at peace for a time. St Rémy is popular with artists today.

Sixteen kilometres (10 miles) west on the D99 is **Tarascon**, its mighty fortress facing that of **Beaucaire** on the other side of the Rhône. Unlike Beaucaire castle, which is in ruins, the château of Tarascon is splendidly preserved, and one of the finest medieval castles in France. It was built to defend Provence's western boundary, and was King René's favourite residence, where he organised splendid festivities and entertained his troubadours. It was later used as a prison. It stands high on a cliff over the river, with fine views from the battlements, and an impressive though bare interior, which you can see on a guided tour. Tarascon is the home of a famous Provençal legend, about a ferocious lion-headed monster from the Rhône called the Tarasque, which regularly emerged to eat children, animals and anyone trying to cross the river. It was finally subdued by St Martha, whereupon Good King René ordered an annual fête and procession to celebrate the town's release. This continues today, with a huge model of the monster paraded through the streets and trying to knock down the onlookers.

South on the N570 and the D33 is **Fontvieille**, a peaceful village known for limestone quarrying and the famous windmill of Alphonse Daudet. The nineteenth-century novelist immortalised the ruined mill in his *Lettres de mon Moulin*, a popular work evoking the Provençal life and countryside. A lovely avenue of pines leads from the village to the mill, which has been restored and holds a small museum of Daudet's life and work. West on the D17 is the abbey of Montmajour, largely in ruins but still impressive, with a mixture of twelfth-century and eighteenth-century buildings. It has a fine large crypt, and cloisters with fascinating Romanesque carved capitals, including a figure of the Tarasque monster.

The tour ends just down the road at **Arles**, an ancient town in a strategic position at the head of the Rhône delta, gateway both to the Camargue and to the Fos industrial complex and port. It is a lovely town, though perhaps less animated than Avignon and less stylish than Aix and it can be hot and humid in high summer. Its main attractions are its Roman and medieval monuments, which are right in the centre and give the place a historic 'feel', and its excellent museums. Arles lives on its past importance, first as capital of Roman Gaul, and later as a major religious centre in the Middle Ages, when it was capital of a Burgundian kingdom. In more recent times it was associated with Van Gogh, who lived here, first alone and later with Gauguin, and painted many views of Arles and the country around. Today Arles is the centre of France's rice production.

Arles' two important Roman monuments are close together in the middle of town — the splendid amphitheatre and the theatre. The first is well preserved, though not quite as intact as Nîmes, and is used for bull-fights and other spectacles. The second was excavated after being completely covered by houses and gardens, and has been partly reconstructed, enough to allow it to be used for shows and festivals. Near to the theatre is the medieval jewel of St Trophime's Church, named after the first bishop of Arles in the early third century. The richly-ornamented west doorway is a masterpiece of Romanesque art, strongly suggesting the Classical influence of a triumphal arch with its profusion of beautifully carved figures while the cloisters are the finest in Provence and possibly in France. They are partly Romanesque (twelfth-century north and east galleries) and partly Gothic (fourteenth-century south and west galleries), with a wealth of superb sculpture. The other Roman remains are the partly-excavated fourth-century baths of Constantine. Three fine museums are the Museum of Pagan Art, the Museum of Christian Art and the Arlaten Museum, the last of these being a famous ethnographic museum created by Frédéric Mistral, the champion of Provençal life and culture, to help preserve its identity and language. He contributed his Nobel award prize money to the collection in 1904. It is housed in the beautiful sixteenth-century Hôtel de Castellane-Laval.

Just outside the old town on the south-east side is a curiosity unique to Arles — a Roman/early Christian necropolis called the Alyscamps, or Elysian Fields. The habit, stemming from Roman times, of lining the Aurelian Way outside the gates with tombs and mausoleums grew in early Christian times to a fever, and coffins were sent from far and wide to be piled high in rows along the route. The popularity of the necropolis declined in the late Middle Ages, and from the Renaissance city councillors began giving away finely-carved sarcophagi to visitors as presents. Some sarcophagi have been preserved in churches and museums, others have disappeared, and only a few plain ones remain today. But the one remaining avenue of the Alyscamps, sombre and tree-shaded, still has melancholy echoes of its past.

Arles is on the edge of the **Camargue**, and is an ideal starting-place for a tour of this fascinating region, unique in Europe. The immense alluvial plain of the Rhône delta, about 800sq km (308sq miles) in extent, is rich in wild life and is now a Regional Nature Park, and part of it a Nature Reserve. It is famous for its wild white horses, black bulls and flamingoes, but there are many other species of flora and fauna to be seen there. Part of it is cultivated, and the Camargue now produces all of France's rice requirements, processed and marketed in Arles. It is a romantic place, but parts of it have become very popular with visitors. The *gardians*, or local cowboys, flamboyant, colourful characters who herd the bulls for the local (harmless) bullfights or *courses*, now make their money leading horse-trekking parties of tourists and the annual gipsy pilgrimage into the sea at **Les-Saintes-Maries-de-la-Mer** is looking more like a pop festival every year (the town itself is sadly over-commercialised). Most of the Camargue is carefully preserving its traditional pattern of life, and there is still plenty of space to explore its hidden delights, as long as you obey the rules (you are not allowed into the Nature Reserve unless you are an accredited naturalist). Do not forget to take your binoculars.

Provençal Cuisine

The phrase *à la Provençale* attached to a dish is widely known to indicate certain quite distinctive ingredients: garlic, olive oil, olives, tomatoes and herbs such as basil, bay, rosemary and thyme. Garlic and olive oil are the basis of Provençal cuisine. Some dishes such as an *aillade*, contain a lot of garlic — usually whole cloves baked in their skins — but when it is well-cooked the taste becomes much milder.

There are three famous Provençal soups: the *bouillabaisse*, which is really a rich and expensive fish stew; the *bourride*, a more normal soup made with white fish and cream; and *soup au pistou*, a vegetable soup flavoured with basil. *Pistou* is the Provençal version of the Italian *pesto*, a garlic and basil paste that is added to many dishes. *Bouillabaisse* is the classic and best-known local dish, and is made with a variety of Mediterranean fish and shellfish (*rascasse*, or hog-fish, gurnet and conger-eel are usually the basics) cooked with olive oil in a *bouillon* and flavoured with onion, tomato, saffron, garlic, herbs, fennel, orange peel, white wine and/or cognac. It is served with *rouille*, a paste of peppers, which is sometimes stirred into the dish and sometimes spread on the bread you eat with it. *Bourride* is usually made with angler fish, sea bass and whiting and is usually served with *aïoli*, a freshly-made garlic mayonnaise.

Other popular fish are red mullet, sea bass and sea bream, often baked or grilled with fennel. Lamb is a popular meat, usually grilled with herbs and garlic. Beef is often eaten in a rich stew, known as *daube Provençal*, braised with onions, garlic, herbs, vegetables and red wine. A kind of tripe called *pieds-paquets* is a speciality of Marseilles, while Arles is known for its sausages. A savoury tart, a variation of the Italian pizza, is called the *pissaladière*, made with cheese, tomato, olives and anchovies.

The most common vegetables are tomatoes and onions (often eaten raw), closely followed by courgettes, aubergines, peppers and fennel. A popular vegetable dish is the *ratatouille*, a stew of courgettes, aubergines, tomatoes, red and green peppers, onions, garlic and herbs. Large tomatoes, peppers and aubergines are sometimes eaten baked, with a savoury stuffing. Fruit is superb in Provence. The most popular are figs, peaches, nectarines, apricots, cherries, grapes, melons and watermelons. Cavaillon melons, the soccer-ball-shaped ones with orange flesh, are delicious. Black Provençal olives, marinated and flavoured with herbs, are a favourite of the connoisseur.

Wine is abundant and varies in quality from the mediocre to the superb. Côtes-du-Rhône reds are excellent, and the whites and rosés can be very good. Others (Tricastin, Ventoux, Luberon, Provence, Bandol) are lighter and more variable in quality. *Pastis*, and the excellent Muscats of Baumes-de-Venise and Rasteau, are favourite aperitifs. Others (Tricastin, Ventoux, Luberon, Provence, Bandol) are lighter and more variable in quality. *Pastis* and the excellent Muscats of Baumes-de-Venise and Rasteau, are favourite aperitifs.

Additional Information

Places of Interest

Grignan
Château
Open: daily, Easter to 30 September.

Vaison-la-Romaine
Roman Remains and Museum
Open: 9am-5pm or 6pm in season.

Orange
Roman Theatre
Open: 9am-6.30pm ex performance days
(info Tourist Office).

Municipal Museum
Open: 8.30am-12noon and 2-6.30pm in
summer, 5pm in winter.

Avignon
Papal Palace
Guided tours at fixed times.

Petit Palais Museum
Open: 9.30-11.30am and 2-6pm, except
Tuesday and holidays.

Calvet Museum
Open: 10am-12noon and 2-6pm, except
Tuesday and holidays.

Villeneuve-lès-Avignon
*Philip the Fair's Tower and Municipal
   Museum*
Open: 10am-12.30pm and 3-7.30pm,
April to September; 10am-12noon and 2-
5pm rest of year; closed February.

Charterhouse and Fort St André
Open: 9am-12noon and 2-6.30pm, closed
Tuesday and February.

Fontaine de Vaucluse
Norbert Casteret Museum (speleology)
Open: 9am-12noon and 2-6.30pm, closed
Tuesday and February.

Vallis Clausa Paper Mill
Open: 9am-12.30pm and 2-6pm; Sunday
10.30am-12.30pm and 2-6pm; summer
9am-7pm. Hand-made paper on sale.

Gordes
Borie Village
Open: daily 9am-sunset.

Château and Vasarely Museum
Open: 10am-12noon and 2-6pm except
Tuesday.

Moulin des Bouillons
Open: 10am-12noon and 4-6pm.

Sénanque
Abbey
Open: 10am-12noon and 4-6pm, 7pm in
season; concerts, exhibitions.

Lourmarin
Château
Open: 9-11.45am and 2.30-5.45pm or
4.45pm winter, except Tuesday October
to April.

Ansouis
Château and Musée Extraordinaire
Open: 2-7pm, 6pm winter, except
Tuesday (château).

Aix-en-Provence
Granet Museum
Open 10am-12noon and 2-5pm, 6pm in
summer, except Tuesday and holidays.

Museum of Old Aix
Open: 10am-12noon and 2-5pm, 6pm in
summer, except Monday.

Cézanne's Studio
Open: 10am-12noon and 2-5pm, 2.30-
6pm summer, except Tuesday and
holidays.

Vasarély Foundation
Open: 9.30am-12.30pm and 2-5.30pm,
except Tuesday.

Salon-de-Provence
*Château de l'Emperi and French Army
   Museum*
Open: 10am-12noon and 2.30-6.30pm, 2-
6pm October to March; except Tuesday
and holidays.

Nostradamus' House
Open: 10am-12noon and 3-7pm, except
Tuesday.

St Rémy-de-Provence
Ruins of Glanum
Open: 9am-12noon and 2-6pm; 10am-
12noon and 2-5pm winter, except
Tuesday.

Alpilles Folklore Museum
In Mistral de Mondragon mansion
Open: 10am-12noon and 2-6pm April to
October, except May, Saturday, Sunday,
Monday only; 10am-12noon and 2-4pm
winter.

Tarascon
Château
Hourly guided tours 9am-5pm or 10am-
4pm winter; except Tuesday and
holidays.

Fontvieille
Daudet's Windmill
Open: 9am-12noon and 1.30-5.30pm.

Arles
St Trophime Church (Cloister),
Museum of Pagan Art,
Museum of Christian Art,
Arlaten Museum,
Roman Arena, Theatre and Baths,
Réattu Museum
All same hours and admission ticket:
Open: 9am-7pm May to September;
9am-12noon and 2-6pm/5.30pm winter.

Tourist Information Centres

Aix-en-Provence
Office de Tourisme
Place Général-de-Gaulle
☎ 42 26 02 93

Arles
Office de Tourisme
Esplanade des Lices
☎ 90 96 29 35

Avignon
Office de Tourisme and Accueil de
    France
41 cours J. Jaurès
☎ 90 82 65 11

Orange
Office de Tourisme and Accueil de
    France
cours A. Briand
☎ 90 34 70 88

Vaison-la-Romaine
Office de Tourisme
Place Chanoine Sautel
☎ 90 36 02 11

Restaurants

R = With Accommodation
Haute-cuisine restaurants include:

Aix-en-Provence
Clos de la Violette
☎ 42 23 30 71

Avignon
Christian Étienne
☎ 90 86 16 50

Hiély
☎ 90 86 17 07

Brunel
☎ 90 85 24 83

Auberge de Cassagne (at Le Pontet) (R)
☎ 90 31 04 18

Les Frênes (at Montfavet) (R)
☎ 90 31 17 93

Cavaillon
Prévot
☎ 90 71 32 43

Nicolet
5km (3 miles) south
☎ 90 78 01 56

Châteauneuf-du-Pape
Host. Château des Fines Roches (R)
☎ 90 83 70 23

Fontvieille
La Regalido (R)
☎ 90 54 60 22

Gordes
Bastide de Gordes (R)
☎ 90 72 12 12

Joucas
Mas des Herbes Blanches (R)
☎ 90 05 79 79

Les Baux-de-Provence
Oustaù de Beaumanière (R)
☎ 90 54 33 07

La Riboto de Taven
☎ 90 54 34 23

La Cabro d'Or (R)
☎ 90 54 33 21

Malataverne
9km (6 miles) south of Montélimar
Domaine du Colombier (R)
☎ 75 51 65 86

Monteux
$4^1/_2$km (3 miles) south-west of
Carpentras
Saule Plaurer
☎ 90 62 01 35

Rochegude
14km (9 miles) north of Orange
Château de Rochegude (R)
☎ 75 04 81 88

Salon-de-Provence
5km (3 miles) north-east
Abbaye de Ste-Croix (R)
☎ 90 56 24 55

Séguret
9km (6 miles) south of Vaison-la-Romaine
La Table du Comtat (R)
☎ 90 46 91 49

St Rémy-de-Provence
Host. du Vallon de Valrugues (R)
☎ 90 92 04 40

Verquières
11km (7 miles) north-east St-Rémy
Croque Chou
☎ 90 95 18 55

Other restaurants, offering good value
for money, include:
Aurel
Near Sault
Au Relais du Mont-Ventoux (R)
☎ 90 64 00 62

Avignon
La Fourchette II
☎ 90 85 20 93

Châteauneuf-du-Pape
Le Pistou
☎ 90 83 71 75

Gigondas
Les Florets (R)
☎ 90 65 85 01

Montélimar
Francis
☎ 75 01 43 82

Rognes
16km (10 miles) north of Aix-en-Provence
Les Olivarelles
☎ 42 50 24 27

Vaison-la-Romaine
Le Moulin a Huile
☎ 90 38 20 67

8

LANGUEDOC

The name Languedoc conjures up different images to different people. To some, it is the place where the wine is red, strong, plentiful and cheap; to others it is a long, flat, sunny coastline of modern resorts and camp-sites; to the explorer it is a land of wooded mountains and valleys, limestone plateaux and deep gorges, underground caverns and remote, forgotten villages; to history-lovers it is the 'other' France, with its own language distinct from that of the north and its tragic past of rebellion, persecution and subjection; and to the sportsman it is rugby football and bull-fighting. In fact, it is all these things, and the traveller in the region can experience something of them all.

The Languedoc is not as precise a region as Provence, and does not have the same clear identity. In the past the name has been applied to the whole of southern France, stretching from the Italian border to the Atlantic. Today it is generally imagined to be that central part, west of the Rhône and east of Toulouse, between the southern slopes of the Massif Central and the sea. But exactly how far its boundaries extend is still not certain. The modern region corresponds roughly to the old province, except that it includes the Catalan-speaking department next to the eastern Spanish border, officially known as Pyrenees-Orientales but usually called Roussillon. It also comprises the de-partments of Gard, Lozère, Hérault and Aude, but excludes the Ardèche and the Ariège. It is the hottest, driest (and dustiest) part of France, with a flat, marshy coastline backed by an undulating plain studded with barren, rocky outcrops, rising to the mountains of the Cévennes in the east and the Causses further west.

Its name derives from the 'alternative French' spoken in the south, which was traditionally distinguished from the northern tongue by the word it used for 'yes'. In Paris and the north they used *oil*, which has developed into the modern *oui*, while in the south they used *oc*. Thus the northern tongue was the *langue d'oil* and the southern languages — Provençal, Catalan, and other regional patois — were collectively known as the *langue d'oc*. Today the letters OC are used as a symbol of the separate identity of southern France, and are seen on cars, road signs, walls and other public places. Southern French languages (excepting Basque) are closer to Latin than northern French, and are more closely related to Italian and Spanish.

Along with its own language, the Languedoc developed its own religious variations from Roman Catholic orthodoxy, which were ruthlessly crushed

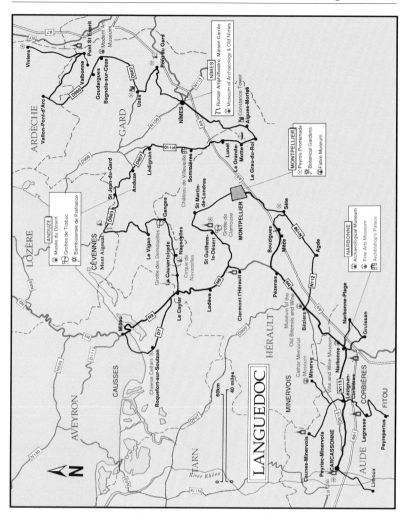

by the north. In the early Middle Ages, the Albigensian or Cathar heresy became widespread, particularly in the south-west, and after a period of tolerance it was eventually stamped out by mass murder and destruction of churches and strongholds. Much evidence of this destruction can be seen in the area today. At the Reformation, many parts of the south turned to the new Protestant faith, and this too was eventually suppressed. Today the south is reasserting its identity by reviving its language and traditions. It is still an area where religious feeling runs deep, though these days its outlets may be its twin passions — rugby football and bullfighting.

This tour covers a fairly extensive area of southern France, and briefly visits a variety of attractive regions, each one of which might make a holiday centre in itself. It is not suggested that you visit them at the same rate, merely that you pick up some ideas for future longer stays. The route zig-zags across the

Languedoc plain from mountains to coast, starting in the Rhône Valley and ending at the walled city of Carcassone.

The Western Rhône Valley

The starting-point is the old cathedral town of **Viviers**, on a rock over the west bank of the Rhône near Montélimar. Traditionally the Midi begins here. The town certainly has a meridional appearance, with its Roman pantiled roofs, old stone buildings with wrought-iron balconies, and avenues of plane trees. It gives its name to an old province, the Vivarais, on the eastern edge of the Massif Central, bordering the Rhône, a large, imprecise area now incorporated in several departments: Ardèche, Loire, Haute-Loire, Lozère and Gard. The medieval town centre is attractive, dominated by an old tower and impressive cathedral façade, and with a terrace above the cliffs giving a good view of the Rhône Valley and the Alps.

Take the N86 south, following the Rhône as far as **Pont St Esprit**, whose long thirteenth-century bridge was once the main crossing point of the area, and whose old streets lie behind a pleasant, wide, shaded main boulevard. Nearby is the charterhouse of Valbonne, a fine Classical-style monastery hidden in the forest, with a superb Baroque church and Burgundian coloured tile roofs. This is a good starting point for a tour of the **Ardèche Gorges**, one of France's most spectacular sights and a very popular holiday area. One of its attractions for the more daring is a canoe trip down the river, which can be a short one-day affair or a two-day traverse of the gorges with an overnight bivouac. The river is also pleasant for swimming, and the views from the Haute Corniche road are breathtaking, but the many camp-sites mean crowds in summer.

Turn off the N86 at St Just onto the D290. After St Martin d'Ardèche the road follows the northern bank of the Ardèche on a high corniche, with many belvederes giving stupendous views of the gorges from different aspects. Below one of these is **Grotte de la Madeleine** a typical limestone cave with stalactites and stalagmites. From here, a short detour to the right on the D590 brings you to the **Aven de Marzal**, one of the many large underground caverns in the area (the whole area is a delight for potholers and speleologists). An *aven* is a large single 'cathedral' chasm, whereas a *grotte* is a series of smaller caves linked by passageways. This *aven* is typical in having a spectacular display of multi-coloured stalactites and stalagmites.

Continue along the corniche, stopping at the viewpoints of Gaud and Serre de Tours for more magnificent views, and descend to the **Pont-d'Arc**, one of France's best-loved (and most-photographed) sights. This huge natural stone arch spans the river at a delightful spot where the gorges flatten out to more gentle slopes. It has good beaches and swimming, and is a starting-point for canoe trips. Unfortunately, it is also the part of the gorges where the tourist hordes are densest. Nearby **Vallon-Pont-d'Arc** is the tourist-ridden commercial centre of the area, while **Ruoms**, a little further north, is equally attractive and less spoilt. At Vallon, cross the river on the D579 to Salavas, and later turn left on the D217 for Labastide de Virac and the south side of the gorges. Here there is no corniche road, but a series of tiny roads running off into the scrubby forest, with sudden surprise views of the Ardèche Valley and plateau. Further on you pass two more *avens*: first, the **Aven de la Forestière**, and later the deepest and most impressive in the region, the **Aven d'Orgnac**. This huge hole in the ground is really a series of three caves, one on top of another, only explored in 1935. It is very deep (788 steps), with magnificent stalagmites in impressive shapes — pine-cones, curtains, stacks of plates, urns, and at the bottom a beautiful red 'city' — and an urn containing the heart of its discoverer, Robert de Joly, displayed in a niche. At the entrance is a small museum and a tasting of Côtes du Vivarais wines.

From the pleasant little village of Orgnac-l'Aven, take the D417 to join the D980 at the head of the **Gorges de la Cèze**. These are much less spectacular than the Ardèche gorges and soon open out into a pleasant valley, passing the pretty village of **Goudargues**, with a stream running through its main street and **La Roque-sur-Cèze**, perched splendidly on a rock with the Sautadet waterfall at its feet. Lower down is **St Gervais**, which produces a very good Côtes-du-Rhône Villages wine, and **Bagnols-sur-Cèze**, a residential town for the workers at the nearby Marcoule atomic power station, but with an attractive old centre ringed by boulevards and a good Modern Art Museum in the old town hall. Not far from Bagnols are some villages producing excellent wines: **Chusclan** (Côtes-du-Rhône Villages red and rosé); **Laudun** (Côtes-du-Rhône Villages red); **Lirac** (fine AC rosé and good red); and **Tavel** (the best, and strongest, rosé in France).

Continue on the N86 for 13km (8 miles) then turn right on the D982 for **Uzès**, a delightful Italian-looking town isolated in the wild yet charming countryside of the *garrigues* — rocky limestone plateaux, shallow gorges and low hills covered with scrub and herbs at the foot of the Massif Central. Uzès is an old duchy, consulate and bishopric whose dukes were once powerful and independent. In the sixteenth century it became a stronghold of Protestantism, and in the reigns of Louis XIII and XIV many of its Huguenot citizens were killed or exiled-it still has a large Protestant population today. It is associated with two famous writers, Jean Racine and André Gide. Uzès is dominated by medieval towers, three of which represent the three powers that rules Uzès: the Clock Tower, belonging to the bishop; the King's Tower opposite; and the Bermonde Tower next to the large Ducal Palace, with its splendid Renaissance façade. The most beautiful is the elegant and unusual Tour Fenestrelle, a round bell-tower in receding storeys with varying Romanesque arched 'windows'. This is the only remaining part of the old cathedral, destroyed in the Wars of Religion. Government grants are helping to restore Uzès' lovely old narrow streets, sixteenth-to eighteenth-century mansions, arcaded square and fountains, which make it one of the prettiest towns in France. There is a colourful market in the old square on Saturdays.

A fast and busy road, the D98, runs from Uzès to Remoulins, passing the **Pont du Gard**, one of the wonders of the Roman world and one of France's most famous monuments. The 275m (892ft) high bridge, spanning the wooded Gardon Valley, was part of a long aqueduct which carried water from Uzès to Nîmes through a duct in the top tier, 49m (161ft) above water-level. It

One of France's most picturesque sites is the Pont d'Arc spanning the River Ardèche

The Pont du Gard, a grand achievement in Roman architecture and engineering

is both a magnificent feat of engineering and an object of beauty, its three tiers of arches being built of large blocks of uncemented stone in a simple but elegant design. You can walk along the top of it, either inside the water-channel or, if you have the stomach for it, along the open, unfenced roof. Although the top is 3m (10ft) wide, the strong breeze and the 50m (164ft) drop make it a nerve-racking experience. If you are not too dizzy, there are wonderful views from the top; but the best view of the bridge itself is from the Château St Privat upstream. A road (one-way) runs along the top of the bottom row of arches. The bridge's harmonious appearance and dramatic setting have great appeal, and it is one of France's most-visited sites, so beware of crowds. There are camp-sites nearby, and good swimming in the clean River Gard.

Avoid the busy N86 Remoulins-Nîmes road and, returning towards Uzès, take the attractive D979 through the *garrigues* to **Nîmes**. This is a busy commercial town (a striking contrast to Uzès), very hot and dry in high summer, but it has fountains, pleasant parks and shaded boulevards encircling its old centre, and a Mediterranean aspect reminiscent of Spain or Italy. Its interest for the visitor is its wealth of Roman monuments, reflecting its importance as a chief city of the *Provincia Romana*, beloved of Augustus himself. There are four main ones to see, which you can visit on a single ticket. The first is the best-preserved Roman amphitheatre in France, a beautiful building with arcades and vaulted galleries around the outside and fine views of the city from the top of its tiered walls. It is still in use for bull-fights and summer spectacles, with capacity for 20,000 spectators. The Maison Carrée claims similar fame as the best-preserved Roman temple. The name 'square house' is a misnomer — it is a 26m by 15m (85ft by 49ft) rectangle — but this first-century BC temple of classic Greek proportions is a wonderful sight, in spite of being hemmed in by surrounding buildings. It houses a small collection of local antiquities. The other two monuments are less impressive: in the attractive Fountain Garden, an eighteenth-century construction with artificial lakes, is a so-called Temple of Diana, a jumble of ruins which were probably part of a larger building; and above the gardens, on top of Mount Cavalier (the highest point in Nîmes), is the Magna Tower, the only remaining part of the old Roman fortifications. There is a fine view from here over the *garrigues*.

South of Nîmes, on the edge of the Camargue, lies a low ridge topped by a string of villages known as the Costières de Nîmes. This area produces pleasant, light wines, formerly called Costières du Gard and now renamed Costières de Nîmes. Further south, in the sands of the Camargue itself, vines are grown successfully and produce popular if rather bland wines called Vins des Sables. The centre for the production of these is a fascinating old walled town in the western corner of the Camargue called **Aigues-Mortes**. It is a perfectly-preserved medieval fortified town, built in a square, with a rectangular pattern of streets like the lines on a chessboard. Virtually the whole town is contained within its ramparts. As you walk round the top of them you get a good view of the town within and the strange landscape of lagoons, salt marshes and vineyards outside. You get an even better view through the wrought iron cage on top of the impressive Constance Tower, a massive circular keep standing in one corner of the walls. The town was built in the thirteenth century by Louis IX (St Louis) — his statue stands in the central square — as a port of embarkation for the Crusades. In those days it was on the sea coast, but later the surrounding water silted up and it became unusable as a port. Another use was found for it as a prison, where southern Protestants were incarcerated, often for long periods (one, Marie Durand, spent 38 years in the Constance Tower).

Aigues-Mortes is a delightful place to visit, whether to wander round the old streets, march round the ramparts, climb the spiral staircase of the Constance Tower, visit the Listel wine cellars just outside the town, or simply sit and eat ice-cream in the lovely Place St Louis. But it is not a coastal resort — it is now isolated 8km (5 miles) inland. The nearest coastal town is the small but busy fishing port of **Le Grau-du-Roi** (good fish restaurants), and on either side the modern holiday complexes of **Port-Camargue** and **La Grande-Motte**. The former, begun in 1969, is simply a man-made port and yacht marina surrounded by anonymous low-rise buildings; but the latter is worth visiting as an example of modern architecture at its most aggressive. Started in 1967, it was the first of the new resorts to be built on the Languedoc coast, after General de Gaulle had ordered the marshes to be drained and cleared of mosquitos in the early 1960s. People seem to love it or hate it. The central core of the town is a group of honeycombed pyramids, though there are other large blocks of holiday flats in a variety of weird shapes. Everything is in concrete, ultra-modern and brash. However, it is spaciously laid out and has every amenity a holiday resort could wish for, with fine sands and a 52-acre marina. It is excellent for water-sports.

The Cévennes

Turn inland from La Grande-Motte on the D61 to Lunel, renowned for its excellent sweet Muscat wine, and then across the undulating plain of the Gard. As you approach each village, the sign advertising the times of Mass will be augmented with one for Culte Protéstante. This is territory that has suffered much for its Protestant faith in the past, and still holds to that faith today. The D34 from Lunel leads to a lovely, quiet town hidden in the *garrigues*, **Sommières**. It is an old fortified town, huddled beneath its ruined castle on the right bank of the Vidourle. The modern bridge, built on top of an old Roman one, leads to the old arched town gate topped by an attractive clock tower. Round the remains of the old walls are pleasant tree-lined boulevards with cafés overlooking the river and inside the walls are narrow streets, elegant Classical mansions and a pretty arcaded square. Just outside the town is the imposing Château de Villevieille, built on a rocky spur, with medieval towers and a Renaissance façade.

From Sommières, the road north runs through a landscape of vineyards, scrub and rocks, past pleasant, sleepy Gard villages (Lédignan, Lézan, Quissac) and with views of the ever-approaching Cévennes, to **Anduze**. This picturesque small town, in a dramatic setting on one of the Gard tributaries, the Gardon d'Anduze, has two titles: the 'Gateway to the Cévennes' and the

'French Geneva'. The first is certainly apt. To the north of the town the river enters a narrow defile where the mountains close in and, following the river road through the defile, you are suddenly in the Cévennes. The town reflects this contrast — to the south the valley is green, broad and pleasant; to the north, steep, rugged and severe. Anduze has an old craftsmen's quarter entered through a gateway from its main boulevard, with narrow streets and old houses leading to a square with a covered market and a quaint fifteenth-century fountain-pagoda in green and yellow glazed tiles, the same colour as its pottery. The town's second title is also appropriate. In the central square, opposite the old clock tower, is the severely-Classical temple, one of the largest Protestant churches in France, and round the corner is a Methodist chapel, both testifying to Anduze's long tradition of Protestant independence.

The teaching of Calvin took hold in the Cévennes and most of the Gard department during the Reformation, and for a while after the Wars of Religion the Edict of Nantes gave French Protestants freedom of worship and political status. But when it was repealed by Louis XIV in 1685, they were brutally repressed by royal forces and became outlaws. In the Cévennes they took to the hills, locally known as the *désert*, worshipping out of doors and living in open rebellion. They waged guerrilla war, attacked royal troops and destroyed churches, calling themselves Camisards — the Languedoc word for the white shirts they wore to identify one another during nightly raids. The War of the Camisards lasted 2 years, from 1702 to 1704, and its leaders, Roland and Cavalier, became local heroes. Roland was eventually caught and savagely executed, but Cavalier escaped to England and ended his career as governor of Jersey. After the war the Huguenots who had not been killed or deported continued to worship in the *désert* until freed by the Revolution.

Just above Anduze the Gardon divides into the Gardon de Mialet and the Gardon de St Jean, each river following its own valley. Higher up they are mountain streams running through rocky gorges, with clear water ideal for swimming amid lovely scenery. Three kilometres (2 miles) north of Anduze in the Mialet Valley, in a huddled village called the **Mas Soubeyran**, is the house of the Camisards' leader Roland, now turned into a museum of French Protestantism, the Musée du Désert. In its evocative setting, this small museum movingly tells the story of the Camisards' War and the history of Protestantism in France. There is a pilgrimage every September, with a large open-air service.

The delightful Mialet Valley holds another curiosity, a park of giant bamboos. In a pretty spot by the river in the village of Générargues, the local microclimate has allowed a tropical garden to be created, the Bambuseraie de Prafrance. Amid a profusion of blooms, a thick clump of bamboos gives you the impression of being in a tropical rain forest. Further up the valley, you can visit the Grottes de Trabuc, a long series of caves with stalactites and stalagmites. The village of **Mialet** itself is tiny but quaint, with its bijou octagonal Protestant temple built in the centre of a cluster of typical Cévenol houses. Further up, the valley becomes a gorge, crossed by a spectacular bridge, the Pont des Abarines. There is superb swimming from granite rocks in the gorge,

with nude bathing in the more secluded spots.

The D50 leads down from the Abarine bridge to **St Jean-du-Gard**, an ※ attractive, typically Cévenol small town that could serve as a base for exploring the southern Cévennes (some good camp-sites). St Jean has tall dry-stone houses with overhanging roofs, throwing the narrow streets into shade. There are two bridges, an old and a new one, spanning the Gardon and there is a colourful market on Tuesdays, when farmers from the remote valleys sell their local produce (honey, *pelardons* of *chèvre* cheese, ham and sausages, jams, herbs, soaps and perfumes). This is where the Scottish writer Robert Louis Stevenson ended the journey he made in 1877 with his donkey Modéstine, after taking a long and tortuous route from Le Puy in the Velais, through the Vivarais, over Mont Lozère, and across the Cévennes. He travelled rough,

(Opposite) Roads meander through the delightful scenery of the Tarn Gorges

Exploration of the Tarn Gorges reveals pleasant, sleepy villages

sleeping in the open and living off the land and local charity and wrote about it in *Travels with a Donkey in the Cévennes* one of the most delightful travel books ever written. He sold Modéstine, after fond farewells, in the market place at St Jean-du-Gard. The town meeting-hall over the market is named the Salle Stevenson in his honour.

The Cévennes are one of France's best-kept secrets. Though there are tourists in summer, the vast size of this National Park and the remoteness of some of its valleys means that there is always plenty of space, peace and freedom. The area has become depopulated over the years, with the decline of some of its traditional industries such as chestnut and silk production, and though the National Park endeavours are trying to revive its culture and way of life, it remains France's wildest and least-explored region — an ideal destination for the adventurous traveller. It is quite unlike the regions to the east and west (the Ardèche and the Causses), which are limestone country of plateaux, gorges and caves. The Cévennes are old granite mountains, thickly-wooded with oaks, pines, chestnut and mulberry trees, broom and herbs, with deep, steep-sided valleys and clear mountain streams. In the north the hills are barer and the weather cooler and wetter, but in the south olive and cypress trees appear and the climate is Mediterranean, hot and sunny by day but pleasantly cool in the evening.

A tour of the Cévennes should include the superb **Corniche des Cévennes**, which begins just north of St Jean-du-Gard, a finely-engineered road along the mountain crests, with magnificent views; and the ascent of **Mont Aigoual**, the mountains' highest peak (1,567m, 5,140ft), with a good road right to the summit. The view from the top is extensive on a clear day (from the Alps to the Pyrénées) but it is often hazy in summer and wet in the autumn (*aigoual* means 'wet'). There are many narrow mountain roads through valleys and over passes — the Col de l'Asclier and Col du Pas are two of the more spectacular — and many places with memories of the Camisards' War. Of the mountain villages, **Lasalle** and **Valleraugue** are particularly attractive. The latter was an important silk-weaving centre, and still has some ruined silk-mills and its old terraces of mulberry trees (mulberry leaves were the silk-worms' diet). North of the Corniche, **Florac** is a pleasant centre for exploring the Causses, the Tarn Gorges and Mont Lozère.

The Grands Causses

Assuming that your Cévennes tour ends at the summit of Mont Aigoual, descend from here on the D48 down the Hérault Valley, with a spectacular view over the valley from L'Espérou. The road winds attractively down, steeply at first and then through gorges carved in the rock, to **Le Vigan**, a small town making bonnets and silk ribbons, with a fine old bridge over the Hérault and an interesting Cévenol folk-museum in an old silk mill. Continue to **Ganges**, at the southern edge of the Cévennes, a town once famous for silk and now for stockings, and a good base for visiting two extraordinary nearby sites. The Grotte des Demoiselles (guided tours only) is more of an *aven* than a *grotte* a superb cathedral-like cavern with beautifully-coloured stalactites and stalagmites in fantastic shapes, including the famous 'Virgin and Child'. It is the scene of a midnight mass every Christmas.

The D25 west from Ganges follows the valley of a Hérault tributary, the Vis, to France's Grand Canyon, the **Cirque de Navacelles**. The road climbs steeply out of the Vis gorge by a series of hairpin bends to St Maurice-Navacelles. Turn right here, crossing the Larzac plateau on the D130, and in 6km (4 miles), at the Baume-Auriol farm, you will get a sudden, staggering view of the cirque below. At the foot of a high, arid gorge, a deep meander in the river has formed an amphitheatre with a conical scrub-covered rock in the centre, surrounded by a green river-bed and the hamlet of Navacelles itself. It is a breathtaking sight from the top, and from the narrow hairpin road that winds down into the gorge and up the other side. At the bottom you can swim from rocks in a lovely clear pool near the village.

Climb out of the cirque to the village of Blandas, from where a road leads to another dramatic cirque at Vissec, and beyond to the deserted village of **La Couvertoirade**, hidden in a hollow on the Causse de Larzac. This settlement, isolated and completely contained within its walls, was fortified by the Knights Templar in the fourteenth century to protect passing pilgrims, and deserted when the wool trade declined in the late nineteenth century. It is now largely in ruins, but some artists and craftsmen have moved in to restore parts of it and benefit from its tourist appeal. The **Causse de Larzac** is the most southerly of the five great Causses, or high limestone plateaux, that cover this south-central part of the Massif Central (the other four are the **Noir, Méjean, Severac** and **Sauveterre**). They are a fascinating area for a holiday or tour, with their wild, deserted uplands, deep, dramatic gorges, *avens* and grottoes, and fantastic rock formations. They have delightful rivers for swimming and canoeing, and large stretches of open heath for walking or pony-trekking. Their most spectacular gorges are the **Tarn, Jonte** and **Dourbie**, their most superb underground chasm the **Aven Armand**, and their most bizarre rock formation the **Chaos of Montpellier-le-Vieux**, a complete 'city' of natural stone. The Causses have an additional attraction: the sheep which roam the broad plateaux at random provide the milk for the world's finest (and most expensive) cheese, Roquefort. You can visit the natural caves at **Roquefort-** **sur-Soulzon** where this sublime cheese is kept at a perfect constant temperature. The nearby glove-making town of **Millau** is a good base for exploring the area.

The Hérault Valley

From La Couvertoirade, join the N9 at **Le Caylar**, a village on the Larzac surrounded by an outcrop of jagged-shaped rocks which look like its walls and castle. Continue south through the eastern edge of the Monts de l'Espinouse, which form the south-western corner of the Massif Central. *Espinouse* means 'prickly', and describes their covering of prickly maquis. They are a wild region of mountains and lakes, part of which form the Haut-Languedoc Nature Park. The road passes the large reservoir of **Lac du Salagou**, a popular centre for boating, wind-surfing and fishing. Nearby is the small town of **Clermont-l'Hérault**, in the centre of the most prolific wine- ✳

producing area in France. Wine from the Hérault Valley was once thought fit only for the EEC wine lake, but recent improvements in production methods have meant that excellent-quality vintages can now be found here, often at bargain prices. Try the Côteaux de Languedoc reds, the sharp, dry and refreshing Picpoul de Pinet white and a pleasant sparkling wine, Clairette du Languedoc. Clermont-l'Hérault is also known for its excellent dessert grapes. The town has a pleasant old quarter of narrow streets, and an interesting fortified Gothic church.

Just above the town, at the village of St Jean-de-Fos, the Devil's bridge marks the beginning of the Gorges de l'Herault. These are not spectacular by the standards of the Causses, but they boast two attractions: the **Grotte de** **Clamouse**, with strange, flowery mineral formations and the beautiful village of **St Guilhem-le-Désert**, squeezed into the narrow side-gorge of the Verdus. The village is picturesque, with narrow cobbled streets rising up the gorge to the shaded square and fountain, old houses with flowery window-boxes, and street signs in the old Languedoc language and lettering. It has a magnificent Romanesque church, founded in AD804 but rebuilt in the eleventh century, with a superb apse, a lovely altar, a restored sixth- to seventh-century carved sarcophagus and the remains of fine cloisters. It owes its name to a Frankish warrior, William of Orange, a friend and chief lieutenant of Charlemagne who, after a distinguished military career, escaped to the wilderness to live the monastic life. Charlemagne gave him a fragment of Christ's cross as a souvenir, and he built the church to house it. Before he died, in fasting and prayer, he saved the village from an invading Saracen and they renamed it after him. The church and its holy relic drew hordes of pilgrims in the Middle Ages, remembered in an annual procession with lighted snail-shells.

At the northern end of the Hérault gorge, the D122 leads off right to **St Martin-de-Londres**, an attractive village with old houses clustered round an early Romanesque church. Nearby is the narrow defile of **Pic-St-Loup**, whose peak is the highest point in the *garrigues*, giving fine views over the Languedoc plain from the Cévennes to the Pyrénées (you can reach it on foot by the GR60). From St Martin descend by the D986 to **Montpellier**, the capital of the Languedoc. This busy, prosperous city is the administrative centre of the region, and a cultural and intellectual mecca with a large university of international repute. Though the suburbs are large and sprawling, the inner town is handsome, with elegant buildings and narrow streets ringed by wide boulevards and lovely, spacious parks. The settlement began as a trading post on the Eastern spice route, thereby developing a reputation as early as the eleventh century for its knowledge of the medical secrets of the East. Its university and medical school were founded in the thirteenth century, and soon became world-famous (Rabelais studied medicine here in the sixteenth century). As an intellectual centre, it embraced religious reform and was strongly Protestant during the Wars of Religion, as a consequence of which it was virtually destroyed. In the seventeenth to eighteenth centuries, it became an administrative capital and southern seat of Parliament, and its fine streets and buildings date from this time, with rich lawyers and financiers building themselves splendid hotels.

Montpellier's main attraction is the Peyrou Promenade, a magnificent feat
of architecture with seventeenth- to eighteenth-century terraces, pools
shaded by plane trees, an equestrian statue of Louis XIV and a triumphal arch
commemorating his victories, a delightful eighteenth-century hexagonal
water-tower at the end of an elegant 880m (2,886ft) long aqueduct with two
rows of arches, and, from the upper terrace, a magnificent view over the coast
and mountains behind. The old town's narrow streets conceal handsome
seventeenth- to eighteenth-century mansions — plain, even forbidding, on
the outside but with richly-decorated inner courtyards, monumental stair-
cases and first-floor galleries. The city's gardens include the oldest botanical
gardens in France; and the Fabre Museum, in part of the Jesuit College, has a
wonderful collection of fine art, particularly of French nineteenth-century
paintings (David, Ingres, Delacroix, Courbet). The old Faculty of Medicine, in
the St Benoit abbey, can be visited. The university is now out of town.

The lower Languedoc coast is largely reclaimed marshland, with littorals,
sand dunes, large lagoons and salt-flats. Montpellier has two modern seaside
resorts at Carnon-Plage and Palavas-les-Flots. Lower down is **Frontignan**,
home of an excellent Muscat dessert wine, and the busy commercial fishing
port of **Sète**, the most important in the Mediterranean. It is the meeting point
of the Midi and Rhône canals, and a lively working port with good fish
restaurants. There are some impressive old buildings lining the canal, which
bisects the town and is the scene of its famous water-jousts, a colourful
spectacle popular with locals and visitors in summer. Behind Sète is an
enormous lagoon, the **Bassin de Thau**, the meeting-point of the two canals
and a leading area for the production of oysters and mussels. From here you
have a choice of two routes from Sète to Béziers: you can either take the N112
along the lido to **Cap-d'Agde**, a seaside resort with the largest nudist colony
in France, and **Agde**, an old port founded by the Phoenicians but now
stranded 4km (2 miles) inland; or the N113 along the inland shore. This passes
the famous Thau oyster-beds and the village of **Bouzigues**, their commercial
centre, which has an excellent Oyster Fair in early August. At Mèze (excellent
shellfish), turn inland for **Pézenas**, a quiet town living off its past as a political
capital of the Languedoc and a cultural centre in the fifteenth to seventeenth
centuries (Molière spent time here entertaining the Prince of Conti's court). It
still has some elegant old houses, a good Arts Festival in July/August, and an
important wine market.

Further on, **Béziers** is a much larger and busier town, the capital of the
Languedoc wine industry. It is a lively working town, whose citizens, called
Biterrois, are passionate about two things — rugby football and bullfighting.
This was the scene of the first, and one of the bloodiest, episodes in the Cathar
saga when, on 22 July 1209, a Crusade was sent by Rome to crush the Cathar
heresy, which had taken hold of the region. Béziers was made an example of,
and its citizens indiscriminately slaughtered. The Canal du Midi, built by a
local landowner, Paul Riquet, passes through the town in a series of locks. The
old fortified cathedral stands imposingly on a terrace over the River Orb, and

close by is an interesting Museum of the Old Biterrois and Wine.

The Aude

From Béziers, continue on the N113/N9 to **Narbonne**, a smaller but more attractive town in the Aude department. Narbonne is set 12km (7 miles) inland at the edge of a series of large *étangs*, or shallow lakes, surrounded by marsh and salt-flats. It is a typical Mediterranean city with a relaxed and sunny disposition (it is the hottest and driest place in France); the old centre with a cluster of religious buildings at its heart is cut by the Robine canal and ringed by wide, tree-lined boulevards. The canal banks are particularly attractive, crossed by foot-bridges and lined by fountains, gardens and terraces with cafés. Narbonne was an important town in Roman times, capital of the original *Provincia*, which was called *Narbonnensis*, and later the Roman capital for a while under the Visigoths. Unfortunately few Roman remains survive intact, as they were either destroyed by invaders or built over but there is a very informative and well-presented display of Roman and other antiquities in the Archaeological Museum, located in the Archbishop's Palace. The central cluster of buildings consists of the Cathedral of St Just, its cloister and, joined by the Anchor Passage, the Archbishop's Palace, housing two museums, of Archaeology and Fine Arts.

The Gothic cathedral, though unfinished, is one of the most handsome in southern France, with a superb choir, beautiful tombs and a fine treasury with a fifteenth-century Flemish tapestry of the Creation (this can only be visited with a joint museum ticket). Surrounding the complex are a maze of narrow streets, with a few fragments of Roman architecture in the Place Bistan. An interesting wine museum, the Maison Vigneronne, housed in a seventeenth-century powder magazine near the tourist centre, reflects the importance of Narbonne today as the commercial centre of the Aude wine trade.

You can make a short round-trip from Narbonne to the coast. Take the D31 to **Gruissan**, a charming fishing village on a peninsula projecting into the *étangs* and overlooked by the ruined Barberousse tower. Along the coast, **Narbonne-Plage** is a typically-anonymous modern seaside resort, with a nearby cave, the Oeil-Doux Chasm. Return by the D168 over the Montagne de la Clape, a pleasant pine-clad range with *dégustation* points where you can taste the good local La Clape wines. Other excursions can be made to the Sigean African Safari Park, south of Narbonne on the edge of the *étangs*; and, by the N113, D613 and a cul-de-sac road, to the beautiful **Fontfroide** Abbey. Set in an isolated, tranquil valley at the entrance to a deep ravine, surrounded by cypress trees, this walled Cistercian abbey has a twelfth- to thirteenth-century church, cloister and chapterhouse of simple elegance, enhanced by lovely floral gardens. It is a haven of peace in the Corbières countryside.

The N9 and the Languedocienne motorway south from Narbonne lead to Perpignan and the Roussillon, the Catalan-speaking department by the Spanish border where the language and traditions of Catalonia are fiercely preserved. Here the atmosphere is Spanish, the buildings look Spanish or Italian, and if you are lucky you will see them dancing the *sardana*, the Catalan national dance. West from Narbonne the N113 leads into the **Corbières**, an area north of the Pyrenées with a pleasant, undulating landscape of hills, valleys, woods and vineyards, which produces fruity, good-value AOC wines (see the Food and Drink section in the Fact File). A good base for tasting these and other local wines is **Lézignan-Corbières**, a quiet little town in the Aude Valley. It lies on the northern edge of the Corbières and the southern edge of the Minervois (another good AOC wine area), and is a commercial centre for both wines. It has an excellent privately-owned Vine and Wine Museum, housed in a wine cellar, which combines a display of old and new equipment for growing grapes and making wine with a tasting of a range of wines from both regions. The town has good camping and swimming facilities.

The Corbières, to the south of Lézignan, becomes wilder and hillier as it approaches the Pyrénées. In the north are some attractive wine villages (Fabrezan, Ferrols-les-Corbières, Montséret, Durban) and the prettily-sited medieval village of **Lagrasse**, ably restored after being partially abandoned, with its fourteenth-century church, fifteenth- to sixteenth-century houses, cobbled streets, shaded squares and artists' studios. An old hump-backed bridge over the River Orbieu leads to its abbey, the oldest part of which dates from Charlemagne's time, but which is mainly a mixture of eleventh- and eighteenth-century buildings. This is now also being restored, by a Byzantine Catholic religious community. Lagrasse, like many villages in the area, has tastings of Corbières wines from private growers and co-operatives. In the south-east, near the Roussillon border, is another good AOC wine area, **Fitou**, with its commercial centre at Tuchan. Nearby **Rivesaltes**, in Roussillon, produces the best-known, if not the best, Muscat Côtes-du-Roussillon Villages (AOC) is an excellent red.

In south Corbières, in the hilly country on the Roussillon border, are three impressive ruined fortresses associated with the Cathars. This sect became the dominant religious group in the Languedoc in the early Middle Ages, thriving under the protection of the Counts of Toulouse. They rejected the Catholic sacraments and appointed their own clergy, of both sexes, known as the 'Perfects'. They believed that only the spiritual world was good, and man and this world were intrinsically evil. Though they were a gentle and tolerant sect, their beliefs were a challenge to Catholic orthodoxy, and in 1208 the Pope launched a crusade, led by the Anglo-French warrior Simon de Montfort, to destroy them. After much bloodshed, they were crushed, but some held out for a while in remote, inaccessible fortresses, like the three in south Corbières — **Quéribus**, **Peyrepertuse** and **Puylaurens**. The first two are the most spectacular: Quéribus held out until 1255, when it was betrayed; Peyrepertuse is the highest and most impressively set. There are magnificent views from the tops, but they entail strenuous climbs!

North of Lézignan is the Minervois, another pleasant area of quiet wine villages nestling under the slopes of the Black Mountains. The old capital is **Minerve**, now merely a village, in a dramatic setting on the side of a canyon hollowed out of the limestone by the River Cesse. Once the chief town of the area, Minerve was another victim of De Montfort's savage repression of the

Albigensian heresy. It was beseiged in 1210, and eventually fell when its water supply was cut off — 150 Cathars chose to die in the fire rather than renounce their faith. The village recalls its past, with remnants of the old walls, a ruined château, a Cathar Memorial Museum, and a small Romanesque church with an old altar (AD465). Two natural tunnels run under the village, and in the canyon you can see the old St Rustique Well, which De Montfort's catapults destroyed.

In the region, **Caunes-Minervois** is an attractive village, with narrow streets and handsome Renaissance buildings. The church adjoins the ruins of an old abbey. In the square, in the abbey refectory, is a display of Minervois wines with generous tastings. Outside the village, in a quiet rural setting, is the beautiful little pilgrimage chapel of Notre-Dame-de-Cros, and nearby are quarries of red and pink marble. There is a delightful and curious eleventh-century Romanesque church at **Rieux-Minervois,** built on a circular plan with a heptagonal belfry. The inside is gloomy as the church is shut in by surrounding buildings, but the capitals on the seven columns holding up the central cupola have fascinating carvings. **Peyriac-Minervois** is a pleasant old village with a good wine Co-operative, and **St Jean-de-Minervois** produces one of France's finest Muscat wines.

Leave Lézignan-Corbières by the N113 and travel west, with the bare Montagne d'Alaric on your left and the Canal du Midi and the River Aude on your right. At Carcassone the Aude, which gives the department its name, turns south towards its source in the Pyrénées, while the canal continues west to join the Garonne at Toulouse and link the Mediterranean to the Atlantic.

The village of Minerve in a dramatic setting on the side of a canyon

Carcassonne, your tour destination, has one of the most impressive, and ✳
popular, sites in France, the upper town or medieval city (the French just call
it La Cité). This is simply the most complete, the biggest, and the most
splendid fortified town in Europe, if not the world. Its first impression is
staggering — as though a fairy story has come to life — and as you walk
through the portcullis and town gates, you feel you really are moving back
through the ages. The crowds are medieval too — just as numerous, noisy and
jostling as they must have been then. The town has been a fortress since Roman
times, and part of the Visigothic walls remain. It was a key fortress against the
Albigensian crusade, but it only held out for a month, though it later rebuilt
its walls and withstood attacks from both the Black Prince and Protestant
forces. After falling into disuse and decay, it was restored in the nineteenth
century by Viollet-le-Duc as his greatest project, and, thanks to him, it remains
as a text-book example of medieval fortifications. It has a double set of
crenellated walls separated by grassy *lices*, round towers with conical turrets,
arched gateways and an inner fortified castle. The cobbled pedestrian streets
of the inner town lead to tree-shaded squares with wells and fountains. The
place abounds with craft and gift shops, cafés, restaurants and *créperies*. The 🍸
St Nazaire Church is splendid — part-Romanesque, part-Gothic, with beau-

---

Cuisine in the Languedoc

Many Languedoc dishes are similar to those of Provence and use the same
ingredients. For instance, *Daube Cévenol* is identical to *Daube Provençal*, though
local wine and olives may be used. Olive oil, garlic, wine and aromatic herbs
are still the basic ingredients for savoury dishes.

For soups, the fish soup *bourride* is common, usually with angler fish (*lotte*).
Boulinade is a variant of *bouillabaisse*. A garlic soup, called in the Languedoc *aigo
boulido*, includes eggs, herbs and croutons. The *ouillade* is still made at the wine
harvest, when two soups, of cabbage and beans, are mixed at the last moment.

Shellfish include the excellent oysters and mussels from Bouzigues.
Écrevisses, or river prawns, are not as common as they were in the mountain
streams, but they are still found. Snails are often eaten, not as in Burgundy, but
en cargolade, that is, stewed in a wine sauce.

Fish is common along the coast. A fish dish from Nîmes is the *brandade de
morue*, creamed salt cod with olive oil and garlic, often served in a feuilleté, or
vol-au-vent. Trout from mountain rivers is popular.

The most common meats are mutton, from the *garrigues*, and pork. Pigs are
often used for the fine air-cured sausages and smoked hams from the mountains. These are used in the classic dish of the Midi, the *cassoulet*. This is a thick
stew of haricot beans and mixed meats, usually sausage and ham, though duck
or goose can be added. It is essentially a winter dish.

The finest cheese is *Roquefort*, a sheep's milk cheese from the Causses. *Bleu
des Causses* is another good blue cheese made with cow's milk. *Pelardons de
chèvre* are round pats of goat's cheese from the Cévennes.

Wines are many and plentiful: Côtes-du-Rhône; Costières de Nîmes;
Côteaux de Languedoc; Corbières; Minervois; Fitou; La Clape; Blanquette de
Limoux. As an *apéritif, pastis* is popular, and the region produces excellent
muscat dessert wines: Lunel, Rivesaltes, Frontignan and St Jean-de-Minervois.

tiful stained glass and statues in the choir (Simon de Montfort is buried here). There are fine views over the new town and the Midi Valley from the ramparts.

The Carcassone lower town, a busy commercial town and departmental capital, is laid out in a grid pattern below the splendid silhouette of La Cité. It is a good base for exploring the area, with the Montagne Noire to the north (heavily-forested on the northern side, arid on the southern), and the upper Aude Valley and gorges to the south. The small town of **Limoux**, 24km (15 miles) south, produces France's oldest, and second most popular, sparkling white wine called Blanquette de Limoux. Some people prefer it to champagne!

Additional Information

Places of Interest

Ardèche Gorges
Grotte de la Madeleine
Open: daily April to October 9.30am-12noon and 2-6.30pm.

Orgnac
Aven d'Orgnac
1 hour guided tours daily.

Bagnols-sur-Cèze
Modern Art Museum
Open: 10am-12noon and 2-5.30pm, except Tuesday.

Nîmes
Roman Monuments — Arena; Maison Carrée; Magna Tower etc
Comprehensive ticket: 9am-12noon and 2-5pm or 7pm according to season.

Museums of Archaeology and Old Nîmes
Open: 10am-12noon and 2-5pm October to Palm Sunday; 3-7pm in summer; closed Sunday mornings.

Aigues-Mortes
Constance Tower and Ramparts
Open: 9am-12noon and 2-6pm April to September; 10am-12noon and 2-5pm October to March.

Sommières
Château de Villevieille
Open: July to 15 September 2-7.30pm; Sunday off-season.

Anduze
Musée du Désert — Protestant Museum
Open: March to November 9.30am-12noon and 2.30-6pm.

Bambuseraie de Prafrance
Open: March to November 9am-12noon and 2-7pm; July to August 9am-7pm.

Grottes de Trabuc
Open: June to September 9.30am-6pm; 15 March to 15 October 10.30am-12.30pm/ 2.30-5.30pm; closed October to March.

Montpellier
Fabre Museum
Open: 9am-12noon and 2-5pm or 5.30pm daily, except Monday.

Béziers
Museum of the Old Bitterois and Wine
Open: 9am-12noon and 2-6pm, except Monday.

Narbonne
Archbishop's Palace
Containing *Archaeological Museum, Fine Arts Museum and Apartments*
Open: 10-11.50am and 2-5.15pm or 6pm; except Monday off season.

Fontfroide
Abbey
Visits daily, closed Tuesday October to March.

Lèzignan-Corbières
Vine and Wine Museum
Visits and tastings daily.

Lagrasse
Abbey
Visits daily except Sunday mornings
and religious holidays.

Minerve
Cathar Memorial Museum
Daily visits.

Carcassonne
La Cité
Guided tour daily except national
holidays; night visits 9.30pm July to
September.

Fine Arts Museum
Open: 10am-12noon and 2-6pm except
Sunday and national holidays.

Tourist Information Centres

Anduze
Syndicat d'Initiative
Plan de Brie
☎ 66 61 98 17

Carcassonne
Office de Tourisme and Accueil de
    France
15 Boulevard Camille-Pelletan
☎ 68 25 07 04

Montpellier
Office de Tourisme
78 Avenue Pirée
☎ 67 22 06 16

Narbonne
Office de Tourisme
Place R. Salengro
☎ 68 65 15 60

Nîmes
Office de Tourisme and Accueil de France
6 Rue Auguste
☎ 66 67 29 11

Restaurants

R = With Accommodation
Haute-cuisine restaurants include:
Béziers
Le Framboisier
☎ 67 49 90 00

Carcassonne
4km (2 miles) north-east
Château St Martin 'Trencavel'
☎ 68 71 09 53

3km (2 miles) south
Domaine d'Auriac (R)
☎ 68 25 72 22

Florensac
Léonce (R)
☎ 67 77 03 05

Montpellier
Le Chandelier
☎ 67 92 61 62

Jardin des Sens
☎ 67 79 63 38

Nîmes
Garons (9km, 6 miles) south-east
Alexandre
☎ 66 70 08 99

St Côme (15km, 9 miles) west
La Vaunage
☎ 66 81 33 29

Port-Camargue
Near Le Grau-du-Roi
Le Spinaker (R)
☎ 66 53 36 37

Roquefort-sur-Soulzon
Grand Hôtel (R)
☎ 65 59 90 20

Other restaurants, offering good value
for money, include:
Bagnols-sur-Cèze
La Coupole (R)
☎ 66 89 61 06

Laville (R)
☎ 66 89 61 32

Carcassonne
Le Languedoc
☎ 68 25 22 17

Fitou
Cave d'Agnès
☎ 68 45 75 91

Issirac
Near Pont-St-Ésprit
Le Vieux Fusil
☎ 66 82 19 09

Lézignan-Corbières
Le Tassigny et Rest. Tournedos (R)
☎ 68 27 11 51

Limoux
Relais Touristique de Belvèze
☎ 68 69 08 78

Montpellier
Le Ménestrel
☎ 67 60 62 51

Orgnac-l'Aven
Les Stalagmites (R)
☎ 75 38 60 67

St Jean-du-Bruel
Midi-Papillon (R)
☎ 65 62 26 04

St Jean-du-Gard
L'Oronge (R)
☎ 66 85 30 34

Aub. du Péras
☎ 66 85 35 94

Tavel
Auberge de Tavel (R)
☎ 66 50 03 41

9

AQUITAINE

The name Aquitaine has a romantic ring. It suggests water, perhaps the sea, a magic land beyond the Ocean. It certainly sounds more glamorous than 'south-west France', which is where it is. The name has been used for this area of France since Roman times, but was given legitimacy in AD778, when Charlemagne officially created the Kingdom of Aquitaine. Since then the name, and the region, have had mixed fortunes.

It is difficult to say where Aquitaine is as the region has had shifting borders over the ages. It is certain that its western edge is the Atlantic Ocean, in the south-east corner of the Bay of Biscay and its southern border is the Spanish frontier — unless you exclude the Basque country and the Pyrénées, as some guides do. The northern border is less distinct, but seems to lie around the Gironde estuary and the upper Dordogne and Garonne rivers. But its eastern edge? This has been variously defined throughout history, when warring factions fought for its possession.

The Romans colonised Aquitaine and made it a prosperous and cultured state. During the barbarian invasions, the Visigoths established their empire here, but their leader, Alaric, surrendered it to the Franks in the sixth century. At about this time, uncolonised Basques or 'Vascons' from the Pyrénées invaded the plain, ravaged it, and established their own colony of Gascony. After its reconquest, Charlemagne gave Aquitaine to his son Louis as his kingdom, but it later fell back into anarchy. In 1152, Eleanor, only daughter of Duke William of Aquitaine and divorced wife of the French king, married Henry Plantagenet, soon to become King of England, and brought the province with her as her dowry. It then remained an English possession for 300 years.

English connections with Aquitaine have existed since then, particularly in the area round Bordeaux and in the Bordeaux wine-trade. English influence is also seen further south, at Pau and Biarritz, and many of the *bastide* towns were founded by the English during the Hundred Years War. Certain freedoms given to the citizens then survive today, and perhaps help to explain the general pro-British attitude to be found in the region.

The main feature of the region, and its chief delight to the visitor, is its variety of landscape, people and culture. It comprises five very different areas. The Bordelais, in the north, is the vine-growing slopes and plains round Bordeaux, producing some of the world's finest and best-known wines. The Landes, just south of here, are the flat, sandy pine forests lying behind the high dunes of the straight Atlantic coastline. Sparsely populated by Gascon 'cowboys', they form the biggest continuous forest in Europe. Inland from here is the Gascon heartland, rolling farmland studded with *bastide* towns that produces the rich fare for which the south-west is famed, including *foie gras* and Armagnac brandy. In the south are the Pyrénées, wild, green and majestic mountains three times higher and wetter than Wales; and the Basque country, a delightful region of mountain and coast with its own language, culture and traditions.

The tour starts at Bordeaux, and after a preliminary detour into the Médoc and Côte d'Argent, takes an inland route through the Garonne Valley, Grandes Landes, Gers, Hautes-Pyrénées and Pyrénées-Atlantiques, ending on the Basque coast at the Spanish border.

Bordeaux and The Médoc

Bordeaux, the capital of Aquitaine and centre of the greatest wine-producing and exporting area in the world, is a good starting point. It has many fine buildings, mainly dating from the eighteenth century when it was the most prosperous French town outside Paris owing to its unique position as a tidal river port. Its main commerce was in wine, chiefly with the British who had dominated the trade since the Middle Ages, both as consumers and producer-traders. The British even had their own name for the red wine, claret, derived from an old French word *clairet*; British names like Talbot, Palmer and Barton appear frequently on labels and English is widely spoken among dealers. This long-time prosperity gives Bordeaux a rather bourgeois appearance, elegant yet formal, with a heavy uniformity of style in its buildings. The crescent of quays fronting the river is an impressive sight, leading to its nickname and symbol, 'Port de la Lune'.

 Bordeaux's centre is a grid of old streets with the Grand Théâtre and Bourse (Stock Exchange) at one end and the cathedral and Fine Arts Museum at the other. These are now a restored pedestrian area, with fine shops, restaurants and bars and an active night-life. At the edge of the old town are two monuments dear to the Bordelais: the Porte Cailhau (Gascon dialect for *cailloux*, or stones), a medieval gateway cum triumphal arch near the spot on the quay where stone ballast was unloaded and the Grosse Cloche, a fifteenth-century belfry erected over an ancient gate. A more modern monument which dominates the town is the Girondins monument, near the quay on the north side — a 50m (164ft) high column topped by a statue of liberty, erected in 1895 to the Bordeaux deputies who were executed during the Revolution in 1792 as members of the Girondin (federalist) party. The eighteenth-century houses are shown to best effect along the quays and around the magnificent Place de la Bourse, flanked by the Stock Exchange and the Customs House. Nearby is another splendid square with fine houses, the Place de la Comédie, in front of one of Bordeaux's finest buildings, the Grand Théâtre. This was built in the 1770s to provide entertainment for the bourgeoisie. Its sumptuous decor is said to have given inspiration to Garnier when building the Paris Opera.

The Cathedral of St André is a fine Gothic building with two tall spires, a separate bell-tower, and superb statuary on the exterior doorways. The town hall and the Musée des Beaux-Arts behind it are both housed in the old Archbishop's Palace. The latter has a splendid collection of painting and sculpture from the fifteenth century onwards, including Titian, Van Dyck and Goya. Other museums include: the Museum of Decorative Arts (life in Bordeaux from the Middle Ages to the eighteenth century); the Natural History Museum; the Contemporary Art Museum; the Jean Moulin Centre (Museum of the Resistance); and the Museum of Old Bordeaux (in the Cailhau Gate). There are plenty of good restaurants and small hotels in the town, and an excellent wine shop, the Vinothèque.

The **Médoc** is the wine region to the north of Bordeaux on the west bank of the Gironde estuary. This is the home of the great Premiers Crus whose names are so familiar to wine-lovers, and of the grand châteaux that embellish their estates. The land is ideal for producing great wine: slightly ridged into narrow valleys, it gives a variety of growing conditions; the light has a special quality and the stony soil retains the heat. The famous vineyards tend to be near the estuary (they say 'the wine is best when the grape can see the water'), so they are all on or near the D2 coast road. However, a word of warning: you need to arrange in advance to visit a château in the Médoc — you may get in at the gate, but it is unlikely (you can see most of the châteaux from the road, but that is hardly the same as a visit). Do not expect much of a tasting — this wine is too valuable to give away! Moreover, the land which is so good for producing wine is less good to look at. Mostly it is flat and dreary, and only the châteaux and the vines that surround them are worth a visit.

Leave Bordeaux by the N215 and bear right onto the D2 just after crossing the motorway. The wine châteaux you can visit, along with other sights, are, in order: **Château Siran**, at Labarde; **Château-Margaux**, a *premier grand cru classé*, one of the great wines of France (cellars only); **Château Lamarque**, a curious lighthouse-shaped bell-tower in the village; **Fort-Médoc**, one of Vauban's defensive forts guarding Bordeaux — a lovely carved gate, good view of the Gironde; **Château Lanessan**, with a museum of horses and horse-transport; **Château de Beychevelle**, prettily ornamented with carved foliage; **St Julien**, famous wines, with châteaux Lagrange, Léoville, Beaucaillou and Talbot; **Pauillac**, centre of the Médoc wine trade, river port (nearby oil refinery), a good Maison de Vin in the village, the oldest co-operative in the Médoc — nearby is **Château-Latour**; **Château Mouton-Rothschild**, famous wine, a *premier cru classé* since 1973, wine cellars, a good museum in superb ancient cellars; **Château-Lafitte**, the most famous *premier grand cru classé* of the Médoc, wine cellars with rare old bottles; **Manoir Cos d'Estournel**, a strange

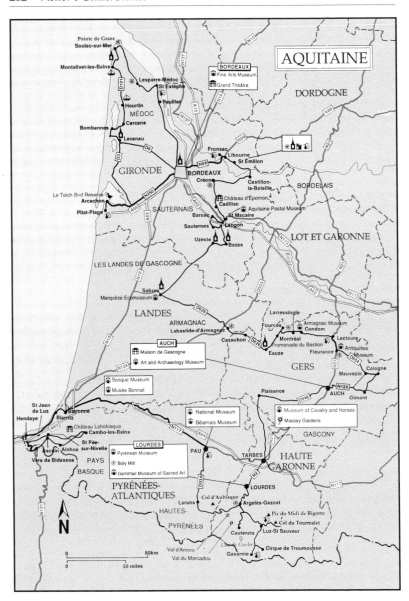

oriental pagoda; **St Estèphe**, market town, famous wines, good views from the old quay with quaint fishermen's huts; **St Seurin-de-Cadourne**, the northern end of the Haut-Médoc appellation.

Inland from St Estèphe, **Vertheuil**, dominated by its ruined castle, has an eleventh-century Romanesque church with a fine doorway surrounded by quaint sculpted figures. **Lesparre-Médoc**, at the end of the D2, has preserved the handsome square keep of its fourteenth-century castle. From here take the N215 north to Le Verdon-sur-Mer, a deepwater port for tankers, and further on to the **Pointe de Grave,** where the ferry crosses the mouth of the Gironde to Royan and the Charente. There is a memorial to the American troops who landed here in 1917, and a lighthouse with a Museum of the Cordouan Lighthouse inside (the Cordouan light is 9km [6 miles] out to sea). Return to **Soulac-sur-Mer,** a family holiday resort with a safe beach and a fine Romanesque church, the Notre-Dame-de-la-fin-des-Terres, which was swallowed up by the dunes in 1757 and only unearthed a century later. Inside are beautiful figured capitals and a polychrome statue of the Virgin. Continue south on the D101 through the dunes and pine forests of the Landes Girondines. There is no coastal road, except for a short stretch at Montalivet: the whole coast from Soulac to Arcachon is one endless straight stretch of white sand backed by dunes, and the beach resorts, most of them new, are reached only by access roads. This is an area for family beach holidays rather than for touring, and many of the new resorts offer a variety of accommodation. **Montalivet-les-Bains** has excellent swimming, and the first naturist beach in France, opened in 1950.

Continue south on the D101 to **Hourtin,** near the eastern edge of the immense Lac d'Hourtin-Carcans. This is a typical Landes lake, with marshes and reed-beds on the inland side and high dunes and pines on the seaward (the dunes are as much as 60m, 197ft, high in places). Hourtin has facilities for sailing and canoeing, with a new beach resort at Hourtin-Plage 9km (6 miles) away across the marsh and dunes. Continue south to Carcans, and turn right to **Maubuisso,** an attractive settlement of fine villas at the southern end of the lake. North from here a dead-end road leads to a pleasant open-air centre at **Bombannes,** with a range of facilities including a swimming-pool, tennis courts, a gymnasium, sailing club and archery range. Nearby, in a wooden lodge, is a Landes Forest Folk Museum. Towards Carcans-Plage, turn left and follow the D6E through the coastal pine forest (the GR8 footpath follows a route along the top of the high dunes) to **Lacanau-Océan,** the largest bathing resort of the Médoc Atlantique. Turn inland on the D6 to **Le Moutchic,** a charming resort at the head of Lac de Lacanau that has become a centre for wind-surfing. The lake, though smaller than Hourtin-Carcans (8km by 3km, 5 miles by 2 miles), is more developed, and is a paradise for water-sports enthusiasts and fishermen. On the eastern side of the lake is the market town of **Lacanau,** in the heart of the Landes pine forest, with a beautiful eighteenth-century church and little port on the lake.

To the south the D3 leads through the sand-beset village of Le Porge to the **Bassin D'Arcachon,** a vast lagoon famous for its oyster farms (good cheap oysters at roadside stalls). It is best explored by boat, as its shoreline is heavily built up and the basin is almost completely emptied twice a day by the tide. Bathing from any of the surrounding resorts is unpleasantly muddy. **Arcachon** is a large resort, smart and animated, with the highest dune in Europe nearby at **Pilat-Plage** (114m, 374ft high — wonderful views from the top). The Le Teich Bird Reserve is worth visiting, with guided tours and good explanatory material, but it is extensive, with long walks, and you need binoculars. The D6 from Lacanau, the N250 or A63 motorway from Arcachon lead back through the vast Landes forest to Bordeaux. En route you can stop at forest clearings for wine-tasting.

The Bordelais

Back in Bordeaux, take the fast N89 to **Libourne**, a former English *bastide* town which owes its name to its thirteenth-century founder, the English knight Sir Roger de Leyburn. Its old ramparts have now been replaced by shady promenades (only the towers by the Grand Port remain) and it has a pleasant town centre with large and charming arcaded market square. Libourne is a river port on the Dordogne and the commercial centre for the second most famous wine region of the Bordelais after the Médoc. This area makes exclusively red wines, using mainly the softer Merlot grape rather than the more tannic Cabernet-Sauvignon which predominates in other Bordeaux reds. Its districts include, from west to east, Canon Fronsac, Fronsac, Pomerol, Lalande-de-Pomerol and St Émilion. Libourne has some good hotels and restaurants, and is a good base for touring the area and wine-tasting.

Just outside the town is the village of **Pomerol**, whose superb red wines reach their peak of perfection with Château Pétrus, possibly the best, and probably the dearest, wine in the world. The production at Pomerol is tiny and the wine expensive; you will find it more affordable at **Fronsac**, where the quality is good and the tastings generous. Fronsac has a ruined hill-fort with fine views over the Dordogne Valley, and there are interesting Romanesque churches in the area at Marcenais, Mouillac and Lalande-de-Fronsac. The most attractive town in the area, in a beautiful setting on the side of a steep hill, is **St Émilion**, one of the gems of France. Still largely enclosed within its medieval ramparts, St Émilion has a harmonious blend of golden-limestone, rose-tiled buildings, narrow, steep cobbled streets leading up to a picturesque market square, an underground church carved out of solid rock, a ruined convent, monastery and castle, and a network of subterranean galleries with catacombs and a charnel-house. The horseshoe-shaped site, a natural amphitheatre, was occupied in Gallo-Roman times and praised by the poet Ausonius (the Château Ausone vineyard is supposed to be built on the site of his villa); but the town is named after a Breton holy man, who founded a monastery here in the eighth century. It is a lovely place to visit, with many interesting sights (including a splendid view from the top of the castle tower); but it is popular with tourists and prices can be high in shops and restaurants.

St Émilion's wines have been renowned since the Middle Ages, when the English King John founded a *Jurade* (municipal council) to control and classify their quality. Today there are about a thousand mainly small producers, most of them quite close to the town, and many of them welcome visitors. There is also an excellent co-operative which sells a huge range of vintage wines, and a wine museum to explain them. The wines are appealingly deep-coloured, rich, fruity and light on tannin, but they do vary greatly in quality according to their grading, so it is not always wise to buy the cheapest. Outlying villages are allowed to combine their village name with that of the town and these can often be good value. Good St Émilion can be bought *en vrac*.

Nearby, on a bluff over the Dordogne, is **Castillon-la-Bataille**, named after the famous battle of 1453 which ended the Hundred Years' War and the British occupation of Aquitaine. There is a memorial to Earl Talbot, the English general who was killed in the battle (his name survives today in the fine Haut-Médoc wine), and the battle is re-enacted every year in August. The local Côtes de Castillon wine is a Bordeaux *supérieur*. The great philosopher Montaigne lived 9km (6 miles) east of here after his retirement in 1570, at **St Michel-de-Montaigne** in the Dordogne region. The library tower where he wrote his famous *Essays* is open for visits.

Leave St Émilion by the D122, crossing the Dordogne at Branne. The wedge of land between the Dordogne and Garonne rivers is known as **Entre-Deux-Mers**, known for its crisp, dry white wines (an excellent accompaniment to Arcachon oysters). This is a gentle land of meadows, orchards, vineyards and tobacco or maize fields, criss-crossed by mill-streams, and of small *bastide* towns (Créon, Sauveterre-de-Guyenne, Cadillac) and Romanesque churches (Blasimon, Haux, Castelvieil). From Branne, take the D936, the D11 and the D239 to **La Sauve**, with the imposing ruins of a Benedictine abbey and a fine parish church, and the D671 to **Créon**, whose *bastide* has a pretty arcaded square. This would be a good base for a longer tour of the Entre-Deux-Mers. Take the D13 south to **Cadillac**, a historic town on a hillside above the Garonne. This *bastide* village has a beautiful gateway, an arcaded square and an imposing seventeenth-century château of the Dukes of Épernon. The nearby chapel has a splendid mausoleum containing their tombs. Cadillac is known for its sweet white wines (you can taste them at the Maison de Vin in the château), and has given its name to the American motor-car.

Take the D10 south-east along the Garonne Valley to **Loupiac**, the site of a Roman villa thought to have been the home of the poet Ausonius, who sang the praises of the local wines. The next village, **Ste Croix-du-Mont,** is perched on a hill surrounded with vineyards, with fine views of the valley and the Sauternais beyond from the picturesque church terrace. The cliffs below are formed from fossilised oyster-shells, which you can see lining their once-inhabited caves. **Verdelais** cemetery contains the grave of the painter Toulouse-Lautrec, who died in a nearby château while **St Macaire** has an interesting Aquitaine Postal Museum, housed in a lovely old arcaded house. This attractive, well-preserved medieval town, on a limestone rock overlooking the river, has three fine fortified gateways, a web of narrow streets and a charming long fifteenth-century arcaded market square.

Cross the river here on the N113 to Langon, an important centre for Côtes de Bordeaux wines, and take the D8 to **Fargues**, one of the five towns of the **Sauternes** appellation. This small, rather unprepossessing area on the west bank of the Garonne is the home of the world's greatest and best-known sweet white wine, named after another of its five villages — the other three are **Barsac**, **Preignac** and **Bommes**. This luscious, honeyed wine is made by a special process, which leaves the grapes on the vine until they have been attacked by a tiny fungus that gives them the *pourriture noble*, or 'noble rot', thus causing a concentration of sugar in the wizened fruit and giving the wine a unique flavour. The signposted 'Sauternais Tour' takes a winding route through the vine-covered hillsides, dotted with famous wine châteaux, the most famous of which is **Château d'Yquem**, home of the fabulously expensive wine which requires one vine to make one glass per year! You can visit the estate and inner courtyard free (no tastings, but a good view of the area from the battlements). The most beautiful is the Château de Malle, a seventeenth-century Classical building with lovely gardens, paintings and furniture. This and other châteaux offer free tastings, and there is a good Maison de Vin at the largest of the villages, **Barsac**, where you can buy and taste half bottles of the delicious demi-sec, Sauternes-Barsac, produced by the local co-operative.

Gascony

North-east of the Sauternais is the other famous Bordelais wine region, the **Graves**, which produces excellent red and dry white wines. To the south and west is the vast, sparsely-populated region of the **Landes**, the flat, sandy forest area that stretches 120km (74 miles) inland from the coast. This is not natural forest: most of it was planted in the nineteenth century, and it needs constant protection to prevent it returning to marshy dune and scrubland. It is populated by 'pioneer' farmers and ranchers, living in small rural communities in isolated clearings in the forest, their houses low, ranch-style buildings of painted wood and patterned brick. They grow tobacco and maize, keep ducks

Medieval cobbled streets and ramparts of St Émilion make an enticing photo-call

and geese, and burn timber for charcoal. The people are Gascons of Basque origin, though they speak a Languedoc patois rather than Basque, and they are keen riders and sportsmen, playing rugby and pelota and following the bullfight and *Course Landaise,* or bull-run. As in the Languedoc, they do not kill the bull, but show their bravery by plucking rosettes from its horns as it charges by. The capital and administrative centre of the region is Mont-de-Marsan, in the south, where they have a colourful Fête de la Madeleine in mid-July, with bullfights and Spanish-style *Corridas* (bull-runs or processions).

Take the D222 south from Langon to the **Château de Roquetaillade**, a restored medieval castle with a fine 35m (115ft) high square keep. South-west on the D932 is **Bazas**, a handsome town at the northern edge of the forest, with its beautiful thirteenth-century Gothic cathedral of St Jean (splendid nave and façade) looking out over a wide cobbled square flanked by old arcaded houses. The town has old ramparts and a gateway with two fifteenth-century towers. Nearby **Uzeste** (10km, 6 miles, west on the D110) has another large, impressive Gothic church. From here, your route takes you into the heart of the **Parc Régional des Landes de Gascogne**, first on the D222 to Préchac, then on the D9 and D4 to **Luxey**, with its former processing plant for resin products (open to the public), and on the D315 to **Sabres**, which has a church with a lovely Renaissance doorway and arcaded bell tower. From here you can find out about traditional life in the Landes by visiting the **Marquèze Ecomuseum** on a small special train (the only way to get there). In a clearing in the forest is a reconstructed nineteenth-century village, with beautiful traditionally-furnished old farmhouses, barns, chicken-houses, watermill, beehives, sheep and horses, illustrating the past economy of the Landes communities.

Rejoin your car at Sabres, leave on the N134 and in 2km (1 mile) bear left onto the long, straight D626 through the southern Landes, via **Roquefort**, a small fortified town, to Labastide d'Armagnac. You are now leaving the Landes and entering the region that produces France's 'other' brandy, Armagnac. This is part of the ancient province of Gascony, peopled by those warlike descendants of the Basques who conquered and colonised the area in the Dark Ages. They lost their original language and now speak French with a strong accent and a Languedoc patois, which they are trying to revive (many road signs and place-names are displayed in the two languages). It is debatable whether Gascony belongs spiritually to Aquitaine or the Midi, but today the people tend to look towards Toulouse rather than Bordeaux as their regional centre, and the main Gascon department of the Gers is not in Aquitaine but in the Midi-Pyrénées region. Gascons have kept their warlike reputation through the ages, often fighting as mercenaries, and their proud symbol is that fiery little warrior, the half-fictional D'Artagnan.

This charming corner of France is still not widely known to visitors, but those who discover it find an attractive countryside of green, fertile plains, low hills and wooded valleys, heavily cultivated with cereals, sunflowers, vines and fruit trees, and with many cows, ducks and geese. The people are friendly and hospitable, and proud of their rich produce and fine cuisine. Their most famous product, Armagnac brandy, is the oldest eau-de-vie in France, the Gascons having probably learnt the art of distilling wine from the Moors across the Spanish border. It is certainly older than its rival, Cognac, and was being distilled by monks in the twelfth century. Armagnac tends to be darker and smokier in taste than Cognac, with a distinct whiff of prunes. It is made by continuous distillation of the weak, acidic white wines of the region, and is aged in oak barrels, sometimes for many years. There are three Armagnac regions: **Bas-Armagnac**, in the west, produces the finest-quality brandies; the central region of **Ténarèze** tends to produce stronger-tasting, more fiery Armagnacs, often with a bouquet of violets; and the **Haut-Armagnac** in the east produces less and poorer-quality brandy used mainly for blending. There are still many small producers and traditional equipment, such as the old pot still, is still used alongside the more recent alembic still. A sweet aperitif called *Floc de Gascogne* is also made, with Armagnac and fresh grape juice.

One feature of the Gascony landscape is the *bastide* town or village. In the Middle Ages this was disputed border territory between lands held by the English and French, and fortified new towns were built by both sides to persuade their supporters to stay and defend the region. The race to build became intense: in 1200 Gascony had about 100 *bastides*, built mainly in the aftermath of the Albigensian débâcle; but in the period before and during the Hundred Years' War the arms race between English and French intensified and by the early fourteenth century there were about 1,000. They were normally square or rectangular in shape, and the pattern was identical except for differences in the terrain they were built on: a square block of buildings on a defensible site surrounded by ramparts, a grid of streets with a large central square containing a covered market and surrounded by arcaded houses. Each house had a small garden, and inhabitants were also given a piece of land just outside the town. Churches were often fortified, and sometimes incorporated within the walls. The new towns were sometimes given merely descriptive names, like Labastide or Sauveterre (redeemed land); others were made more enticing to prospective settlers by sponsorship from major cities throughout Christendom: Cologne; Fleurance (Florence); Valence (Valencia in Spain); while others reflect the name of title of the founder: Hastingues; Montréal (Mount-Royal).

Bastide towns were models of town planning in their day, and are often pleasant places to visit and explore. Sometimes they have become run-down, but many are being attractively restored, their central squares charmingly decked with flowers, their arcades sheltering pavement cafés or craft shops. Such a one is **Labastide d'Armagnac**, founded in 1291 by Bernard IV, Count of Armagnac. With its lovely central Place Royal, surrounded by old arcaded stone and wood-panelled houses embellished with colourful window-boxes, it is a good place to start a *bastides*-and-brandy tour of Gascony. Rejoin the D626 at Cazaubon, where there is a left turn for the small spa town of **Barbotan-les-Thermes**, a treatment centre for rheumatism, prettily set in a wooded valley near to the Uby reservoir (fishing, sailing, Courses Landaises, swimming, good camping, tennis). There are some good restaurants in the area. Continue to **Eauze**, a lively, attractive town with a picturesque main square flanked by its impressive southern Gothic cathedral, whose stones include some from the old Gallo-Roman city of *Elusa* which stood on this spot. In the arcaded square is a fine half-timbered house with wooden pillars, named after Jeanne D'Albret, the mother of Henri IV, who stayed here with Queen Margot in 1579. Eauze is the capital of the Bas-Armagnac, and the main commercial centre for its brandy. It is surrounded by top-quality Armagnac-producing houses, and is an ideal place for a visit and tasting (Marquis de Caussade; Societé des Produits d'Armagnac).

Take the D29 from Eauze to **Montréal**, a typical *bastide* town founded in 1255 and set handsomely on a promontory. Nearby is an important Gallo-Roman villa with mosaics at **Séviac**. North of Montréal on the D29 is **Fourcès**, an unusual *bastide* in that it is circular rather than square. Founded by the English in the thirteenth century on the base of an old stronghold, it is highly picturesque, its low timbered houses with red-tiled roofs and arcades surrounding a large square with a copse in the middle. Take the D114 and 278 to **Larressingle**, a ruined thirteenth-century fortified village with massive walls, a fortified gate, a dungeon, church and several restored houses (you can climb up the three-storey dungeon by a spiral staircase). It is a charming, peaceful little village, with local products for sale. Take the D15 into **Condom**, passing as you enter an excellent co-operative selling both Armagnac and local wines. Condom is the main town of northern Armagnac with a brisk trade in its brandy. It is a busy market town, with an attractive centre of old houses clustered round its abbey cathedral, a fine Flamboyant Gothic early sixteenth-century building with a lovely cloister, and a small Armagnac Museum in its bishop's palace. The large Armagnac distillery of Janneau in the town gives an interesting visit with tastings.

South of Condom on the D930 is **Valence**, another *bastide* town with an old church and arcaded square. Nearby is Flaran Abbey, with only its chapter, cloister and fine church remaining of the former Cistercian abbey. Tastings of Armagnac from the nearby production centre of Cassaigne are given during the tour. Take the D142 west from Valence to St Puy, then the D42 to **Lectoure**, an old walled town perched dramatically on a promontory over the River Gers, with wonderful views from its Promenade du Bastion of the Gers and the distant Pyrénées. It has an interesting Antiquities Museum with a collection of twenty, third-to fourth-century altars for ritual bull sacrifice found in the area, along with many other Roman remains. South on the N21 is **Fleurance**, one of the loveliest *bastide* towns in the Gers (founded 1280). It has a striking main square with a covered stone market in the centre, and an elegant southern Gothic church with beautiful stained glass windows. Fleurance is a clean, well-preserved town, decked with flowers in keeping with its name. From here take the D654 to **Mauvezin**, a graceful, quiet town with a lovely wide arcaded main square and an excellent restaurant, La Rapière. East of here is the charming, typical *bastide* village of **Cologne**, and the attractive lake of Thoux-St-Cricq with excellent boating and wind-surfing and good camping. This is the Haut-Armagnac, not a region for brandy-tasting but ideal for another Gascon delicacy, *foie gras*. Many farms in the area produce it and will gladly let you sample this and other products of the duck and goose (magrets, confits, hearts, gibiers, pâtés).

From Mauvezin, take the D12 south to **Gimont**, the *foie gras* capital of the Gers and another *bastide* town. This one has an unusual feature of the main road running through the centre of its covered market! Just outside the town is the ruined Gimont Abbey, and nearby an excellent restaurant at the Château de Larroque. From here the fast N124 runs west to the capital of Gascony, **Auch**, proudly set on a hill over the Gers. This large but dignified town is the essence of Gascony — as you climb the monumental staircase to the central square, you are overlooked by a large statue of D'Artagnan and in the main square you are confronted on one side by the superb large pale-yellow cathedral, on the other by one of the best restaurants in France, André Daguin's Hôtel de France. The cathedral is late Gothic, with an impressive Classical façade and fine wrought iron gates, and inside magnificent carved choir stalls and beautiful stained glass. The pedestrianised old town has many fine buildings (one housing the Tourist Office), and many shops selling local products. But to sample the fine things of Gascony, you must visit the Maison de Gascogne (open daily), housed in a large modern ranch-style building. Here you can spend an afternoon tasting 100-year-old Armagnac, local wines like Jurançon, Madiran and Côtes de Gascogne, the local Kir Gascogne (made with *mûr*, or blackcurrant liqueur, rather than the Burgundian *cassis*), *floc*, *foie gras*, pâtés, fruits in brandy, and many other delicacies. You will be greeted at the door by a D'Artagnan lookalike, and treated with warmth and enthusiasm throughout your visit.

The High Pyrénées

Leave Auch by the N124 going west, and in 5km (3 miles) turn left onto the D943 to follow the scenic **Route des Bastides et Castelnaux**. This runs over hills and across river valleys, passing through a number of pretty *bastide* towns — Barran, Montesquiou, Bassoues, Beaumarchés — to **Plaisance**, an aptly-named *bastide* town slumbering quietly in the Bas-Armagnac plain. You will eat superbly here at the fine Ripa Alta restaurant. North of here is **Castelmore**, supposed birthplace of Dumas' eponymous hero (D'Artagnan), and **Termes d'Armagnac**, with a tall keep giving a fine view of the area. Turn south from Plaisance on the D14 to Maubourguet, then on the D935 to **Tarbes**. As you approach, you will see the Pyrénées rearing up to meet you, and their full height and power are felt as you reach the town. Tarbes is busy both with industry and agriculture and has little to interest the visitor except the attractive Massey Garden, which contains some medieval remains. The town is the home of the National Stud, and there is a Museum of Cavalry and Horses in an Italianate villa. Leave the town on the N21 to **Lourdes**, a stronghold of the county of Bigorre on the Gave de Pau (*gave* is a Pyrénean word for river). Its

Château of the Counts of Bigorre dominates the town and, though restored, is impressive, with an interesting Pyrénean Museum.

But this is not why Lourdes is world-famous and why people flock to it in their millions. Until 1858 it was a quiet hamlet; then an ailing, uneducated peasant girl called Bernadette Soubirou claimed to have had eighteen visions of the Virgin and discovered a miraculous spring in the Massabielle Cave. The devout, the sick and the simply curious visit, turning it into a strange mixture of holy shrine and commercial phenomenon. It is a tremendous enterprise, with hotels, campsites, an underground basilica, two huge above-ground basilicas, one on top of the other (the lower is neo-Romanesque, the upper neo-Gothic), a splendid esplanade, baths for immersion, a megavision slide show, a large hospital, and many administrative buildings. It is well organised, with enough space to avoid the feeling of oppression that large crowds can create. Though the religious supermarkets in the town, with their plastic bottles of holy water and cheap statues, are a matter of taste, there is no denying the atmosphere of hope and cameraderie that the place engenders. Though the underground basilica resembles a huge car-park, the two main churches are impressive, and the Massabielle Cave is a popular attraction. There is a fine view from the calvary, several museums in the town and Bernadette's birth- ✳ place, the Boly Mill.

The valley south of Lourdes leads into the **Parc National des Pyrénées**, the

The majestic granite cliffs of the Pyrénées

highest and wildest part of the whole mountain range. There are a number of valleys reaching deep into the range, but no way through into Spain at this point — all the valleys end at the blank wall of the huge *cirques* whose crests line the border, the greatest and best-known of which is the **Cirque de Gavarnie**. It is an area of incredible natural beauty, severe and awe-inspiring in places, but some of the mountain roads are not for the faint-hearted driver: they are narrow, twisting and precipitous on their outer edges, and French drivers tend to take them too fast, and are reluctant to give way (there are a number of deaths from cars going over the edge each year). South of Lourdes is **Argelès-Gazost**, a pleasant spa town and holiday resort in an open, green valley, with plenty of hotel accommodation and good camping at Arcizans-Avant and Arras-en-Lavedan.

Argelès-Gazost would make a good base for exploring the area. It has an attractive old centre in the upper town, with a superb view from the orientation table on a terrace in the main square. With its position at the junction where the rivers Cauterets and Gavarnie combine to form the Haut Gave de Pau, it is an ideal starting point for any of the many excursions that can be made into the surrounding valleys. South of the town is the pretty village of **St Savin**, with an impressive fortified early Romanesque church, and nearby **Arcizans-Avant** has a splendid twelfth-century château dominating the valley. On the other side of the river, **Beaucens** has a ruined medieval château housing a falconry museum, the Donjon les Aigles. A 20km (12 mile) drive on the Hautacam mountain road gives superb views over the valley from the top.

Drive south to **Pierrefitte-Nestalas**, a village with some attractive old houses at the entrance to the Luz and Cauterets gorges; take the left fork on the D921 through the spectacular Gorge de Luz to **Luz St Sauveur**. This lively little spa resort, set in a beautiful, isolated high mountain valley, has an attractive old sector of neat whitewashed houses with wrought-iron balconies and slate roofs, and a quaint late twelfth-century Romanesque church, fortified by the Knights Hospitaller, with a fourteenth-century-crenellated surrounding wall and a fine carved doorway. Luz was for centuries the capital of a self-governing mountain canton, the Pays-Toy, which maintained its independent links with Spanish mountain valley communes. There is a nearby winter sports centre at Luz-Ardiden. From here you can follow the **Route du Tourmalet**, a spectacular drive eastwards on the D918 (one of the Tour de France's most arduous sections). You pass through the spa village of **Barèges** (treatment of bone diseases), now a winter sports resort with a cable car to the Lienz plateau, a funicular to the Pic d'Aire (2,418m, 7,931ft) and some good mountain walks. Climb to the bare and desolate **Col du Tourmalet**, one of the highest (and hairiest) passes in the Pyrénées (2,115m, 6,937ft), from where you get a superb panorama of high peaks and glaciers. The GR10 footpath leads from here to the Massif de Néouvielle. From the pass you can follow a toll road (open June to October) to the Pic du Midi de Bigorre (the last 200m, 656ft, by cable-car), which gives one of the most incredible views in the Pyrénées, over the Gascony plain and the high mountain peaks (2,865m, 9,397ft). The Observatory and Geophysical Institute can be visited.

From here you can make a round trip via the Col d'Aspin, Arreau, Bagnères-di-Bigorre and Lourdes, or retrace your steps to Luz St Sauveur. The latter will give access to the two *cirques* of Gavarnie and Troumousse. From Luz, take the D921 south over the 65m (213ft) high Napoleon bridge into the **Gorge de St Sauveur**. Pass the largest HEP station in the Pyrénées at Pragnères, and fork right at Gèdres, passing through the Chaos de Coumély, a wilderness of rocks that George Sand called 'hell'. At the village of **Gavarnie** (tombs and statues of famous Pyrénéistes in the cemetery), leave your car and walk, or hire a horse or donkey, for the last 5km (3 miles) to the foot of the *cirque*, for probably the most spectacular, and certainly the most famous, view in the Pyrénées. This natural amphitheatre, 10km (6 miles) in circumference, 1,500m (4,920ft) high, is a breathtaking sight which becomes ever more awe-inspiring as you approach its base. Waterfalls crash down from the snows above over the sheer granite faces of the majestic cliffs (one drops over 420m (1,378ft) without touching rock), and the contrast of the surrounding pine-wooded hills with the huge bleak wall of rock is ravishing. You will not be alone, however as hordes of refugees from Lourdes make the trip but you can avoid most of the crowds by taking a superb high-level track starting behind the hotel.

The whole area is a vast botanical garden containing more than 400 species of Pyrénean plants. A good road from the village leads up the side of the *cirque* to the Spanish border at the Port de Gavarnie or Boucharo Pass, though there is no road through into Spain. This road, giving lovely views, especially from the Pic de Tantes, a short steep climb from the road, was once a pilgrim route to Santiago de Compostela. Return to Gavarnie and back through the *chaos* to Gèdre, then turn right into the Gave de Héas, to visit the other natural amphitheatre, the **Cirque de Troumousse**. This is accessible by car right to the foot (toll road from Notre-Dame de Héas), and much less crowded than Gavarnie. The sight is almost as spectacular, too, with some lovely walks for the more energetic.

Return via Luz to Pierrefitte-Nestalas for an excursion to the Cauterets Valley. The D920 leads through a narrow gorge to **Cauterets**, one of the busiest and best-known spas and ski resorts in the Pyrénées. It is a lively, modern resort appealing to the younger age group, and hectic in winter. Beyond the town, just past the thermal baths, is the beautiful Cascade de Lutour, a waterfall in a rocky, pine-clad valley. Further on at Pont d'Espagne (another lovely waterfall), the road ends, and you have a choice of footpath. The gentler but longer walk takes you into the charming Marcadou Valley, with its picturesque variety of scenery, leading to the Wallon refuge (1,866m, 6,120ft). The steeper walk, which can be alleviated by a spectacular chair-lift, takes you to the delightful Lac de Gaube, a mountain lake shimmering beneath the high, glaciated Vignemale (3,298m, 10,817ft). The GR10 leads beyond the lake to more spectacular, but difficult, mountain walks.

Return to Argelès-Gazost and turn left on the D918 into the Azun Valley (this route can be avoided by returning to Lourdes and Pau via the D937). At

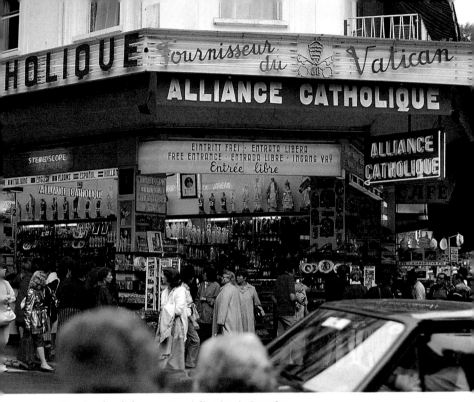

Tourism has led to commercialization in Lourdes

The Lac de Gaube, seated at the bottom of Vignemale mountain

Arras-en-Lavedan, whose walled thirteenth-century château Castelnau d'Azun has a ruined keep, the D103 side-road leads down the wild, glacial Labar-de-Bun valley to a moraine lake, the Lac d'Estaing, with the surrounding wooded slopes reflected romantically in its waters. The GR10 continues from here into the National Park, where the izard (Pyrenean mountain goat) still roams free. Continue along the Azun Valley to **Arrens**, a holiday centre and gateway to the National Park via the **Val d'Arrens**. This wild valley is green and picturesque in its lower section, savage and bare beyond the Tech dam. Return to Arrens (church with fifteenth-century crenellated wall) to start your climb over the **Col de l'Aubisque**, a spectacular run along a corniche road with a sheer drop on one side. Cyclists may be seen toiling up the hairpin bends in training for the Tour de France, which passes along here. From the high col (1,710m, 5,609ft) there are superb views over the mountains of the Béarn, which you have just entered. Descend past the ski resorts of Gourette and Eaux-Bonnes to **Laruns**, a busy market village in the scenic and spectacular Vallée d'Ossau. The D934 left leads to the Col du Portalet and into Spain; turn right and descend the valley to Pau.

Pau, a large, handsome town popular with the British, is a university town, an army base, a market centre and the capital of the Pyrénées-Atlantiques region. It stands high above the Gave de Pau, dominated by its restored twelfth-century château, which contains two museums: the National Museum, with superb tapestries, and information about King Henri IV, who was born in the town; and the local Béarnais Museum. Pau is famous for its stupendous view of the Pyrénées, best seen in winter when the peaks are snow-covered.

The Basque Country

The N117 runs along the Gave de Pau Valley to Orthez, then via Peyrehorade to Bayonne, gateway to and capital of the French Basque Country. This is one of France's fringe areas, and perhaps the most fascinating. The Basques are a strange race, with an incomprehensible language full of consonants (they say it took the Devil 7 years to learn three words), an obscure origin (there are several theories as to where they came from, or whether they were here in the first place), and their own colourful folklore, arts and crafts, beliefs and practices which they jealously guard (they have a strong sense of their own identity). Most of the Basque country is in Spain, and differs from the French in that it is industrialised, heavily populated and politically dissident. French Basques live peaceably, mainly in small villages, in the pleasant green foothills of the Pyrénées or along a small strip of coast swept by the Atlantic winds. Of the seven Basque provinces, three are in France: the Labourde, nearest to the coast, which is the most picturesque and typical, the Basse Navarre and the Soule, which are heavily forested and lightly populated.

The Basque country near the coast is dotted with lovely villages, each with its round-topped fronton wall (for playing *pelota*), its church with its cemetery full of curious little round gravestones with strange crosses like swastikas, and its picturesque squat houses with their whitewash, rust-painted timbers, shutters and alpine-type roofs. The people are strongly religious and traditional in outlook, with their own dances, musical instruments, costume (the Basque beret and the espadrille), and folk-plays and masques. High summer in the Basque country is a continual round of traditional fêtes, dances and theatrical events which are colourful and entertaining to visitors even if they can not understand their significance. Perhaps their most entertaining spectacle is their traditional game of *pelote-Basque*, a kind of 'fives' played by two teams catching a ball with a curiously-shaped wicker basket and throwing it against the fronton wall. This is an exciting game to watch when played at a high standard.

The best place to find out about the Basques and their culture is the Basque Museum in **Bayonne**. This beautifully housed and presented museum is one of the finest in France: it displays their dress, furniture, crafts, decoration and artefacts, such as the *pelota* baskets, or *chisteras*; and it tells of their history, customs and beliefs, such as their cult of the dead and fear of witches. Bayonne is a large, busy port and industrial town at the junction of the rivers Adour and Nive, famous for its smoked ham, chocolate and *touron* (nougat with pine nuts), and for giving its name to the *bayonet*. It is a lively, pleasant town, though it could be smarter, with attractive quays and bridges along the Nive and a bustling arcaded main shopping street. Its ancient ramparts still encircle the town, and its Ste Marie Cathedral throws up its slender twin spires in the centre. The cathedral is fourteenth- to fifteenth-century Gothic, though the spires are nineteenth-century additions; it has some fine Renaissance stained-glass, and a handsome thirteenth-century cloister. As well as the Basque Museum, Bayonne has a splendid fine arts museum, the Musée Bonnat, with works by famous artists donated by a local painter.

Bayonne's alter ego is **Biarritz**, which is almost a suburb of the Basque capital. The contrast between old, industrial Bayonne and genteel, residential Biarritz is striking. The latter has no particular Basque character, although until the mid-nineteenth century it was a small whaling village, and it still has a tiny fishing port. It became one of the first of the internationally-fashionable resorts in the late nineteenth century, frequented by the Empress Eugénie, who built a sumptuous villa (now the Hôtel Palais), and by many other wealthy Europeans. Today it has a rather faded air, and attracts mainly the genteel retired community, although it is also popular with young surfers. It has a superb natural setting, with rocky headlands separating three beaches swept by the strong Atlantic waves, which provide great swimming and water sports. There are two casinos, and fine views of the Basque coast from the spectacular promontory, the Virgin's Rock.

The Basque coast from Biarritz is a succession of sandy beaches, cliffs and rocks, good for surfing but sometimes dangerous for swimming (the waves can be fierce and the undertow strong — watch for the 'danger' cones). Bidart and Guéthary are pleasant small resorts with some Basque character. **St Jean de Luz** is a much more attractive resort than Biarritz. It is still an active fishing port, specialising in tuna, and its picturesque harbour is surrounded with artists, craft shops, art galleries and colourful cafés. Its centre is the Place Louis XIV, with a bandstand and café terraces overlooking the quay. This is lively at night, especially when one of the many fêtes is in progress, like the *toro de fuego*, where a 'fire-bull' runs through the street spouting fireworks. Louis XIV was married here in 1660 — you can visit the Château Lohobiac where he lived while waiting for his bride to arrive. The Church of St Jean Baptiste, where the wedding took place, is typically Basque in style, with wooden galleries round the walls, a painted wooden vault, and a splendid large gilt altarpiece. Many of the old houses in the picturesque Barre Quarter are also typical of the Basque style of architecture, with painted wooden beams. In this mainly pedestrianised area are good restaurants, fashionable shops and art galleries. St Jean de Luz has a fine sandy beach in a safe, sheltered bay.

Across the harbour is the quiet fishing village of **Ciboure**, with a fortified sixteenth-century church and more fine old Basque houses. The composer Maurice Ravel was born here in 1875 (at number 12 on the quay). From here the D912 running along the edge of the cliff-top to Henday-Plage is known as the Basque Corniche, offering fine views of ocean and coast. **Hendaye-Plage** is a quiet coastal resort with an old-fashioned charm, while inland **Hendaye** is a busy border town and rail terminus beside the River Bidassoa.

Before ending the tour, a round trip can be made from here to some of the inland villages of the Basque Country. Return to St Jean de Luz on the N10, then take the D918 inland to **Ascain**, a pretty village with a traditional Basque church and old houses. **St Pée-sur-Nivelle** and **Espelette** are also typically Basque. St Pée has a ruined sixteenth-century château, and Espelette has old discus-shaped tombstones in the churchyard, and a winter fair of Basque ponies, or *pottoks*. **Cambo les Bains** is a pleasant, flowery spa and winter resort. From Espelette take the D20 to **Ainhoa**, one of the most typical Basque villages, with its Romanesque church, fronton and seventeenth-century houses. From here the D4 leads to **Sare**, perhaps the prettiest of all the inland villages. It has a lovely church with wooden galleries, and at the head of the St Ignace Pass nearby is a rack railway to the top of the **Rhune**, the highest peak of the area (900m, 2,952ft). From here you can either return via Ascain, or cross the border to the attractive, typically Basque Spanish village of **Vera da Bidassoa**, then return along the Bidassoa valley to Hendaye, to conclude your tour.

Cuisine in the Aquitaine

Though some dishes are common to the different regions of the Aquitaine, each has its own specialities:

The Bordelais and the Landes

This is a region known for its fish and shellfish: oysters from Arcachon, usually served with bread, butter and small sausages, and washed down with *Entre-Deux-Mers*; lamprey, shad and eel from the Gironde, often stewed in a wine sauce with shallots and mushrooms; salmon and, rarely, sturgeon. A popular meat is salt-meadow lamb from Pauillac. Beef is good, and *entrecôte* steak cooked *à la bordelaise*, with bone marrow, shallots, *cèpes*, tarragon and red wine. Ideally the steak should be grilled over vine-twigs.

Corn-fed 'yellow' chickens are popular, and wood-pigeons and ortolans (a small bunting, now a protected species). Products of the goose or duck are highly-rated: the *magret*, or fresh breast meat off the bone; a *confit*, any piece preserved in its own fat; and, of course, the fattened liver, or *foie gras*, a great delicacy and very expensive. *Paté de foie gras* is cheaper. A popular dish in season is mushrooms and *cèpes à la bordelaise*. Bordelais wines are renowned for their quality and variety.

Gascony and the Pyrénées

For fish dishes, trout and salmon from Pyrénean rivers are excellent. The *garbure* is the traditional starter in Gascony. It is a thick country soup made with seasonal vegetables, enriched with duck, goose or pork *confit*, served in a big tureen. A popular dish is the *poule au pot*, a boiled chicken served with vegetables; also *pot au feu*, or boiled meat and vegetables. *Confits*, *magrets* and *foie gras* are also a speciality of this region. The *salmis*, a kind of rich game stew with wine, is popular.

Ewe's milk cheeses are popular both in Gascony and the Pyrénées. The *tome des Pyrénées*, a rich, firm cows' milk cheese, is known throughout France. Fruit tarts and gâteaux, often with prunes steeped in Armagnac, are popular. Armagnac brandy, *floc de Gascogne*, and the wines of Madiran, Jurançon and Côtes de Gascogne are widely drunk. *Kir Gasconge* is made with *mûr*.

The Basque Country

Fish dishes are popular here: tuna from St Jean de Luz, sea bream, turbot or whiting. *Ttoro*, the Basque *bouillabaisse*, is a fish stew usually containing eel, monkfish and gurnet. Little squids, or *chipirones*, are often cooked in their own ink (*à l'encre*), though they can be grilled or stuffed. Sardines are usually grilled, or fried with egg yolk. Hake and other white fish are often served in a 'green sauce', ie a white sauce with parsley.

Basquaise sauce is a common accompaniment to a number of dishes; it usually implies the use of red peppers, with onion, garlic and sometimes Bayonne ham. Perhaps the best-known Basque dish is the *pipérade Basquaise* — scrambled eggs with tomatoes, green or red peppers and onions.

Charcuterie is good and common, the best-known being Bayonne ham (the traditional type is cured simply by being rubbed with salt). The Basques often fry this with eggs. Small garlic sausages are called *loukinkos*, and the local black pudding, made with mutton, is called *tripotcha*.

For dessert, the *gâteau basque* is popular throughout France, usually decorated with cherry jam. Bayonne chocolates and *torron*, a rich marzipan with nuts, and macaroons from St Jean de Luz, are all highly regarded. A local wine is Irouléguy, either red, white or rosé — the red is best. *Izarra* is a local liqueur, distilled in Bayonne (visits welcomed).

Additional Information

Places of Interest

Bordeaux
In old Archbishop's Palace
Fine Arts Museum
Open: 10am-12noon and 2-6pm daily,
except Tuesday.

St Michel-de-Montaigne
Montaigne's Library Tower and Château
Open: 9am-12noon and 2-7pm; closed
Monday, Tuesday and 6 January to 19
February.

Cadillac
Château d'Épernon
Open: daily except Tuesday.

St Macaire
Postal Museum of Aquitaine
Open: 2-6.30pm daily April to 15
October; Saturday, Sunday, national
holidays only out of season.

Sauternais
Château de Malle
Open: 3-7pm daily except Wednesday,
late March to mid-October.

Château de Labrède (Montesquieu's Birthplace)
Open: 9.30-11.30am and 2.30-5.30pm,
except Tuesday, mid-March to mid-
November; 2.30-5pm Saturday, Sunday
in winter.

Roquetaillade
Château
Open: 9.30am-12noon and 2-7pm daily,
July to September; 2-6pm Sunday out of
season; closed 15 December to 15 January.

Sabres
Marquèze Ecomuseum
Open: June to mid-September daily; end
March to May and mid-September to
end October, Saturday afternoon,
Sunday and national holidays; closed
early November to March.

Séviac
Gallo-Roman Villa
Open: daily in summer; guided tours.
☎ 62 28 43 18

Condom
Armagnac Museum
In old Bishop's residence
Open: daily except Sunday and Monday
and national holidays out of season.

Lectoure
Antiquities Museum
Open: daily.

Auch
Art and Archaeology Museum
In Jacobin convent
Open: 10am-12noon and 2-8pm or 4pm
winter; except Sunday, Monday, na-
tional holidays.

Tarbes
Museum of Cavalry and Horses
Open: 10am-12noon and 2-6pm daily,
except Monday, Tuesday and national
holidays.

Lourdes
Boly Mill (Ste Bernadette's Birthplace)
and *Gemmail Museum of Sacred Art*
Open: daily except Saturday, Easter to
15 October.

Pyrénean Museum
In Château of Counts of Bigorre
Open: daily except January.

Beaucens
Donjon des Aigles Falconry Museum
Open: daily, afternoons April to Octo-
ber.

Pic du Midi du Bigorre
Toll road from Col du Tourmalet
Open: 1 July to 10 October.

Pau
National Museum and Béarnais Museum
In Château
Open: daily 9.30-11.45am and 2-5.45 or
6.45pm.
Also *Fine Arts and Bernadotte Museums.*

Bayonne
Basque Museum
In sixteenth-century house
Open: 9.30am-12.30pm and 2.30-6.30pm

daily in season except Sunday and national holidays; 10am-12noon and 2.30-5.30 low season.

Bonnat Museum
Open: 10am-12noon and 4-8pm daily except Tuesday in season; 10am-12noon and 3-7pm daily except Tuesday, Saturday and Sunday low season.

St Jean de Luz
Château Lohobiaque
Louis XIV's pre-marriage residence
Open: afternoons 8 to 15 June and July to 21 September daily except Sunday afternoons.

Tourist Information Centres

Auch
Office de Tourisme
Place Cathédrale
☎ 62 05 22 89

Bayonne
Office de Tourisme
Place Liberté
☎ 59 59 31 31

Biarritz
Office de Tourisme
Square d'Ixelles
☎ 59 24 20 24

Bordeaux
Office de Tourisme and Accueil de France
12 cours 30-Juillet
☎ 56 44 28 41

Lourdes
Municipal Office de Tourisme
Place Champ-Commun
☎ 62 94 15 64

Pau
Municipal Office de Tourisme
Place Royale
☎ 59 27 27 08

St Émilion
Office de Tourisme
Place Créneaux
☎ 57 24 72 03

St Jean de Luz
Place Maréchal-Foch
☎ 59 26 03 16

Restaurants

R = With Accommodation
Haute-cuisine restaurants include:
Ainhoa
Ithurria (R)
☎ 59 29 92 11

Auch
France/A. Dagoin (R)
☎ 62 05 00 44

Biarritz
Palais (R)
☎ 59 24 09 40

Miramar (R)
☎ 59 41 30 00

Bidart
La Table des Frères Ibarboure
☎ 59 54 81 64

Bordeaux
Le Chapon Fin
☎ 56 79 10 10

Le Rouzic
☎ 56 44 39 11

La Chamade
☎ 56 48 13 74

Jean Ramet
☎ 56 44 12 51

Pavillon des Boulevards
☎ 56 81 51 02

Le Vieux Bordeaux
☎ 56 52 94 36

Le St James (R)
At Bouliac
☎ 56 20 52 19

Eugénie-les-Bains
Les Prés d'Eugénie (R)
☎ 58 05 06 07

Gaillan-en-Médoc
Near Lesparre-Médoc
Château Layauga (R)
☎ 56 41 26 83

Grenade-sur-l'Adour
Pain Adour et Fantasie (R)
☎ 58 45 18 80

Langon
Claude Darroze (R)
☎ 56 63 00 48

Pau
Le Viking
☎ 59 84 02 91

Poudenas
Near Condom
La Belle Gasconne (R)
☎ 53 65 71 58

Ségos
Near Aire-sur-l'Adour
Domaine de Bassibé (R)
☎ 62 09 46 71

St Jean Pied de Port
Les Pyrénées (R)
☎ 59 37 01 01

Urt
Near Bayonne
Auberge de la Galupe
☎ 59 56 21 84

Villeneuve-de-Marsan
Francis Darroze (R)
☎ 56 45 20 07

Other restaurants, offering good value
for money, include:
Argelès-Gazost
Miramont (R)
☎ 62 97 01 26

Le Relais (R)
☎ 62 97 01 27

Bayonne
François Miura
☎ 59 59 49 89

Bidarray
Pont d'Enfer (R)
☎ 59 37 70 88

Castéra-Verduzan
Florida
☎ 62 68 13 22

Francescas
Near Condom
Relais de la Hire
☎ 53 65 41 59

Gavarnie
La Ruade
☎ 62 92 48 49

Hendaye (town)
Chez Antoinette (R)
☎ 59 20 08 47

Lectoure
De Bastard (R)
☎ 62 68 82 44

Margaux
Auberge Le Savoie
☎ 56 88 31 76

Mauvezin
La Rapière
☎ 62 06 80 08

Moncrabeau
Near Condom
Le Phare (R)
☎ 53 65 42 08

Pau
St Jacques
☎ 59 27 58 97

Plaisance
La Ripa Alta (R)
☎ 62 69 30 43

Sévignac-Meyracq
Bains de Secours
☎ 59 05 62 11

St Émilion
Logis de la Cadène
☎ 57 24 71 40

St Jean de Luz
Le Petit Grill Basque
☎ 59 26 80 76

St Savin
Viscos (R)
☎ 62 97 02 28

10

OTHER SUGGESTED TOURS

The nine tours described in detail do not cover the whole of France. The following is an outline of a number of tours to other interesting regions which you could explore for yourself.

THE LOIRE VALLEY
A trip along France's longest river, with some deviations to its tributaries, while admiring some of the most beautiful castles, delving back into her history, and sampling some of her finest food and wines.

(Opposite) The Alps boast some of France's most spectacular scenery

The Loire Valley is renowned for its châteaux

From Nantes to Sancerre
Nantes; Angers; Montgeoffroy; Cunault; Saumur; Fontevraud; Candes; Chinon; Ussé; Azay-le-Rideau; Villandry; Langeais; Tours; Chenonceaux; St Aignan; Loches; Amboise; Chaumont; Blois; Cheverny; Chambord; Beaugency; Orléans; St Bénoit-sur-Loire; Sully-sur-Loire, Gien; Pouilly-sur-Loire; Sancerre.

ARDENNES — CHAMPAGNE
A trip along the wooded but war-torn Belgian border, then a tour of the region where they make one of France's most famous and delicious products.

From Laon to Reims
Laon; Thiérache; Charleville-Mezières; Sédan, Bar-le-Duc; St Dizier; Colombey-les-Deux-Églises; Brienn-le-Château; Bar-sur-Aube; Les Riceys; Troyes, Sézanne; Chalons-sur-Marne; Épernay; Montagne de Reims; Reims.

THE JURA
A tour round a little-known region on France's Swiss border with a long tradition of independence and community spirit; an attractive area of high plateaux, dense forests, waterfalls and superb cheeses and wines.

From Montbéliard to Bourg-en-Bresse
Montbéliard; St Hippolyte; Maîche; Besançon; Ornans; Pontarlier; Salins-les-Bains; Arc-et-Senans; Dole; Poligny; Château-Chalon; Baume-les-Messieurs; Lons-le-Saunier; Lac de Chalain; Champagnole; St Laurent-en-Grandvaux; Clairvaux-les-Lacs; St Claude; Bellegarde; Nantua; Bugey; Bourg-en-Bresse.

THE ALPS
France's most dramatic region, with Europe's highest mountain, spectacular scenery of snowy peaks, glaciers and alpine lakes, mecca of the skiing world; but also a tranquil land of villages, flowery meadows and streams.

From Evian-les-Bains to Briançon
Evian-les-Bains; Thonon-les-Bains; Abondance; Morzine; Plateau d'Assy; Chamonix-Mont Blanc; St Gervais-les-Bains; Megève; Le Grand Bornand; Thônes; Annecy; Aix-les-Bains; Le Bourget-du-Lac; Chambéry; Albertville; Bourg-St Maurice; Col du Mont-Cenis; Le Maurienne; Pontcharra; La Grande Chartreuse; Grenoble; Le Vercors; Vizille; Le Bourg d'Oisans; Col du Lauteret; Briançon.

THE RHÔNE VALLEY
A wine and food route that runs from the Beaujolais, through France's second city and gastronomic capital, to the vineyards of the sunny south.

From Villefranche to Die
Villefranche; Lyon; Vienne; Condrieu; La Côte Rôtie; St Étienne; St Genest-Malifaux; Bourg-Argental; Annonay; Lalouvesc; Tournon; Romans-sur-Isère; Valence; Privas; Aubenas; Vals-les-Bains; Crest; Die.

THE AUVERGNE
France's remote rural heartland with a reputation for stubborn self-sufficiency; a strange, beautiful land of volcanic cones and broad, bare mountains where traditional dance and song can still be seen and heard.

From Nevers to Le Puy
Nevers; Bourbon-Lancy; Moulins; St Pourçain-sur-Sioule; Vichy; Ambierle; Roanne; Montbrison; St Bonnet-le-Château; Ambert; Thiers; Clermont-Ferrand; Riom; Châtelguyon; La Bourboule; Le Mont-Dore; Murol; St Nectaire; Besse-en-Chandesse; Murat; St Flour; Brioude; La Chaise-Dieu; Le Puy.

THE DORDOGNE
The land of prehistoric art in limestone caves, of deep gorges, majestic rivers and dense forests and a gourmet's paradise.

From Bourges to Angoulême
Bourges; Châteauroux; Argenton-sur-Creuse; La Châtre; Boussac; Montluçon; Evaux-les-Bains; Guéret; La Souterraine; Oradour-sur-Glane; Limoges; Aubusson; Ussel; Mauriac; Aurillac; St Cèré; Rocamadour; Souillac; Sarlat-la-Canéda; Les Eyzies; La Bugue; Bergerac; Périgueux; Brantôme; Angoulême.

THE ATLANTIC COAST
A region of warm, sandy beaches and gentle rolling countryside, of large offshore islands and picturesque marshlands, a stronghold of religion and royalism, good food and, of course, cognac.

From the Île de Normoutier to Royan
Île de Normoutier; St Jean-de-Monts; Les Sables-d'Olonne; La Roche-sur-Yon; Luçon; Le Marais Poitevin; Maillezais; Fontenay-le-Comte; Bressuire; Loudun; Richelieu; Châtellerault; Poitiers; Parthenay; St Maixent-l'École; Niort; La Rochelle; Rochefort; St Jean d'Angély; Cognac; Saintes; Île d'Oléron; Royan.

MIDI-PYRÉNÉES
A tour that starts in the heart of the Massif Central and ends in a remote fastness in the Pyrénées, with an incredible variety of scenery en route — a land of Cathars, troubadours and the Langue d'Oc.

From Mende to Andorra
Mende; Espalion; Conques; Figeac; Cahors; Villefranche-de-Rouergue; Rodez; Sauveterre-de-Rouergue; Albi; Castres; Mazamet; Toulouse; St Gaudens; St Bertrand-de-Comminges; Bagnères-de-Luchon; St Girons; Foix; Pamiers; Mirepoix; Lavelanet; Quillan; Font-Romeu; Aix-les-Thermes; Andorra.

THE CÔTE D'AZUR
A trip along the famous coast taking in all the glamorous and not-so-glamorous resorts, with a detour inland to upland Provence, and a final spectacular drive along the Grande Corniche to the Italian border.

From Marseille to Menton
Marseille; Cassis; Bandol; Toulon; Hyères; Le Lavandou; St Tropez; Port Grimaud; Ste Maxime; Draguignan; Gorges du Verdon; Castellane; Grasse; Fréjus/St Raphaël; Cannes; Antibes; Nice; Monaco/Monte-Carlo; Menton.

France Fact File

Accommodation

Hotels

Tourism is big business in France, and hotels are nationally inspected and supervised. They are graded with stars into five categories: one star is simple but comfortable, four stars (L) is luxury. Prices rise according to category. Rates are usually given for two, and single rooms, if you can find them, may not be much cheaper than double. A third bed will normally cost about 30 per cent extra, though many hotel chains now offer a free bed for a child under 12 in the same room as the parents.

Breakfast is not usually included in the price of the room. Most hotels offer special rates for *pension complète* (room with full meals) or *demi-pension* (room, breakfast and one other meal). You cannot by law be refused a room if you do not want *pension* arrangements, though some hoteliers may expect you to take them. If you do, check that the *pension* menu offers you the same choice as other restaurant menus. You can eat in hotel restaurants without staying there.

The family-run hotel is still the norm in rural France, but hotel chains have sprung up, and are now common in towns and industrial areas. They cater particularly for conferences or coach parties, and although they can offer good value, they tend to be more standardised and impersonal than the traditional *auberge* or *logis*. Some of the family-run hotels are now organised into chains. The best-known and largest of these is the Logis et Auberges de France chain, whose hotels are simple, usually in the countryside, and known for local cuisine and quality of welcome. Other smaller chains of similar type are France-Accueil and Relais Bleu.

Lists of approved hotels are produced by the French Government Tourist Office, and by local Syndicats d'Initiative. Guide books usually give selected lists, their choice often being influenced by the type of reader they are aiming at. Bookings can be made direct to the hotel by phone (though you may have to send a deposit, or *acompte*, which you may lose if you cancel), or through a group central booking service for hotels in a chain. Book well ahead and remember to confirm your booking on your day of arrival if you are likely to arrive late (after 7pm).

Other Types of Accommodation

The most popular type of non-hotel accommodation in France is the *gîte*. This is a self-catering holiday home in or near an inland country village. It may be a small cottage, village house, flat in the owner's house or part of a farm; the owner will not be living in it at the time, but may be on hand nearby. *Gîtes* are rented for a week or longer (two weeks in peak season) and are reasonably priced. This is one reason for their popularity, and why you should book early. They are all inspected and graded, and are usually in good condition. They are often in beautiful countryside, but sometimes remote from civilisation.

Not to be confused with *gîtes* are *gîtes d'etape* (short-stay centres for those on a walking or horseback tour) and *gîtes d'enfants* (centres for groups of children on an outdoor activities holiday). These are really types of hostel, like the *auberges de jeunesse*, or youth hostels. These are worth considering for a short stay: they normally take younger adults as well as children, and they often provide meals and beds, usually in bunkhouses. Another possibility for budget accommodation is the *chambre d'hôte*. This is a room with bed and breakfast in the house of a family in residence, usually in the country and often on a farm. It is a good way of meeting the local people and sampling their produce. Tourist information centres produce the pamphlet *Youth Welcome* listing youth hostels (*auberge de jeunesse*). Other useful addresses are:

Fédération Unie des Auberges de Jeunesse
27 Rue Pajol
75118 Paris
☎ 42 41 59 00

UCRIF (Union des Centres de Recontres Internationales de France)
21 Rue Béranger
75003 Paris
☎ 42 77 08 65

Camping and Caravanning

If you take your own accommodation with you, in the form of a tent, trailer-tent, caravan or camping-car, you have the choice of camping *au sauvage* (in the wild) or on a camp-site. Many French people do the former, but make sure the *camping sauvage* is not *interdit* (prohibited), and get permission from the local farmer or landowner. He may make a small charge for this, but should provide in return access to some basic facilities like running water. He may indeed make regular provision for *camping à la ferme* (camping on small farm sites) in which case he should provide toilets and washing facilities and may have farm produce for sale.

French camp-sites are well organised, regularly inspected and classified with stars into five categories (including ungraded). Stars are nearly always displayed at the site entrance, and are a good guide to the amenities offered, though this does not necessarily mean that the site will be to your taste. At the top of the range, four-star *grand confort* sites should be spacious and attractively landscaped, with your own clearly-marked pitch, an electrical hook-up, and comprehensive amenities, including a restaurant and hot food takeaway, bar, supermarket, laundry, full washing facilities with free hot water, and sports facilities. Some of these are in the Castels et Camping Caravaning chain, whose sites are attractively located in the grounds of châteaux or other historic buildings. Further down the range, a two-star site will still offer basic amenities, which should include hot water and a shop or *buvette* with basic food requirements.

The star grading is not always a reliable guide to the quality of a site. It refers to the amenities the site offers, not to the way it is run. If a site is badly managed (too lax in enforcing the rules, unhelpful and impersonal service) it can still have a high grading, though it may lose this eventually.

Booking

To get onto a beach camp-site or one in a popular tourist area in high season (early July to late August), you will need to book. The same is true of other forms of accommodation. This is normally done direct by telephone or letter, but there is now an alternative in some *départements*, which have set up officially-backed booking services under the name of

Loisirs-Accueil. They usually charge no fee and have an English-speaking operator. They can reserve hotels, *gîtes* and camp-sites, as well as special activity or sports holidays. 'Gîtes de France' also have their own 'Loisirs-Accueil' programme. Contact the French National Tourist Information Centre (see page 243-44) for further details.

Additional Information

In this section the addresses and opening times of places of interest are arranged chapter by chapter under the order as in the main guide. The addresses of tourist information centres and restaurants are listed alphabetically under town/city names.

Annual Events and Festivals

These are some of the regular annual events:

January: Monte Carlo Car Rally; Feast of St Vincent, Vosne-Romanée.

February: Paris Fashion Shows *Prêt-à-porter*; Cannes International Bridge & Chess Festival; Menton Lemon Festival; Nice Carnival.

March: Dunkirk Carnival; Le Touquet Motorcycle *Enduro des Sables*; Black Pudding Festival, Mortagne-au-Perche, Normandy; Malo-les-Bains Carnival; Paris Agricultural Show; Paris Caravanning and Open-Air Show (Le Bourget); Junk Fair, Châtou, near Paris; SMTV (Tourism & Travel Show); Paris Marathon.

April: Daffodil Festival, Gérardmer, Lorraine; Corsica Car Rally; *Foire de Paris*; Le Mans 24hr Motorcycle Race.

May: Bordeaux 'Musical May' Concerts; Cannes Film Festival; Saintes-Maries-de-la-Mer Gipsy Festival; Monaco Grand Prix; Paris International Tennis.

June: Strasbourg Music Festival; Le Mans 24hr Car Race; Django Rheinhardt Jazz Festival, Samois-sur-Seine.

July: Tour de France; Grand Prix de France, Magny-Cours Circuit, Nevers; Bastille Day: Nice Jazz Festival; Motorcycle Grand Prix, Magny-Cours Circuit, Nevers; Avignon Festival; *Fêtes de Cornouailles*, Quimper; Antibes Jazz Festival; Aix-en-Provence Festival; Orange *Corégies* Festival.

August: Paris Festival *Estival* (mid-July to mid-September); Celtic Festival, Lorient; Deauville Grand Prix; Cannes Fireworks Festival; Blue Fishing Nets Festival, Concarneau; Assumption Day celebrations, Brittany.

September: Wine & Beer Festivals in Alsace; Le Castellet *Bol d'Or* Motorcycle endurance race; Paris Autumn Festival (mid-September to mid-December).

October: Paris Harvest Festival in Montmartre; *Grand Prix de l'Arc de Triomphe*, Longchamp, Paris; Paris Motor Show; Gastronomic Fair, Romorantin; Fair of Contemporary Art, Paris; Paris Jazz Festival.

November: Dijon Gastronomic Fair; *Trois Glorieuses* Wine Fair and Auction, Clos de Vougeot, Meursault, Beaune (Burgundy); Beaujolais Nouveau released.

December: Paris Dance Festival; Paris International Boat Show; Christmas crib festivities, especially in Provence.

Business and Shopping Hours

Banks have restricted opening hours: 9am-12noon and 2-4pm weekdays and closed either Saturdays or Mondays. They close early on the day before a bank holiday. For Post Offices, see page 239.

Food shops are usually open from 7am to 6.30/7.30pm, while other shops open 9am-10am to 6.30/7.30pm. Many shops are closed all or half-day on Mondays. Many bakers and some other food shops open on Sunday mornings. Shops in small towns are usually closed from 12noon to 2pm. Most hypermarkets open until 9am or 10pm Monday to Saturday (closed Monday mornings).

Climate

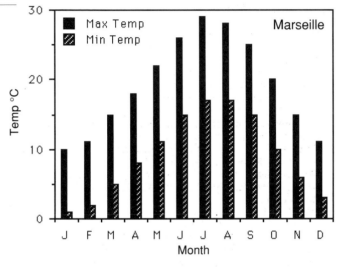

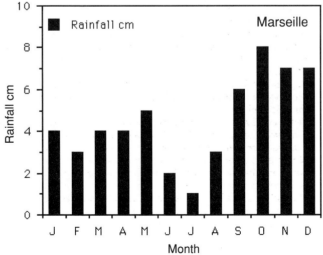

France is the only country in Europe with the continent's three climates — oceanic, continental and Mediterranean.

The north coast, Brittany and the west coast have a maritime climate, similar to that in most of Britain except perhaps the east coast. This is cooler in summer, warmer in winter, and gently rain-bearing. The average winter temperature on the Cotentin peninsula in Normandy is the same as in Nice, on the Riviera. Brittany has the most equable climate, being very mild in winter but rather cool in summer. Of course, the further south you go down the west coast, the warmer the average temperature; but it can still be remarkably cool on occasion in midsummer down as far as the Basque coast. What you cannot guarantee in these areas are sunshine and clear skies.

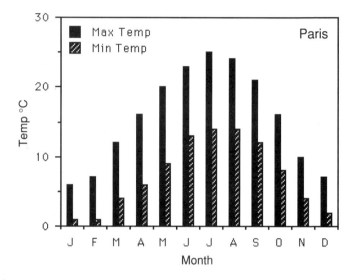

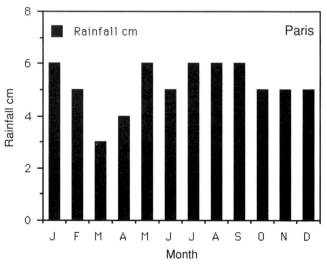

The further east you go, the more continental the climate becomes, that is colder in winter, hotter in summer. The east and the Massif Central tend to have a similar type of climate, with extremes of temperature. Winters tend to be dry, with more rain in summer, often coming in storms. The Massif Central is particularly notorious for storms. The Auvergne has the record for the greatest variations in temperature in France.

As you drive down the Rhône Valley, it is not uncommon to experience a sudden magical change in climate. This usually happens round about Valence — the sky suddenly clears or takes on a bluer tinge, the air becomes hotter and drier, even the smell of the air changes. This is the 'southern syndrome': you are entering the Mediterranean climate zone. The Mediterranean climate is dry and sunny, with low rainfall (more in winter) and hot summer weather. It is usually mild in winter, though cold spells can occur, and the winters are usually short. The climate is the main reason why the south-east is the most popular tourist area of France, though high summer can be hot, and the more discerning tourists go in spring or autumn rather than in July or August.

But French weather is more subtle than this. Because of the variety of scenery a large number of regions have their own microclimates. The high mountains of the Alps and Pyrénées experience extreme climatic conditions, with heavy snowfalls in winter and high temperatures in summer. The nearness of the sea and mountains in the south-east produces atmospheric turmoil that gives rise to the *Mistral*, a cold, dry north wind that howls down the Rhône Valley into Provence for days on end. Sometimes hot, dry winds come from the south, bringing Saharan dust with them. Alsace, squeezed between the Vosges mountains and the River Rhine, often experiences stifling summer weather. The Alps and the Massif Central in particular have a bewildering variety of microclimates. Alpine valleys can be unpleasantly hot and sticky in high summer and the area round Mont Blanc is notorious for its unpredictable weather.

Credit and Eurocheque Cards

All major credit cards are accepted in shops, hotels, restaurants, most fuel stations and some, though not all, hypermarkets. Check the amount shown on the receipt, and note that the division between *francs* and *centimes* may be marked by a comma or not shown at all. You can draw cash from a bank with a credit card, but you will pay interest on it from the moment of drawing, and will be charged a commission. You can gain or lose on the use of credit cards, depending whether the rate of exchange has risen or fallen between the time you use the card and the time your bill is calculated.

Eurocheque cards are widely used and convenient (you can draw money with them as well as pay for goods); but you must apply for the card from your bank at least a fortnight before you leave, and you pay both for the card and a commission charge on each cheque you use.

Currency and Travellers' Cheques

It is wise to take some French money with you when you go. French *francs* can be obtained in banks, change-shops and some hotels, restau-

231

rants and shops, either for currency or travellers' cheques. The most favourable rates of exchange are obtained at banks, whether in France or in your home country. Unlimited currency may be taken into France and only bank-notes to the value of 50,000FF or more need be declared if they are likely to be re-exported. When shopping around for favourable exchange rates, take into account any commission charges that may be added. The French *franc* (abbreviated F or FF) is divided into 100 *centimes*. Current coins include 5, 10, 20, and 50 *centime* pieces as well as 1, 2, 5, and 10 *franc* pieces. Bank notes come in denominations of 20, 50, 100, 200 and 500 francs.

Travellers' cheques in French francs cost more than Sterling ones initially, but may offset a poor rate of exchange and high commission charges for changing your cheques in France. Do not let anyone charge you for changing franc travellers' cheques — ask in advance, and try another bank if they do.

Disabled Holidaymakers

The French Government Tourist Office issue a special information sheet for disabled visitors to France. This is available on application with a stamped addressed envelope.

The Liason Committee for the Transport of Disabled Persons (Comité de Liaison pour le Transport des Personnes Handicapées) 34 Avenue Marceau Paris 8c and the Ministry of Equipment, Housing, Transport and the Sea (Ministère de l'Equipment, du Logement, des Transports et de la Mer) 92055 Paris La Defense cédex 04 publish a transport guide for the disabled.

The French National Committee of Liaison for the Re-Education of the Disabled (Comité National Français de Liaison pour la Réadaptation des Handicapées) 38 Bld Raspail Paris 7E sells two guides for the use of people with a handicap: *Paris-Guide to Cinemas, Theatres, Concerts* and *Paris-Museums, Libraries, Cultural Centres and Workshops*. A list of *gîtes* which accommodate for disabled travellers and regional numbers of the APF (Association des Paralyses de France) can be obtained from the central office at:

17 Boulevard Auguste-Blanqui
75013
Paris
☎ 140 78 69 00

Another useful address to contact for information is
Red Cross
Croix Rouge Paris
1 Place Henri Dunant
75384
Paris
☎ 1 44 43 11 00

Embassies and Consulates

Foreign Embassies and Consulates in France are:

UK
Embassy
35 Rue du Faubourg Saint-Honoré
75008 Paris
☎ 42 66 91 42

Consulate
16 Rue d'Anjou
75008 Paris
(same telephone number)

USA
Embassy-Chancellery
2 Avenue Gabriel
75008 Paris
☎ 42 96 12 02

Australia
Embassy and Consulate
4 Rue Jean-Rey
75015 Paris
☎ 40 59 33 00

Canada
Embassy-Chancellery
35 av Montaigne
75008 Paris
☎ 47 23 01 01

The Foreign Office leaflet *Get it Right Before you Go* gives advice about how to behave in France, and provides information about the services offered by the Consulate. This is obtainable from the French Government Tourist Office.

Eating and Drinking

Food Shops
The place to buy your savouries is a *charcuterie*, or pork-butcher's, where they sell a wider range of cooked foods than this name suggests: pâtés, cooked meats, salads, cooked dishes for reheating, quiches and pizzas, sausages, spit-roast chickens and local delicacies. Their sausages will be the cooked or cured type (*saucisson*) — the uncooked type (*saucisse*) is sold in the *boucherie*. The food will be of better quality than in a supermarket, though probably more expensive.

The butcher's shop, or *boucherie*, is mainly for uncooked meat, game and poultry, though they do sell some home-made pâtés, and cooked meats and chickens. They will recommend the best types of meat for the barbecue, and they will always trim the fat off the meat before weighing it. *Poissoneries* (fishmongers) sell uncooked and cooked fish and, near the coast, a wide variety of shellfish. Oysters and mussels are very popular, and the fishmonger will gladly open your oysters for you.

Though supermarkets sell bread, most people get it from a *boulangerie*, or bakery. Normal French bread is white, unsliced, and in the form of a stick — either small (*ficelle*), medium or normal size (*baguette*), or large (*gros pain* or simply *pain*). It is crusty and only the large size has much of a soft middle, so if you like your bread soft, buy a *pain* or half-*pain* rather than one of the smaller loaves. Though it is delicious when fresh, French bread goes stale quickly. If you tire of the normal bread, you can try one of the longer-lasting loaves that French bakers are producing in greater variety today — the large, heavy and crusty *pain-de-campagne*, the brown *pain complet* or the *pain-de-seigle* (rye bread).

Boulangeries also sell pastries like *croissants*, *brioches* (with or without chocolate in the middle) and a limited range of cakes. For a greater variety of these, you should go to a *pâtisserie*, or cake shop. French cakes are enticing and delicious, but expensive.

Other groceries, including cheese, are sold in an *épicerie* (literally 'spice-shop', ie grocery), or in a general food store or *alimentation*. As well as its wines, France is renowned for the variety and quality of its cheeses, and the best place to buy these is in a supermarket or hypermarket, or on a market stall on market day. French hypermarkets can be enormous, with a vast range of goods, and are generally, though not always, cheaper than smaller shops. An exception to this is fruit and vegetables — these are usually cheaper in specialist shops or on the market, and you are allowed to pick your own.

Cafés and Bars
These are a well-known feature of the French way of life. Some people seem to spend a major part of their holiday sitting with their drink at some pavement or boulevard café table, watching the world go by. The French café or bar is not for eating in — unless it is a *restaurant-bar*. The French are not known for their snacks, and those they have are not very appetising. The French sandwich is half a *baguette* with no butter and a meagre filling; and the *croque-monsieur* is a rather dull toasted ham-and-cheese sandwich (which can be livened up with a fried egg on top, to turn it into a *croque-madame*). Other snacks are usually in plastic packets.An exception to this is the *salon-de-thé,* or teashop. These elegant, rather genteel establishments are often attached to *pâtisseries* and sell their own products. They do not sell alcoholic drinks, which are the province of the *cafébar*. Here the main drink is beer, which is either in a bottle or on draught (*à-la-pression*). *Pression* beer is less gassy than bottled, and, unless you ask for a *grand*, is served in a *demi* measure of just under half a pint.

Coffee is served black and strong in a small cup unless you ask for a *café-au-lait* (very milky) or a *café-crème* (less milky). For a large measure, ask for a *grand*. Tea is without milk unless you ask for it; and other infusions or herbal teas, called *tisanes*, are popular. Fizzy drinks and mineral water are served in small bottles, and are expensive (much cheaper from large bottles in supermarkets). The French equivalent of a fruit squash, but sweeter, is a *sirop*, of which there is a large selection. Most spirits, or *eaux-de-vie*, are drunk after the meal, but the most popular is drunk diluted with water as an aperitif. This is *pastis*, the aniseed-flavoured spirit that has spread from its native Provence to conquer the whole of France.

Most French bars have two prices for drinks: the cheaper price at the *comptoir*, or bar, and the dearer one at a table, or *salle*. Fetching your own drink from the bar to a table will not qualify you for the cheaper price! It is normal to pay for all you have consumed when you leave. You can also buy stamps, cigarettes and cigars in many bars.

Restaurants
When choosing a restaurant use a combination of three methods to ensure a good meal at the right price. The first is to consult the guide books, preferably in advance. The second is to ask, at hotel, camp-site, local Syndicat d'Initiative or bar, for a recommendation. The third is to study the menus which all restaurants must display, with their prices, outside their premises. These will show one or more menus, or fixed-price meals, as well as a list of *à-la-carte* dishes. Menus are always better

value than going *à-la-carte* in French restaurants unless you want only one dish (the *plat du jour*) or a light snack. They offer three or more courses at a range of prices, from the cheaper *menu touristique* to the expensive and copious *menu gastronomique*. Gourmet restaurants may also offer a *menu dégustation*, which gives you a chance to taste smaller portions of a larger number of the chef's specialities.

The first course is usually a starter: often soup, pâté, cold meats or *crudités* (raw salad vegetables). In a four-course meal the second course will usually be a fish dish, and the third course a meat dish. This may be lightly garnished with vegetables, or they may be served as a separate course. If you want a steak well-done, ask for it *bien cuit* or even *brulée* (burnt). *À point* is rare-to-medium, *saignant* (bloody) or *bleu* is hardly cooked at all. The fourth course will be either cheese or a sweet, or both if you are lucky. If so, the cheese will be served before the dessert. A choice of both cheeses and sweets is offered, with the *tarte maison*, or house fruit-flan, an alternative for dessert. Cheaper menus often include a drink in the price.

French restaurants are usually friendly and casual. Children are welcomed and accommodated, often with special menus. The French like to take their time over their meals, and there is sometimes a wait between courses. Lunch, often their main meal of the day, is taken early, at around 12noon, and is finished by 2pm — so get there in good time. Dinner starts at about 7.30pm, but you can go much later. Sunday lunch is the most popular eating-out time for the French, so you should book in advance for this. Sunday evening is very quiet and many restaurants are closed then.

At the other end of the scale, a good place for an *en-route* lunch is a transport café or *relais routier*. They are popular with the general public, and provide a simple but substantial meal at a reasonable price. You can easily recognise them by the distinctive blue and red circle displayed outside.

Wine

French wine, like its food, is unparalleled for quality and variety. The great wine regions of Bordeaux, Burgundy, the Rhône and Loire valleys and, of course, Champagne, produce some of the best-known and most expensive wines in the world; while in other areas there are hundreds of local 'country' wines, of variable quality but rivalling at their best all but the *grands crus* of the prestige vineyards. One of the most exciting developments of recent years is the improvement in the production methods, and therefore quality, of French country wines.

It is customary to pay a mark-up in a restaurant for cellarage, corkage and service. But in French restaurants the prices sometimes seem to bear no resemblance to the cost of the wine outside: you can often expect to pay at least treble the retail price for the more well-known names. The exception is local wines: here the prices are much more reasonable and the wines are often better examples of the local vintage. Choose the house wine or one of the local *crus* in preference to one of the *grandes marques* when dining out.

Wine-tastings at a *cave co-opérative*, a *maison de vin* or a private property are widely available and are usually free, though there may be an implied obligation to buy, particularly if the sign says *dégustation-vente*. The obligation may vary with the establishment: a *co-opérative*, which makes and sells wine from the blended produce of a number of local growers, is staffed by paid employees and is usually generous with its samples than an individual *vigneron*; a *maison de vin*, which is usually established by a local town or village to market the wines of its area, may make a small charge for the tasting but thereby remove the obligation to buy.

Most wine-growing areas have a clearly-marked *route du vin*. It should be an attractive, winding road among the vineyards and wine villages, taking you off the beaten track into the real France. Before you start, get a plan of the route from the local Syndicat d'Initiative and visit the local *maison du vin*, to learn about the wines in the region.

Wine Categories
The wine label will tell you certain things about the contents of the bottle, such as producer, merchant, year, grape variety, alcohol content and character of the wine. It will also grade the wine into one of four categories: the highest, *Appellation Contrôllée* (AC); *Vin Delimité de Qualité Supérieur* (VDQS); *Vin de Pays*; and *Vin de Table*. An AC grading is highly-prized and its allocation strictly controlled. It will guarantee that the wine comes from a certain area or vineyard and that it is produced with approved methods and grape varieties. It can, however, be misleading — an AC from a wide area guarantees nothing like the same quality as that of a single vineyard, and it may not be applied at all in certain areas, like Alsace, or to certain wines, like Champagne (though the quality of these wines is also carefully controlled). It is a useful guide to quality, remembering that the more specific the *Appellation*, the better the wine should be.

VDQS wines are also carefully controlled, and in some areas may be the highest category allowed. They are often a good buy, being less expensive than AC wines and often just as good quality. *Vin de Pays* wines can also be good value — this category guarantees the origin of the wine and often the grape variety. They are perhaps best in areas which have no AC or VDQS appellations. *Vin de Table* wines have no guarantee of quality, and can be very variable. They may blend wines from different districts or even countries.

In the top-quality wine areas there is a classification above the AC called the classed growth, or *cru classé*. These *crus* vary in name and significance from region to region, and range from names like *Premier Grand Cru Classé* at the top to the modest *Cru Bourgeois* at the bottom. They are often named after an individual château, but this in itself does not guarantee their quality.

Better quality wines also tell you the year they were made — their vintage. There is no easy way to read vintages — you should either ask the experts or become one yourself. Meanwhile, it is comforting to remember three points: age matters more with red wines than white wines and with wines of Bordeaux and Burgundy rather than those of other regions and most wine other than the very best should be drunk within 3 years of production.

Most French white wines, and all reds, are dry. A sweet white wine should be labelled *moelleux*, unless it is too well-known to need the label, like Sauternes or Montbazillac. Semi-sweet wines may be labelled *demi-sec*, unless they are sparkling wines — then *demi-sec* means sweet, *sec* means semi-sweet and *brut* means dry. The word *doux*, also meaning sweet, is usually reserved for very sweet fortified wines drunk as aperitifs, like the Muscats of Rivesaltes or Baumes-de-Venise. The label can also tell you the degree of sparkle in a sparkling wine. *Mousseux* is the fizziest, *crémant* a little less fizzy, and *pétillant* or *perlant* only slightly so.

Other Drinks

No wine is produced in northern France; in the north-east, beer is the local drink, while in Normandy and Brittany it is cider. Called *cidre-bouché* this is corked like sparkling wine, mild and fairly sweet. Fruit-based alcohols are popular throughout France, though each region has its own favourite fruit. Other dry spirits, or *eaux-de-vie*, are made from cherries (*kirsch*), William pears, stawberries, raspberries and walnuts *eau-de-noix*.

France is also famous for its sweet spirits, or liqueurs. The best-known are Bénédictine, from Fécamp in Normandy; green and yellow Chartreuse from the famous monastery north of Grenoble; Cointreau; and Grand Marnier. Green Chartreuse is the strongest of these, made with local herbs from an old secret recipe. A popular aperitif, is *kir*. This is white wine with a little *cassis* added; variations are *kir royal*, which has sparkling wine instead of still, and *kir Gascogne*, which replaces the white wine with red and the *cassis* with a blackberry liqueur called *mûr*.

Three other drinks must finally be mentioned: the delicate herb-flavoured dry Vermouth from Chambéry in the Alps; the famous brandies of Cognac and Armagnac; and the rough, strong alcohol called *Marc*, distilled from grape skins discarded after the *vendange* (gathering and pressing of grapes).

Electricity

Though 220 volt electricity is almost universal now, a thin-pronged 2-pin plug is used. An adaptor is needed both for 3-pin and 2-pin plugs.

Maps

The *Michelin Motoring Atlas of France* is recommended for its detail (1:200,000). If you do buy the Michelin atlas, make sure you get the spiral-bound version, as it is more durable. It contains a planning map, a map of French departments, plans of major towns and cities and a gazetteer.

For route planning, the *Michelin Map 911* is invaluable. It contains information on motorways and alternative routes, distances and jour-ney times, 24-hour service stations, and peak travel periods to avoid. This can be supplemented by the red *Michelin Map 989*, an excellent road map for getting from A to B. Its scale is 1:1,000,000, and it lists all the N (National) and many D (Departmental) roads. It also marks the French *Départements* in black and the detailed Michelin map numbers in blue. The AA also produces a clear and uncluttered road map of France (1:1,000,000), with a folding/colour coding system and showing toll and toll-free motorways. This is also available in 'Glovebox Atlas' form. The AA/Baedeker map is slightly more detailed (1:750,000) and has city-centre plans of main towns.

When you get to your destination, you may need a more detailed map than the 1:200,000 Michelin yellow. The French equivalent to the British Ordnance Survey map is the IGN, or *Institut Géographique National*, with a scale of 1:100,000. Even larger-scale maps are the IGN Orange (1;50,000) and the IGN Blue (1:25,000). These are useful for walkers and climbers, showing contours, footpaths and many other details. The IGN also has a range of planning maps.

Measurements

The metric system is used in France. Conversions are:
1 kilogram (1,000 grams) = 2.2lb
1 litre = $1^3/_4$ pints
4.5 litres = 1 gallon
1.6km = 1 mile
1 hectare = $2^1/_2$ acres approx.

Medical Advice and Assistance

To obtain the medical insurance that is now your right under EEC
regulations, obtain form E111 from your social security office. French
pharmacies with a green cross dispense first aid and medical advice,
and they have a rota for night opening. Addresses available from
Gendarmeries (police station). Vaccinations are not normally required
from mainland Britain.

Milk and Water

Pasteurised milk (*lait frais pasteurisé*) is available everywhere in France.
Water is generally safe to drink unless the tap is marked *eau non potable*.

Museums, Art Galleries, Monuments, Prehistoric Caves

National museums normally close on Tuesdays (except for the Musée
d'Orsay, Versailles and the Trianon Palace, which close on Mondays).
Entrance fees vary with a 50 per cent reduction on Sunday. Under-18s
are admitted free, 18-25s and over-60s half-price. Municipal museums
close on Mondays. They offer free admission on Sundays (except for
temporary exhibitions), and to under-7s and over-60s. Most museums
are closed on public holidays. Group visits should be arranged in
advance.

Paris and a few other cities (Nîmes, Arles) offer joint admission
cards to a number of museums, monuments etc. The Paris *Carte Musées
et Monuments*, valid for 1, 3 or 5 days, gives free admission to 65 monuments and museums in Paris and its environs.The *carte* can be bought
from tourist offices, *métro* or museum ticket offices.

Passports and Visas

British Nationals, and visitors from EEC countries, the USA, Canada,
New Zealand and a number of other countries, do not require a visa
when visiting France for stays of up to 3 months. British Nationals
require either a full British Passport, a Visitor's Passport (valid one
year) or a British Excursion Document (valid for one month for trips of
up to 60 hours at any one time — obtainable from Post Offices).

Postal Services

French postal and telephone services are state-controlled. The sign for a Post Office is PTT — Poste et Telécommunications. Post Offices are open 8am-7pm on weekdays and 8am-12noon Saturdays. Post Offices in small towns may close for 2 hours, usually 12noon-2pm, at lunch-times. Letters can be sent to you for collection c/o Poste Restante, Poste Centrale in any French town. You will need proof of identity to collect — there is a small fee.

Public Holidays

France has 13 days of Public Holidays, most of them on fixed dates:
New Year's Day: 1 January
Easter: 2 days, movable
Labour Day: 1 May
VE Day: 8 May
Ascension Day: movable
Whitsun: 2 days, movable
Bastille Day: 14 July
Assumption Day: 15 August
All Saints' Day: 1 November
Remembrance Day: 11 November
Christmas Day: 25 December

Regions of France

Today there are 95 departments grouped into 22 regions. Departments are often named after a dominant physical feature of the department, such as a river or mountain range. Examples are Marne (river) and Jura (mountain range). Others simply describe the location of the depart-ment, for example Nord.

Each department has a *chef-lieu* or chief town, and some of these towns are also regional capitals. For instance, Bordeaux is both the departmental capital of the Gironde and regional capital of Aquitaine. If you are staying in an area for any length of time, it is a good idea to get to know the names of your regional and departmental *chef-lieux*, as you may need to use them.

Sports and Pastimes

Boules
This game is played all over France — in village squares, by the road-side, in parks and camp-sites. A serious game of boules is played with the proper heavy metal *championnat boules*. This is the real game of *Pétanque*. Remember — when you throw you either *pointe* (place the ball) or *tir* (fire hard at the opponent's ball) and the loser, the one furthest from the *cochonnet* ('little pig' or jack) always throws next.

Canal and River Cruising
The most popular canal in France for cruising is the Canal du Midi. This runs from Toulouse to the Mediterranean coast, but the journey can be extended across the Bassin de Thau and through the Camargue

via the Canal du Rhône à Sète to Beaucaire on the Rhône. Other popular waterway cruises are on the River Charente and the Burgundy canal. It is possible, if you have time, to traverse the whole of France by waterway.

Creative Holidays

There are plenty of opportunities in France to 'express yourself' or develop a hobby or creative skill. You can study any subject either on a formal course or in a more relaxed 'house party' atmosphere. You can receive tuition, guidance and inspiration from established practitioners in the arts and crafts; and you will have every opportunity to practise your chosen craft in stimulating surroundings.

Health cures or fitness holidays range from the usual 'taking the waters' at a spa or sweating it out at a health farm to special types of therapy, such as thalassotherapy (sea-treatment) or aromatherapy. If you want to throw off all inhibitions, you can join a naturist group. Although nudity is technically illegal, the police have long ago turned a blind eye to it in out-of-the-way places, and many beaches now have a section for those who wish to be totally nude.

Cycling

The Tour de France is an annual event and the high-spot of world cycling. Held in the first 3 weeks of July, it covers virtually the whole country. Cycling is popular as a pastime, as well as a sport, and a pleasant way of taking a holiday. You can either take a package cycling holiday, with travel, food and accommodation thrown in, or hire a bicycle in France, by the day or the week. It is not a good idea to take your own bicycle: unless you are cycling all the way from the channel port, you will encounter transportation problems.

Football/Tennis

The most popular French sports are football in winter and tennis in summer. Though the French are quite keen on soccer, tennis is a passion with them. Both public and private tennis courts are numerous and usually in good condition. Rugby football is a sport that attracts fanatical if patchy support, mainly in Paris and the south-west. In the Midi, it has become almost a religion — there are even churches dedicated to local teams and heroes!

Golf

Golf was until recently a minority sport in France, played only by the élite. But in the last few years it has erupted into popularity, with golf courses springing up all over. New courses are well constructed, usually in attractive locations, and with excellent facilities. It is especially popular with young people, and a third of all players are female. The golf boom has been called 'the second French Revolution'.

Hiking and Climbing

Whether you are a serious hiker or prefer the odd half-hour stroll, the varied countryside of France contains some ideal walking country. The higher stretches of the Alps and Pyrénées are for practised climbers or, at least, for those with strong stomachs and even stronger thighs: while some of the flat lands of north and central France, particularly the corn-belt south of Paris, have too little variety of scenery to make walking worthwhile. The Massif Central is ideal hiking country.

The French are highly organised walkers. They have a system of footpaths called *Grandes Randonnées* which stretch right across the country. These are magnificent walks, carefully planned to include the best scenery, and studded with places to stay such as *gîtes*, camp-sites and Logis de France hotels. Each GR has a number, so that you can base your holiday on following one. For the more adventurous, there are the *Hautes Randonnées*, taking the high road and each locality has its own secondary footpaths called *Sentiers*. These are usually prepared by the local Syndicat d'Initiative. These are usually colour-graded 'easy', 'moderate' or 'severe' and colour-coded, so that you follow the route by looking for the appropriate colour on trees or rocks as you go. It is sensible to pick up one of these from the Syndicat d'Initiative and follow its routes, to avoid accidents or falling foul of local landowners.

You should climb only if you are an expert or with a guide. Climbing in the Alps is known as *Alpinism*, and the French centre for this is Chamonix, where local guides can be hired from the Bureau des Guides.

Horse Riding

An exciting and 'different' way of seeing France is on horseback. Expert or beginner, you can find equestrian centres all over the country to give you a day's riding or to provide a base for a longer excursion. Basic training is usually available for beginners. If you are a keen rider, special package holidays of a weekend or longer are available, with food and accommodation in *gîtes d'étape, fermes auberges,* hotels or the occasional château. The horses are well kept, well trained and docile and you are usually in the saddle for about 6 to 7 hours a day. Popular areas for horseback tours are the Camargue, Dordogne, Burgundy, Limousin and the Loire Valley (with château visits thrown in) — but most tourist regions offer them. More specialist courses including dressage and jumping are available, particularly in the Camargue. An alternative, especially for the saddle-sore horse-lover, is to hire a horse-drawn caravan.

Motor Racing

One sport for which France has long been known is motor-racing. The French are great motor-car enthusiasts and are particularly fond of old cars. They often hold vintage car rallies, and they have excellent automobile museums. The main races attract world interest: the French Grand Prix at Magny-Cours, near Nevers, the Monaco Grand Prix, the famous Monte-Carlo Rally, and the legendary Le Mans 24-Hour Race. Le Mans is the home of France's best-known racing circuit, part of which is normally open to traffic. Motor-cycle racing is also popular, both on race-track and across-country (known as *motorcross*). The leading motor-cycle races are at Le Mans (the 24-Hour Race), Le Touquet and Le Castellet (the Bol d'Or).

Mountain Pastimes

The dominant mountain sport is skiing, and the French Alps are a leading centre for this. They have some of the finest ski slopes in the world, which attract leading sportsmen and international competitions (for example, the Winter Olympics in 1992). The main resorts are well-known: Chamonix, Megève, Bourg St Maurice, Courchevel, Val d'Isère, Serre Chevalier; and the Massifs of Mont Blanc, La Vanoise and Les Écrins are covered with ski trails, pistes, lifts and mountain railways.

Though skiing is mainly a winter sport, summer skiing on glaciers is increasingly popular and resorts in all three Alpine departments cater for it. The Pyrénées are also a popular area for skiing, though not so highly developed and with less certainty of good snow than the Alps and ski resorts can be found in the Jura, the Auvergne and other mountainous areas.

The skiing season only lasts 4 months, and so ski resorts are now trying to improve their image and broaden their appeal by providing a wider range of activities to attract the summer visitor.

Pelote Basque

In the Basque Country, the game of *Pelote Basque* is not just a spectacle for tourists — it is a serious sport with its own professional players, competitions and league tables. This is the national sport of both the French and Spanish Basques, and every town and village has its round topped pelota-wall or *fronton* . At top standard it is an exciting and colourful game to watch, even if your not sure of the rules.

Watersports

No European country can equal France in the provision of holidays involving water. Its long and varied coastline, its profusion of inland waterways, and its many mountain lakes and *étangs* make it the ideal country for a variety of watersports and pastimes.

You can swim in fresh or salt water all over France. The sea is cleaner on some parts of the coast than others — parts of the Mediterranean are getting particularly murky. The Mediterranean suffers from having no tide, so that the beaches and the shallow off-shore water can quickly become dirty and debris-laden, while the sea further out keeps its azure sparkle. The Atlantic, though less blue and clear, has cleaner beaches and firmer sand and the sea, though colder, is more fun, with big waves and a strong undertow in places. Some parts of the Atlantic coast forbid bathing in bad weather: this edict should always be obeyed. Some of the inland lakes and rivers provide the best swimming, however.

Underwater swimming is widely practised, particularly on the rockier parts of the Mediterranean coast. You need to be qualified before you can hire equipment for deep-sea diving, but snorkelling can be a pleasant alternative.

The most popular canoeing river is the Ardéche, with its centre at Vallon Pont d'Arc. But this can be crowded in high summer, and is best avoided in favour of some of the lesser-known rivers of the Massif Central, Jura or Provence. Less strenuous canoeing can be had on the Loire, Charente or Dordogne, where holidays are combined with visits to châteaux, caves and scenic villages. Some of these holidays can also be taken by small groups in inflatable rafts.

Taxis

For longer journeys out of town, it is best to agree a price beforehand. Taxis are only allowed to pick up from taxi-ranks or *stations de taxi*. Check that they have a meter. You will pay according to rates posted on the cab window and not just the price indicated on the meter. Extra charges may be made for luggage.

Telephone Services

Telephoning in France is very simple. There are only two regions, Paris and the Provinces. All subscribers have an 8-figure number, and to dial from province to province, or from Paris to Paris, you simply dial that number. From Paris to province you dial 16 then the 8-figure number; from province to Paris, dial 16 (1) then the 8 figures. All Paris numbers should begin with a 4, and in the outskirts a 3 or a 6.

Telephoning France from the UK, you start with the international access code (01033) then (1) plus the 8-figure number for Paris and its outskirts, or simply the 8-figure number for anywhere else in the country.

Telephoning the UK from France, you dial 19, wait until the continuous tone recurs, then dial 44 followed by your STD code minus the first 0, and then your number, eg 19-44-21-345-2850. To phone the USA from France 19-1, Canada 19-1, Australia 19-61 followed by the telephone number.

Cheap rates give you 50 per cent extra time: on weekdays between 10.30pm and 8am, and at weekends starting 2pm on Saturdays.

Phonecards, called *télécarte*, operate in most booths. You can buy them from post offices, tobacconists, newsagents, and where advertised on telephone booths. Buy them in the UK from Voyages Vacances Int, 34 Savile Row, London W1X 1AG ☎ 071 287 3171.

Incoming calls can be received at phone boxes with a blue bell sign shown.

Emergency Numbers
Fire 18; Police 17; Operator 13; Directory Enquiries 12.

Tipping

Most restaurants make a service charge, either included in their prices or added on at the end. Cafés include it in the price of drinks if you sit at a table. Tips are customary to taxi-drivers and helpful hotel porters. When public toilets are guarded, an entrance charge will usually be made. When garage attendants clean your windscreen and check your oil, they will welcome, but not expect a tip.

Tourist Information Centres

Larger resorts will have an Office de Tourisme, smaller ones a Syndicat d'Initiative, and their staff are usually only too willing to dispense local information, help and advice. Brochures are usually attractively produced, and often in English. Some of the major tourist offices now have an Accueil de France (Welcome to France) facility to help you with hotel bookings. For a small cover charge they will make hotel bookings for you throughout France on the same day you call or up to 8 days in advance. They are open from 9am to 8pm every day of the year except 25 December and 1 January. Tourist offices at main railway stations in Paris and a few other large towns are open daily except Sundays and Bank Holidays (8am-9pm Easter to October, 9am-8pm in winter).

Main French tourist offices are:

Australia
Kindersley House
33 Bligh Street
Sydney
NSW 2000
☎ (2) 231 5244

UK
French Government Tourist
Office
178 Piccadilly
London WIV 0AL
☎ 071 491 7622

USA
610 Fifth Avenue Suite 222
New York NY 10020-2452
☎ 212 757 1683

Canada
1981 Avenue McGill College
Tour Esso Suite 490
Montreal
Quebec H3A 2W9
☎ 514 288 4264

Travel

By Sea

The way most people get to France from the UK is via a cross-channel ferry or hovercraft. The shortest, cheapest and most popular of these is from Dover to Calais/Boulogne, though you may have to take the time and cost of extra road travel each side of the channel into account in your budgeting. Even so, you should find that this is the most economical way of getting there, as the large number of travellers who use this method testifies. Costs can be even further reduced by taking advantage of one of the special offers that the ferry companies make, or by the special discounts that some companies offer to shareholders. Most companies also operate a 'tariff' system, with cheaper tariffs for midweek, night-time or out-of-season crossings.

The Dover-Calais route is the most popular, and ferries now leave by the hour in peak season. You can usually get onto one of these without booking, except for the most popular daytime or weekend crossings in midsummer. Even then, if you turn up at the port and the next boat is full, you should get onto the following one quite easily. The crossing only takes an hour and a quarter, and there are motorways or express roads both sides of the channel to help you get to or from the ports quickly. The *Autoroute* from Calais is, like most French motorways, *péage*, i.e. toll-paying, but you can now avoid Calais and get onto it direct from the port. This is well worth while, and you can reduce toll charges by only staying on the *Autoroute* for a stage or two. Because of the volume of traffic, customs operations are usually more streamlined at these ports, too, and delays tend to be less.

The hovercraft crossings from Dover and Ramsgate to Boulogne and Calais are even quicker (35 minutes) but are more expensive, and space is more limited. Cars may be transported, but not caravans. Other ferries operate from Dover/Ramsgate to Dunkerque ($2^1/_2$ hours); Newhaven to Dieppe (4 hours); Portsmouth to Caen ($5^1/_2$ hours) to Le Havre ($6^1/_2$ to 9 hours), to Cherbourg (5 hours), Poole to Cherbourg ($4^1/_2$ hours); Weymouth to Cherbourg (4 hours); Plymouth to Roscoff (6 hours).

The effect of the impending Channel Tunnel on ferry crossings is not yet known, but the competition should bring down the costs, which are currently higher than in other European countries. In the meantime, it pays to shop around as there are significant variations in price between operators and according to time and season.

By Air

Another way of getting to France is to fly. You can do so to one of the major Paris airports — Roissy-Charles de Gaulle or Orly — or to a regional airport. Direct flights from the UK are available, though sometimes only in season, to: Biarritz, Bordeaux, Caen, Clermont-Ferrand, Deauville, Le Havre, Lille, Lourdes/Tarbes, Lyon, Marseille, Montpellier, Morlaix, Nantes, Nice, Paris, Perpignan, Quimper, Rennes, Strasbourg and Toulouse. There are also good internal French air services, most run by Air Inter.

If you fly to one of the Paris airports, shuttle buses and trains run regularly to rail and metro stations in the city, and there is a helicopter shuttle service between Roissy and Orly, and also to a heliport at the Porte de Sèvres in Paris.

By Rail

Many travel agents offer inclusive rail-and-sea journeys to many destinations in France. These involve travelling by a combination of British Rail, ferry or hovercraft, and French Railways (SNCF). You may, however, have to make your own way across Paris, which is best done by underground or *métro*. Paris has a high-speed cross-city train (RER) from the Gare du Nord to the Gare de Lyon.

Rail travel in France is usually pleasant and efficient. Many lines use the Corail trains, which are comfortable and air-conditioned; some major lines use Trans Europe Express trains, which are first-class only; while the famous and splendid T.G.V. (*Train de Grand Vitesse*, or high-speed train) covers long distances in much shorter times than other trains and with an amazingly smooth ride. You can reach Marseille from Paris by T.G.V. in 4 hours and 40 minutes. However, local opposition to the construction of further T.G.V. lines may delay the extension of this system.

On longer routes, sleeping facilities are available, either in couchettes, with 4 to 6 beds to a compartment, or in private single, two-berth or three-berth compartments. Food is served on most trains, either in your seat or in the restaurant or bar.

An additional service in France is the Motorail car-carrying train, which has services from Calais to Biarritz, Avignon and the Mediterranean, and further services from Paris.

Rail Services

A number of services are offered by:
French Railways
Piccadilly
London W1V 0BA

Motorail
Information and bookings ☎ 071 409 3518
24-hour brochure hotline ☎ 071 499 1075

France Vacances Pass
Rail rover tickets for unlimited rail travel on any 4 days within 15, or any 9 days within 1 month, 1st or 2nd class.
These are available from: International Rail Centre, Victoria Station, London; ABTA travel agents; French Railways, London (personal application only).

Journeys to and within France
Tickets by personal application from:
Continental Shipping and Travel Ltd
1st floor, 179 Piccadilly
London
☎ 071 499 2153

Group Travel
Savings for school and adult parties:
Group Travel Section
French Railways
☎ 071 499 2153

By Road

Preparing the Car
Before you set off, you need to be sure that the car is in good condition
and fully equipped to meet French requirements. Have the car serviced
before you go, and carry a few spares of essential small items like
plugs, points, fan-belt, and a full set of light bulbs. As oil and distilled
water are more expensive in France, you could carry a small supply of
these too.

Two items you will need to meet French traffic regulations are: a red
warning triangle, which you must place on the road 30m (98ft) behind
your car if it breaks down and has no hazard warning lights (it is a
good idea to use it anyway); and a headlight converter kit. This has the
dual effect of adjusting your headlight beams for right-hand drive and
changing the light to amber. A clip-on converter is the easiest way of
doing this. You are required by law to adjust your headlamp beams
and, though changing the colour to amber is not compulsory for tourist
vehicles, it will make you more popular with French
drivers, and you will not be constantly 'flashed' while driving at night.

You are required to carry with you the original of the vehicle's
registration document, a full valid national driving licence and current
insurance certificate. If the vehicle is not yours, you must have a letter
from the owner authorising you to drive it. An international distin-
guishing sign (i.e GB plate or sticker of black letters on a white oval
background) should be displayed near to the number-plate on the rear
of the car, and on any caravan or trailer you are towing.

Insurance
You should consider taking out three types of insurance: ordinary
travel insurance to cover you for loss of possessions and money, and
for medical expenses; special motor insurance to cover you for acciden-
tal damage to your car, and to other cars or people; and breakdown
insurance, to give you extra protection against the expense and incon-
venience that can result from the car breaking down.

Personal Insurance
This is a good idea but not essential. Unfortunately there have been
quite a few reports in recent years of cars being broken into and possessions taken, so insurance here is a wise precaution. Do not forget to
report any incident to the local *Gendarmerie* straight away, or your
insurance will not be valid. Keep any personal money with you at all
times — do not leave it in your car.

Medical Insurance

Some medical insurance is now your entitlement under EEC regulations — the same as that enjoyed by insured French nationals. You will need to obtain form E111, which you can do from your local social security office. This will save you roughly four-fifths of your medical expenses, but to claim the other one-fifth you will need to take out additional personal medical insurance.

Motor Insurance

Ordinary UK motor insurance gives you only the legal minimum requirement for France. This is much less than the cover you would normally have at home, so although the Insurance Green Card (motor insurance certificate) is no longer a legal requirement, it is still important to provide this extra cover and to give evidence that you are fully insured. Get your Green Card from your car insurer well before you go. If you are towing a caravan or trailer, it should be endorsed for this at no extra cost.

Breakdown insurance can cover you for such things as freighting spare parts from Britain (spares for right-hand-drive cars may not be easy to find abroad); a hire car to continue your journey; or hotel costs while awaiting repairs. Some policies increase cover to stolen cars or to drivers who fall ill, but you are not normally covered for the cost of parts or for labour charges. These policies are usually called 'vehicle protection' or 'vehicle security', and are available from the AA, RAC, Europ Assistance, and the Caravan Club (to members only).

Though this type of insurance is useful if you have a major breakdown, are immobilised and need spare parts, it is not really necessary for minor problems, which can usually be solved by a local garage. Whether the insurance is worth the expense is for you to decide.

Accidents

One way to reduce the chances of an accident is not to drive too long without a rest. But if you do have one, you must inform the police, particularly if someone is injured. An accident statement form (*constat à l'aimable*) must be completed in all cases and signed by both parties (if appropriate). Any disputes should be taken to a local bailiff who will prepare a report, called a *constat d'huissier*.

Motoring Offences

On-the-spot fines are payable for a number of motoring offences including speeding and exceeding the drink driving level, payable in cash on the spot. The French have random breath testing and penalties are extremely severe. Therefore do not drink and drive.

If you do not consider that you are at fault, you will be asked to pay a deposit, or *amende forfaitaire*. This varies according to the offence you are charged with. The police must issue a receipt showing the amount paid.

Regulations

Apart from those mentioned above, there are some vital points about driving in France which you need to observe to avoid a hefty on-the-spot fine or worse. These are:

1. No driving on a provisional licence.
2. The minimum age to drive in France is 18.
3. Seat belts must be worn by the driver and front and back-seat passengers.
4. Children under 10 years old may not travel in the front — unless the

car has no back seat, or if the child is in a specially-approved back-facing seat.

5. You must stop completely at stop-signs. Creeping slowly in first gear is not allowed.

6. No stopping on open roads unless the car is driven completely off the road.

7. No overtaking on the brow of a hill, where there is a solid single centre line, or where a 'no overtaking' sign is shown.

8. Use full or dipped headlights in poor visibility or at night. Use sidelights only when the car is stationary.

Rules of the Road

In France you must drive on the right hand side of the road. You will be reminded by signs, at first in English as you leave channel ports and later by the common and important sign *serrez à droite*. This means both 'keep to the right' and 'keep in the right-hand lane' on dual carriage-ways.

Another important road sign is *Priorité à droite*. The rule in France is that, unless there is an indication to the contrary, traffic coming from the right always has priority. This applies particularly in built-up areas. The exceptions are either Stop or Give Way signs, where minor roads meet major roads. The sign *passage protégé* means that you are on a major road that has priority over side roads. On a major road, a tilted yellow square means that you have priority; when there is a black bar crossing the diamond, you no longer have priority. One particular danger occurs at roundabouts — although the *priorité à droite* regulation no longer applies here, many Frenchmen still drive as though it does. They **should** give way if you are on the roundabout and they are approaching but they may not! It pays to watch traffic coming from the right at all times.

Other Road Signs

Other common road signs are: *toutes directions*, indicating the route for through traffic; *poids lourds*, the recommended or sometimes *obligatoire* route for heavy vehicles; and *centre ville*, indicating the town centre. It does not always pay to follow 'through traffic' signs — they may take you on a long detour, and you may miss seeing the town centre; but they are useful if you are in a hurry and wish to avoid inner-city congestion. It is best to decide beforehand whether you want to see the town and, if so, ignore the through traffic signs and head for the *centre ville*. Of course, if you are a *poids lourds*, ie if you are towing a caravan or trailer, you should normally follow the sign (except possibly at very quiet periods — lunchtimes, evenings, Sundays). Caravans are sometimes prohibited from town centres. In towns, watch also for the signs *sens interdit* (no entry) and *sens unique* (one way).

One sign that the driver in France comes to dread is *déviation*. The diversion may be brief, or on occasion it may take you miles further than you want to go. Unfortunately there is no way of knowing beforehand about the length of the detour.

You should heed signs telling you of road hazards. Common ones are: *gravillons* (loose chippings); *chute de pierres* (falling rocks); *chaussée déformée* (uneven or bumpy road, temporary surface); *côtés non stabilisés* (unsafe or uneven road edgings); *sortie de camions* (hidden works entrance — lorries emerging); *nids de poules* (potholes). It is advisable to reduce your speed until the danger is past. Sometimes you are warned of a longer-lasting hazard: *virages sur 5 kilometres* (bends for 5 kilometres). Watch out particularly for the *chaussée déformée* signs if you are towing a caravan — a bumpy road could do serious damage here.

Though French road signs are usually pretty good, pointer-sign-posts can sometimes cause drivers frustration and confusion. It is not always clear which way they are pointing — they often seem to point across the road indicated, rather than towards it. The best procedure is to take the road nearest to the arrow-head showing your destination. Another problem can be hidden road signs. These can be sited on a wall, often half-way round the corner of the road you are looking for; or they can be hidden by other signs. When you are looking for a road, it is wise to travel slowly enough to be able to respond to a late sighting of a pointer-sign. It helps, too, to study the map well before setting off, or to have a good map-reader with you!

Route Planning

The *Bison Futé* system can be a boon for holiday drivers. Loosely trans-lated 'crafty bison' or 'wily buffalo', it is devised by the French Ministry of Transport to help you avoid the worst traffic jams by showing alternative routes. Maps of these are available free at fuel stations, roadside information centres and from the AA. Road signs usually indicate *Bison Futé* roads with a green arrow, sometimes accompanied by the letters 'Bis'. These roads not only avoid traffic black spots, but they are often scenically attractive, too.

More general route planning advice is available from the AA and RAC. The AA Overseas Routes Service also produce a useful European Through Route Map for each channel port, showing recommended routes to places throughout Europe.

Do not be afraid to use minor roads in France. These are often straight and well surfaced, and are usually much less busy than the main trunk roads. It can be fun to plan your route on minor roads, using the detailed Michelin maps where they are coloured yellow. Note, however, that there will be fewer services, snacks etc and fewer town by-passes than on trunk roads.

Roads and their Classification

French roads are classified A (*autoroute* or motorway), N (National road) and D (Departmental road). Signs for motorways are usually coloured in blue, while other roads are in green. Take care when ap-proaching motorway entrance points: the signpost may indicate the same destination in the two colours, and to stay on the trunk road you must follow the green sign.

Most French motorways are toll roads or *Autoroutes à Péage*. They vary in price per kilometre, but they can be expensive, especially if you use them for long distances. They have emergency telephones, 24-hour fuel stations and *aires de repos* (rest-places). These *aires de repos* are usually equipped with picnic facilities and toilets, and are sometimes attractively sited among trees.

You can find short stretches of motorway that are free. These are indicated on the Michelin maps with marker points and distance numbers coloured in blue rather than the normal orange. They can be useful in getting you into or through large towns like Paris, Marseilles or Lyon.

The main trunk roads are National, with the number usually indi-cating the importance of the road. Thus single number roads (N1 to N9) are usually wider and longer than double, which in turn are more major than three-figure roads. Single-number trunk roads are often almost as fast now as motorways; they are often dual-carriageway for long stretches, by-pass most towns, have restricted entry points and special services. The one drawback though, as with all French roads other than motorways, is traffic-lights. The French have a passion for these, and they can cause considerable delay if you are passing through a large built-up area on an ordinary road.

Departmental roads are often very good — well surfaced and maintained, and relatively traffic-free. They tend to vary in quality according to the prosperity of the department. They are usually narrower, but often better maintained, than three-figure or even sometimes two-figure N roads.

There is often confusion over the numbering of D and N roads. The French Government, responsible for national roads, has handed over responsibility for many to the Departments, which has led to renumbering. If you have an old map, the numbers may be out of date. For example, a road numbered N63 on your map may now be D363. Normally the last two numbers have stayed the same, but an additional 3, 6 or 9 has been added or substituted for the first number. You may find the numbering changing from N to D from one village to the next, depending on whether a local authority has altered its signposts.

Speed Limits
These are lower in wet weather and low visibility than in dry conditions. In dry, unless otherwise posted, they are:

	Dry conditions	Wet conditions
Toll Motorways	130kmh (81mph)	110kmh (68mph)
Dual carriageways and non-toll motorways	110kmh (68mph)	100kmh (62mph)
Other roads	90kmh (56mph)	80kmh (50mph)
In towns	50kmh (37mph)	50kmh (37mph)

The limit starts with the town name, and the derestriction sign is the town name cancelled with a bar. The warning sign *rappel*, meaning 'slow down', means 'continue the restriction' when used in conjunction with a speed limit. There is a new minimum speed limit of 80kmh (50mph) for the outside lane of motorways, but only in daylight, on level ground and with good visibility. Drivers may not exceed 90kmh (56mph) for the first year after passing their test. Speeding offences may be fined on the spot.

Fuel and Garage Services
Essence, or fuel, comes as *ordinaire* (two-star), *super* (four-star), *sans plomb* or *vert* (lead-free), or *super sans plomb* (super lead-free). Unleaded fuel is widely available. Diesel fuel (*gazole* or gas-oil) is both widely available and much cheaper than normal fuel, the difference being considerably greater than in Britain. Vehicles equipped to run on LPG gas (Gepel/GPL) may be imported, and many LPG filling stations can be found in France, especially on motorways. You can get a map showing their location free from LPG stations.

Fuel prices vary, being highest on motorways, average in normal garages and lowest in hyper- and supermarkets. Though it is more economical, buying fuel in supermarkets has its problems — they may be closed at lunchtimes and on Sundays, they may have awkward access and long waits, they will not have toilets or offer other services, and some supermarkets do not take credit cards. There are no fuel coupons in France.

Most normal filling stations are now self-service, but someone should be available to *vérifier*, or check, the *huile, eau ou pneus* (oil, water or tyres), or to *nettoyer le pare-brise* (clean the windscreen). You are advised to tip for these services and you will usually have to pay for distilled water. Some garages make a small charge for air for tyres.

Winter Driving
This is not severely restricted in France, even in the mountains. Snow chains can be hired from tyre specialist garages or bought in hypermarkets. To check road conditions, ring Paris on a 24-hour number C.N.I.R. ☎ (1) 48 94 33 33

Car or Bicycle Hire
If you go by air, fly-drive arrangements for hiring a car are available with the major airlines. Otherwise, you can make your own arrangements with one of the major car rental companies, which have offices in nearly all towns. It is best to do this in advance from your own country. If it is more convenient, you can usually arrange to collect your car in one place and leave it in another, with no extra charge. To hire a car you must have a valid driving licence (held for at least one year) and your passport. The minimum age varies accordingly to the hiring firm but in general you have to be 21.

Central Booking Offices:

Avis	**Thrifty**
☎ (1) 46 09 92 12	☎ (1) 46 56 08 75
Hertz	**Budget**
☎ (1) 47 88 51 51	☎ (1) 46 86 65 65
Europcar	**Mattei**
☎ (1) 30 43 82 82	☎ 91 79 90 10 or (1) 43 46 11 50
Citer	**Eurorent**
☎ (1) 45 67 97 43	☎ (1) 45 67 82 17

Alternatively, you may consider it more healthy and close-to-nature to go by bicycle. Bicycle hire is widely available in France (ask at the local Office de Tourisme or Syndicat d'Initiative for details) or there are facilities at some 200 French railway stations. Some package holidays offer a combined travel and cycling-tour holiday in various parts of France. When hiring for yourself, you are advised to take out insurance before you leave.

INDEX